HOW TO
cheat
IN Maya
2014

Tools and Techniques
for Character Animation

Kenny Roy

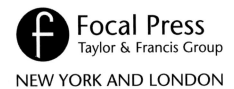

Focal Press
Taylor & Francis Group

NEW YORK AND LONDON

First published 2014
by Focal Press
70 Blanchard Road, Suite 402, Burlington, MA 01803

Simultaneously published in the UK
by Focal Press
2 Park Square, Milton Park, Abingdon, Oxon OX14 4RN

Focal Press is an imprint of the Taylor & Francis Group, an informa *business*

© 2014 Taylor & Francis

Library of Congress Cataloging in Publication Data

Roy, Kenny.
How to cheat in Maya 2014 : tools and techniques for character animation / Kenny Roy.
pages cm
Includes index.
ISBN 978-0-415-82659-4 (pbk)
ISBN 978-0-203-52730-6 (ebk)
1. Computer animation -- Computer programs.
2. Maya (Computer file)
I. Title.
TR897.72.M39R69 2013
006.6'96
dc23
2013020655

Publisher's Note
This book has been prepared from camera-ready copy provided by the author.
Printed in the United States Of America by Courier, Kendallville, Indiana

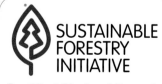

Contents

Contents

How to Cheat and Why

The truth about cheating

When we hear the word cheating, we usually think of something negative; deception, trickery or chicanery. However in this book, cheating is a good thing. If you've watched someone who's a master of something work at it, it can seem unreal, almost like they're... cheating! But really they just have experience and in-depth knowledge of how to achieve something. They know the most efficient way to do a task and make their tools work for them.

That's the goal of this book: to give you in-depth knowledge of animating with Maya so you can skip over the trial-and-error, constant web searches, and pouring through internet forums. Since Maya can be a technical minefield of complex menus and settings, you need someone to help you navigate this sophisticated program and get right down to the most important thing: performance. When it comes down to dodging discouragement, avoiding adversity, and side-stepping setbacks, you want all the cheats you can get! Our goal is for you to come to view this book as your on-hand reference guide as you study the art of motion.

The philosophy

Throughout our teaching experiences, one of the methods we found to be extremely effective in quickly transferring knowledge to someone else was isolation of a concept; really honing in on a single task and practicing until the knowledge is engrained. This may seem obvious but it's rare to come across an animator who didn't learn by studying performance while simultaneously wrestling all of the technical concepts in their student work. Although trial-by-fire can be an effective learning method, it makes for some very discouraging times. This books takes an approach that will give you a firm grasp on the technical concepts of animation, one at a time.

You will understand how to employ Maya's tools faster and concentrate instead on making your animation look amazing, rather than why that prop keeps popping out of the character's hand.

As luck would have it, the How to Cheat series is perfect for this style of learning. Every page spread is geared toward a specific concept, which allows you to go through the book cover-to-cover, or skip around to the things you want to know about. The choice is yours.

Scene files and examples

Just about all of the topics have an accompanying scene file. Most of the topics
enable you to follow along, employing the given technique in a prepared animation.
Once you understand the technique and have practiced using it in an animation, it
will be very easy to transfer it over to whatever you're working on. For chapters that
are one long project, scenes are included in a progressive order, so you can jump in
anywhere and learn what you want to learn without having to start at the beginning.
Having the scene files for an animation book should prove extremely useful, as
you can take a look under the hood and examine the curves and see the movement
for yourself. As great as books can be, you really have to see an animation in motion
in the end.

Throughout the book, we use multiple character rigs that have been stress
tested by students and veterans alike. We've found them to all be very fast, stable
rigs, and all have just the right number of advanced features without getting too
complicated.

The scene files are included for Maya 2014. If you're using an older version of
Maya, just have "Ignore Version" checked in the File > Open options.

What you need to know

While this book starts at the beginning as far as animating is concerned, it does
assume a basic knowledge of getting around Maya. You should be able to navigate the
viewports (orbit, pan, dolly in 3D space), understand the interface, and be comfortable
using the move, rotate, and scale tools. This information is covered in countless places
on the web and in other materials, and we'd rather keep the book focused than rehash
what's easily found elsewhere.

Going further

Visit the book's website at www.howtocheatinmaya.com. There you can find all the
scene files for using the book, as well as previous material from the 2010 and 2012
editions that couldn't be included here due to space. Happy animating!

Kenny Roy

Acknowledgements

We'd like to thank the following artists for agreeing to let us use their rigs in this edition of How To Cheat in Maya.

"Cenk"
Özgür Aydoğdu

"Nico"
Chad Vernon

"Goon"
Sean Burgoon

"Groggy"
Zubuyer Kaolin

"Moom"
Ramtin Ahmadi

"Morpheus"
Courtesy of Josh Burton and cgmonks.com

And a very special thanks to Sonya Ballas for your technical support writing this book.

Note about installation: The animation files provided in this book generally have the rigs imported into each scene. A few of the scenes have the characters REFERENCED (see Chapter 10). If you open a scene and the rig produces an error, simply copy the rig from the "3D/Assets/Rigs/" directory to the chapter's directory and reopen the scene.

The "Cenk" rig requires the python script jlCollisionDeformer.py found in the Chapter 11 project directory. Open the "Readme" file for instructions on installing this script to your Maya program directory.

All of the rigs provided are for educational purposes only. You are free to use these scene files and rigs in any non-commercial use.
Do not redistribute.

How to Use This Book

We've designed this book so that you can use it in the way that best serves your needs in learning to animate with Maya. You can start at the beginning and read it straight through if you like, as the chapters are ordered progressively. The first few talk about fundamental concepts: the principles of animation, workflow, and how animators think about the tools available in Maya. Then we start practicing some techniques in the context of animations already started for you, finally moving on to guiding you through doing projects in blocking, cycles, polishing, lip sync, and much more.

If you've been animating for a while, but need some new tips or approaches to problems you've been having, you can simply go to any topic that interests you, and pick it up right there. Even the chapter-long projects include a series of progressive files so you don't need to start from the beginning. We've also completely updated the book for Maya 2014, and cover all the exciting new animation tools and how to use them.

Throughout the book we use the abbreviation "f01" to mean frame 1, or whatever frame number we're talking about. Frame numbers are also included on every screenshot where they're relevant, to make things as clear as possible. In the upper right corner of each cheat you'll see a download icon (⬤) whenever there are accompanying files, which is almost always. Underneath it the file names are listed for easy reference, and you can download all the scene files, rigs, and material from the previous edition from the book's website.

The projects are separated by chapter, and some of the projects also have QuickTime movies of the chapter's final result. Also included is the Goon rig in several versions (regular, ninja, and demon). For additional info and updates, be sure to check out the website:

www.howtocheatinmaya.com

1

Squash and Stretch

STAGING Anticipation

straight ahead POSE TO POSE

OVERLAPPING ACTION

follow through

Slow In / Slow Out

secondary ACTION

T-I--MI-NG

EXAGGERATION

SOLID DRAWING

Appeal

1
Animation Principles

THE PRINCIPLES OF ANIMATION, identified and perfected by the original Disney animators, guide us when we make technique and performance choices in our work. They are not rules, but rather guidelines for creating appealing animation that is engaging and fun to watch.

These seemingly simple concepts combine together to inform the most complex animation and performances on screen. Though some translation of these principles must occur for animators to utilize these concepts in Maya, this chapter offers a clear explanation of them and shows you how you can begin applying them in your own work.

Squash and Stretch

AUDED AS THE MOST IMPORTANT PRINCIPLE, *squash and stretch* gives characters and objects a sense of flexibility and life. Also, this principle dictates that as characters and objects move and deform, their volume generally stays the same. Some of squash and stretch can be dictated by the object actually smooshing into something, such as a ball bouncing on the ground. With characters, squash and stretch can mean many different things. It can be combined with anticipation to make a character "wind up" for an action in a visually interesting way.

One example would be as a character prepares to move, he may squash his spine, making his figure bulge out. Then as he springs into motion, his form elongates and stretches thin to retain the same volume. Whenever possible, use squash and stretch on your characters to give a sense of strain (a character reaching for something high overhead), or to give a sense of fear (a character squashes into a little ball in a corner to avoid being seen by a predator). Start looking for squash and stretch in professional animation and in life, and you'll see quickly how much this simple principle adds to the illusion of life we give objects and characters.

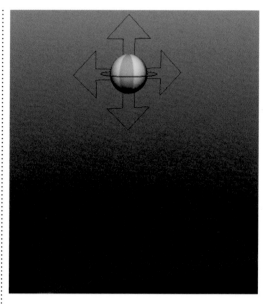

1 Open squash_Stretch_start.ma. We have an animated bouncing ball with the squash control keyed at 0 on f01 and f16. Hit play on the timeline and see how the ball seems neither alive, nor like it's made from rubber. This lifeless plastic ball is in need of some squash and stretch!

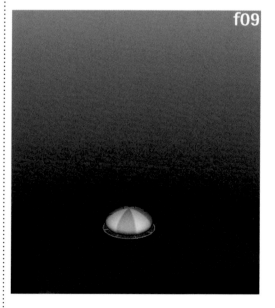

f09

4 At f09, the momentum continues downward through the ball, making it squash even more into the ground. Set the squash to -0.4 and key the control.

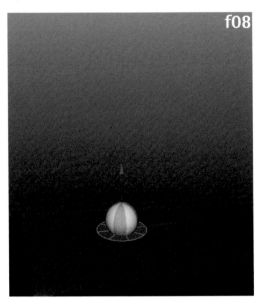

f08

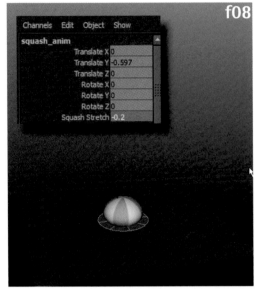

f08

squash_Stretch_start.
ma
squash_Stretch_finish.
ma

2 Go to f08, and check out this dead ball! When it hits the ground, we expect a ball made from rubber to react! It needs to squash, so select the middle squash_anim control and translate it down in Y to the base. The location of this control determines where the ball squashes from.

3 Adjust the Squash Stretch amount in the channel box and key the entire control. The ball contacts for 2 frames, so this frame will be the start of squashing, about −0.2 or so. Also notice that as the ball squashes down in Y, it bulges out in X and Z, retaining its volume.

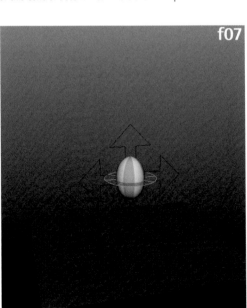

f07

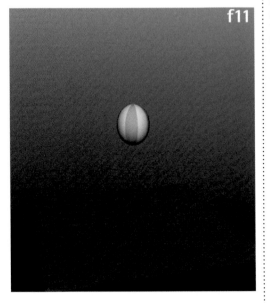

f11

5 Go back to f07. As the ball falls, it would stretch out from the air resistance and the anticipation of hitting the ground. Translate the control back to the middle of the ball (Y is 0) so it stretches from its center, adjust the stretch control, and set a key.

6 At f11, center the squash control in Y, stretch the ball slightly and key it. Since the first and last frames are set to 0, the ball returns to its shape at the top of the bounce. Play back the animation with the controls turned off and watch this principle shine.

Anticipation

ANTICIPATION IS THE PRACTICE of moving a character in a certain way to prepare the character and the audience for the action. Most often, anticipation means moving the character a small amount in the opposite direction of the main action. Since a lot of animation is very physical, many times anticipation is a necessary part of getting the correct physical performance out of the character. For instance, a character jumping must bend his knees first. A pitcher must bring his arm back before he throws the ball. This natural motion that occurs in everyday life is what makes anticipation as an animation principle so effective. We are very accustomed as humans to tracking fast-moving objects by taking a cue from its anticipation, and then looking ahead of the object in the opposite direction. So as animators we must take advantage of this hard-wired trait of humans and use it to our advantage. We can make it so that the audience is always looking at the part of the screen that we want them to, by activating the visual cue of anticipation.

Anticipation also serves a purpose in fine-tuning your performance choices. Disney animator and animation legend Eric Goldberg is known for relating anticipation directly with thought itself. This makes perfect sense; if we see a character really "wind up" for an action, it is clear to us that the character has planned the action well in advance, and is thinking about how to move. On the other hand, if a character moves instantaneously and without warning, the motion comes across as unplanned. Think of the difference between the apparent thought process of Popeye swinging his arm back to punch an unsuspecting Brutus, and Brutus's head when the fist hits him on the back of the head. Popeye was planning to wallop the big bully, but Brutus was not thinking at all of the fist about to hit him! So as you are working, pay close attention to how much anticipation you are using in your animation. It may just mean the difference between a thinking, planning, and intelligent character, and a character simply reacting to the world around him.

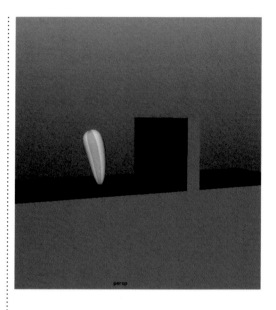

1 Open anticipation.ma. In this scene, a bouncing ball looks at a wall, and then deftly hops over. Play it a few times and see if you can spot the anticipation before the jump.

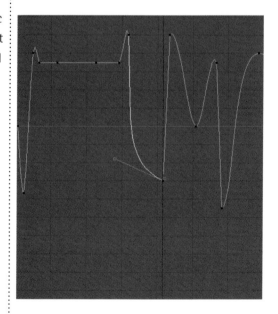

4 Now play with the handle itself! Drag it way out towards the left and playback the animation. See what a different impression you get as to the thought behind the jump? Subtle changes in anticipation can have incredible results.

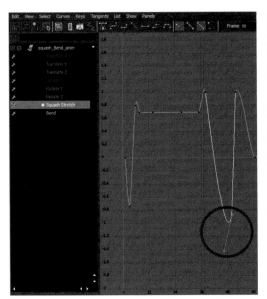

f50

anticipation.ma

2 If you select the squash_Bend_anim control on the ball, you will see there is a keyframe on the Squash Stretch control at f50 with an unlocked tangent. This is the frame of anticipation. We are going to play with this anticipation and see what looks best.

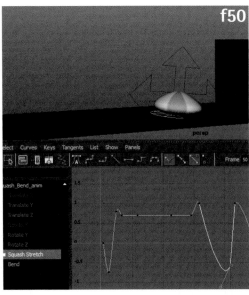

3 Select the squash_Bend_anim control, and open the Graph Editor. See that keyframe with the unlocked tangent handles? Try moving that key up and down and finding a good size of squash for this anticipation. Watch the animation over and over again to see what looks best. Remember, it's up to you!

HOT TIP

Play your animation at speed! We know that timing is vitally important in animation. You get so much more information playing your animation at speed than you do if you just scroll through the timeline.

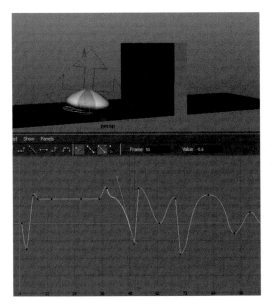

f03

5 Or does this look better? Remember, if you keep the number of keyframes you use to a minimum, you can spend more time making adjustments and less time wrestling with technical trouble. What new impression does this anticipation give you? What is the ball *thinking*?

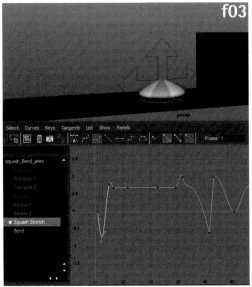

6 At f03 is another little anticipation that I sneaked in. Play with the size and timing of this one as well, and start training your eye to hone in on the most powerful and engaging performance.

Staging

STAGING IS A FUNDAMENTAL that encompasses a mass of artistic sensibilities. Staging involves framing the camera in a way to best capture the action. It involves making sure your animation has been planned to best communicate the motion, the character arc, the story. Simply put, staging is how you create the scene.

Ideally staging starts with your planning phase. Thumbnailing your poses is the best way to make strong pose choices at the start of a shot. If you are not a strong drawer, then perhaps you rely more on photo or video reference to give you cues to begin your work. At this very early phase, staging means you are thinking about how your posing and the layout of the scene is going to clearly show the motion.

As you begin your scene, staging becomes more complex. How are you going to maintain the high level of communication throughout the life of the shot? Will you be able to hit all of the poses that you'd like, or are the poses going to have to be changed to work when the character is in motion? Staging means that you are thinking about the entire action at this point. Adjusting the camera, making tweaks to the layout, and finding just the right balance in the composition all improve your staging of the scene. When you are finished blocking, generally the major staging decisions are decided. This does not mean that staging is over!

As you finish the animation, there are still staging considerations you must be aware of. Where is the audience's eye going to be looking at every moment of the shot? If you've animated the scene correctly, you have a very good idea of what the audience should be paying attention to at every second. As your shot is finished and moves through the rest of the pipeline, other decisions that hone in the audience's focus are going to come into play: lighting, effects, and editing. As animators, our staging choices have far-reaching impact on the success of a shot in communicating an idea. We'll practice these staging concepts by repositioning a bouncing ball animation, the camera, and some lights to find the greatest impact.

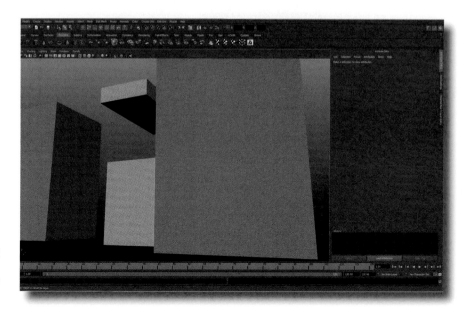

1 Open staging_start.ma, and set one of your panels to look through "renderCam". Yikes. This scene has a lot of staging problems. The camera is in a position where it cannot see any of the action, the ball has been positioned very oddly, and the light is casting a shadow on the entire main action. Let's make some adjustments.

2 Rotate, pan and zoom the camera around until you've found an angle that shows off the animation nicely when you scrub through the timeline. This is a nice angle for me.

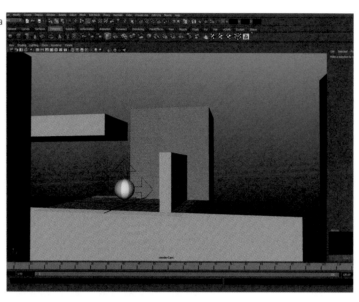

staging_start.ma
staging_finish.ma

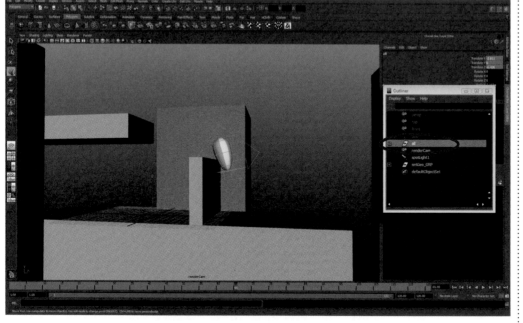

3 Let's adjust the position of the animated ball to make the action read clearer, shall we? Grab the "all" group in the Outliner, and scrub through the animation. See how the ball is pushed far towards the edge of the set, and hits the wall on f65? Let's reposition it to be a little more centered, and to not hit the set on its path.

Staging (cont'd)

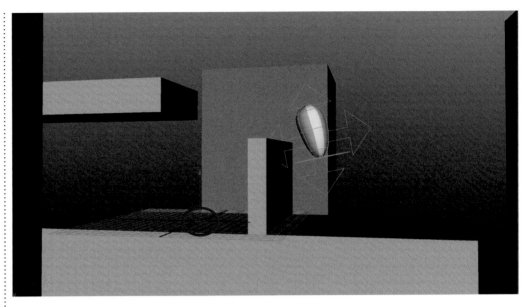

4 Much better. I moved the group back to the world origin, and the animation is working much better to camera.

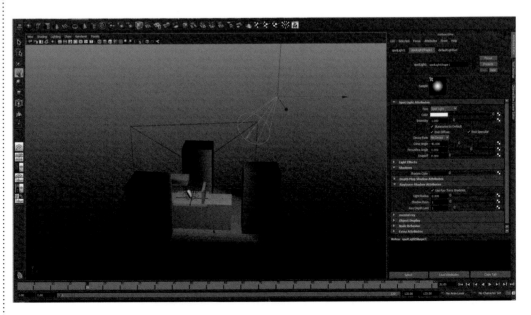

6 In a perspective panel, press the **7** key to enable the lighting, and make sure Show > Lights is enabled in the viewport menu. Select the light and transform and rotate it until it gives a nice ¾ lighting angle. The action should be lit so that we get a fully lit view of the scene, but also so that the shadows are angled so they show the detail and depth of the set.

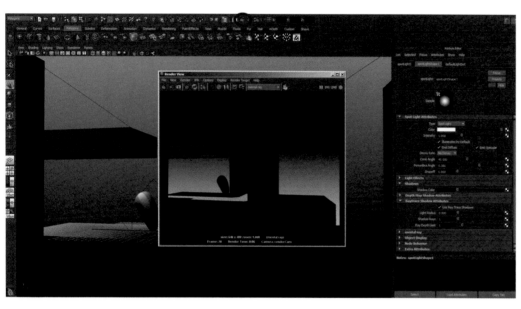

5 Hit the render button to see how the lights are positioned. Uh oh, the main action is happening in deep shadow!

If you select a spotlight, and then go to the "Panels" menu in any panel and choose "Look Through Selected", it will create a temporary camera view that matches the view as seen from that spotlight. Many Maya users find using Maya's in-panel camera moving tools to position lights is a fast and easy way to stage the scene. Maya even gives you an in-panel preview of the light's Cone Angle!

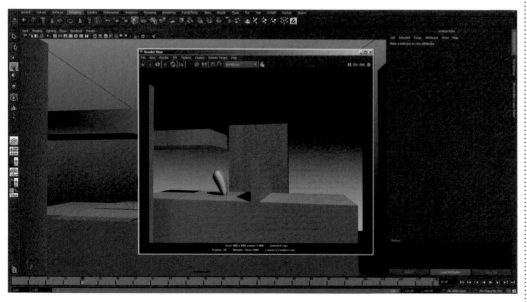

7 Now click render when you have repositioned your light. Beautiful!

Straight Ahead/Pose to Pose

THIS FUNDAMENTAL DESCRIBES the two basic approaches to block in a piece of animation. Straight ahead means that an animator creates the base animation by posing the animation in a frame, then moving forward one or more frames and posing again. This approach is akin to stop-motion animation, in which you have to pose every one or two frames because the camera needs to capture that frame on film before moving forward. Pose to pose means that you create the key poses, and then essentially time the rest of the animation by inserting blank or "hold poses" in between your key poses. This is akin to a non-linear approach in which you can test different timings of a shot by simply sliding poses around on the time slider. Both approaches have their advantages and disadvantages.

Straight ahead animating should be used when the action is very mechanical or physical. This is because the ability to perceive the motion as you frame through the animation in slow motion is far greater than trying to imagine what pose the highly mechanical or physical movement is going to hit. Let's take an overlapping antenna, for instance. With this kind of highly physical action it would be impossible to imagine where the antenna is going to be without framing through the animation and adjusting the pose as you go. This is what we'll do to practice this concept.

Pose to pose animating should be used for creating character performances. Unlike highly physical actions, the key poses a character hits are going to tell the story. So in order to be sure that you arrive at these golden moments, you should pose them out and retime them as necessary to make the motion work. We bias our work in performance animation to feature the pose because, without a strong sense of the character's body language, the emotional story gets lost. We're going to create a pose and retime it using Maya's Dope Sheet.

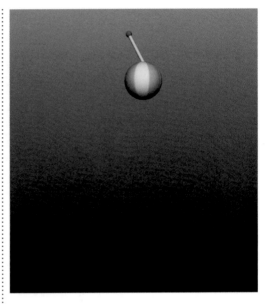

1 Open straightAhead_start.ma. This bouncing ball looks familiar, but now it has an antenna on top. Let's practice animating straight ahead and make the antenna flop back and forth.

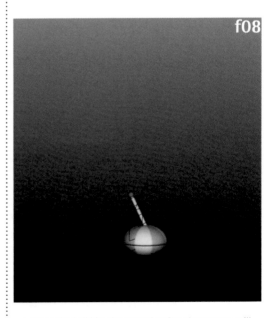

4 When the ball hits the ground at f08, the antenna will not react yet because the momentum needs time to travel up through the ball. Key the antenna straight up.

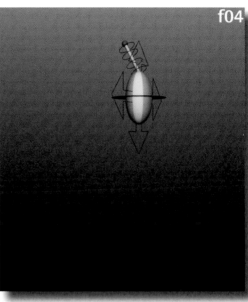

f01

2 On f01, the ball is at the top of its arc, so the antenna will be travelling upwards, trying to catch up. Select all the antenna controls, and key them upwards.

3 Go to f04. The ball has started falling and so the antenna will continue to move upwards as it catches up with where the ball was a few frames earlier. Keep an eye on the squash and stretch for a cue. Key the antenna a bit more up.

f10

f15

5 Now at f10, the ball is traveling upwards again, but the antenna will still be moving down from the impact of the ball hitting the ground a couple frames earlier. Key the antenna bending downward.

6 Finish the scene by copying f01 to the last frame (f15) as you do with all cycles.

straightAhead_start.
ma
straightAhead_finish.
ma

HOT TIP

As we demonstrated in this example, straight ahead usually works best when there is a frame of reference to judge the movement by. In this case, we knew what the antenna should do because of where the ball was. Don't confuse animating straight ahead with animating blindly. That rarely turns out well, even for experienced animators. Always have a good plan for what you are going to animate beforehand!

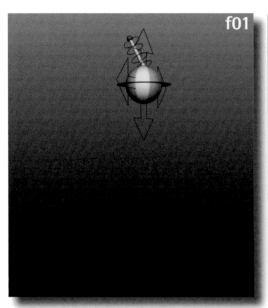
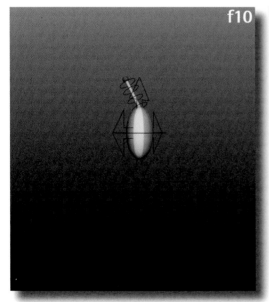
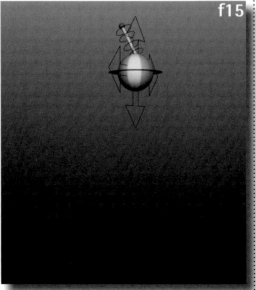

13

Pose to Pose (cont'd)

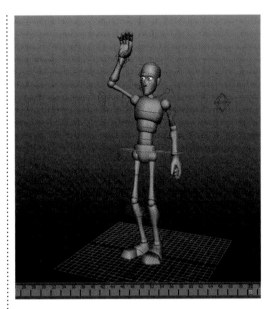

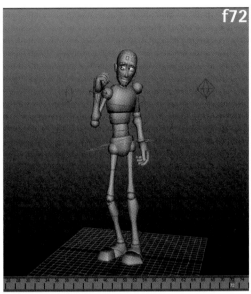
f72

7 Open pose_to_pose_start.ma. This character is waving to someone he thinks he recognizes, but then he realizes he doesn't know them! He retracts into an embarrassed pose, and looks away.

8 Let's create his embarrassed pose on f72 and then adjust the timing using the Dope Sheet. Select all of the controls in the body and hit **S** on f72. Pose Goon with his face and body exhibiting embarrassment.

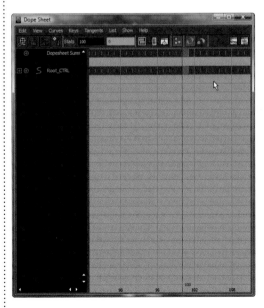

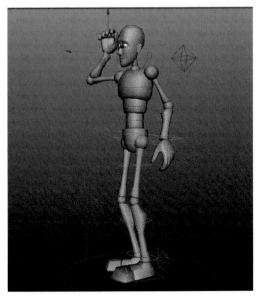

10 F72 is too soon for this final pose. Select the block on f72 in the Dope Sheet and MMB drag it to a later frame, whatever looks good to you! I chose 100 and I like how Goon slinks into this embarrassed pose.

11 Goon now needs a breakdown to define the arc of this movement and make it less linear. Rotate the camera to his profile. See how the arm comes very close to his face? It is common to need to add breakdowns when you retime animation created pose to pose.

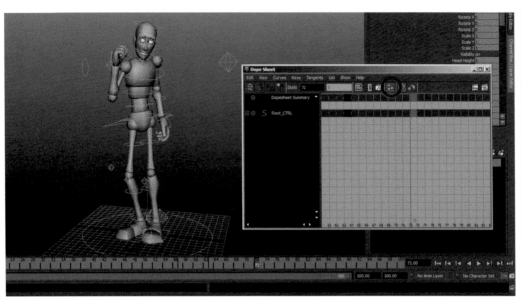

pose_to_pose_start.ma
pose_to_pose_finish.
ma

9 Open the Dope Sheet and find the Hierarchy/Below button and click it. Now if you choose Goon's root_CTRL in the panel you will notice all of the keyframes load into the Dope Sheet. The Dope Sheet is a good tool for broad retiming of a scene.

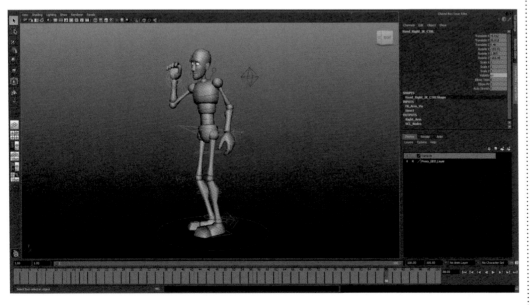

12 On f88, grab Goon's Root control and move it forward just a little. Also add a little bit of bend throughout the spine, and lastly move his hand forward so that it takes a nice arced path from the pose above his head to the pose near his face.

Overlapping Action/Follow-through

OVERLAP AND FOLLOW-THROUGH are the two most intuitive fundamentals in animation. Both basically deal with the principle that it takes energy to move objects and also to slow them down. Overlap is what we call it when an object "lags" behind the main action. Follow-through is what we call it when an action overshoots or goes past the end pose.

Overlap instills a fluidity to character animation. When added to your character's gestures, overlap makes the animation feel like the character has a natural limber quality to it. When a character swings his arm, the bending of the wrist creates a nice organic quality. Natural rise and fall in the spine in a walk cycle makes it feel calm, while an extreme amount of overlap in the spine in a walk can make the character look depressed and sad. In this way we can see overlap has a very major impact on the performance of a character.

With follow-through, the main thing you can show is a sense of weight with your character. The heavier the weight, the more energy it will take to stop the character. Use follow-through to emphasize this in your characters.

We've already had some practice with overlap in the last section, but let's get some more practice with a simple animation of Goon landing from a jump.

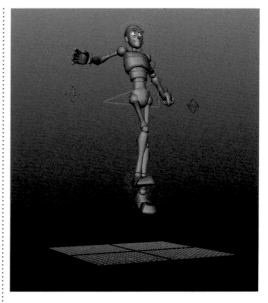

1 Open overlap_start.ma. Playing back the animation, you can see the Goon is landing on the ground from a jump. See, though, how his spine looks very stiff and unnatural. This scene needs some overlap and follow-through.

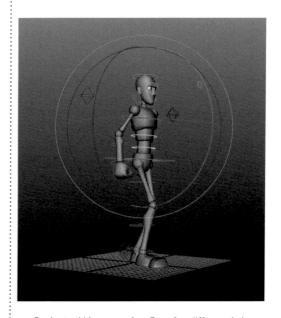

4 Don't stand him up too fast. Try a few different timings and sizes of pose at the end here as well. You'll notice that the weight of the character changes drastically with only a few frames of difference!

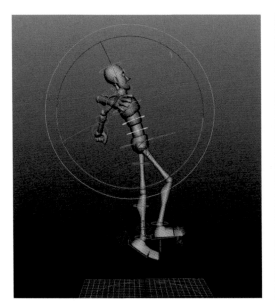

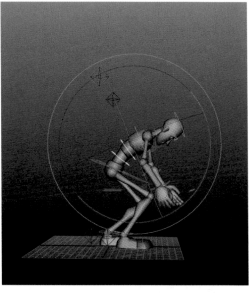

overlap_start.ma
overlap_finish.ma

2 Select the controls in Goon's spine and set a key on f01. Just like the antenna that you animated in the last section, we are going to have his spine "lag behind", or overlap as he falls. As Goon falls, set a key on the spine, having him straighten up a bit. I like this pose.

3 When he hits the ground, we need the action to follow through. This means bending Goon back over as he lands. Try a few different choices of pose and a few different timings as well.

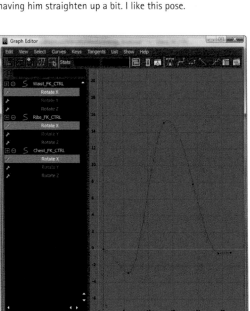

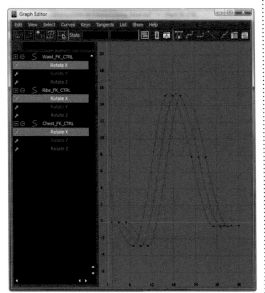

5 Let's also offset the overlap to get even more natural follow-through in this action. Select the controls of the spine, and open the Graph Editor. Isolate just the Rotate X channels; it should look like this.

6 Offset the ribs by moving them two frames forward, and offset the chest by moving them four frames forward. Now play the animation back, and you have even nicer, fluid overlap in the spine!

17

Slow In/Slow Out

S LOW IN AND SLOW OUT, also called ease in and ease out, refer to the spacing of the keys when an action comes to a stop, changes direction, or a character transitions from pose to pose. This principle means to animators that we typically decelerate objects as they come to a stop rather than have them come to a dead halt instantly ("slowing in" to the pose). It also means we should gradually accelerate objects as they begin to move and not have them instantly be at full speed ("slowing out" of a pose). In the Graph Editor of Maya, this principle is simply illustrated by flat tangents. It is easy to see how an object slows in to a change of direction in the Graph Editor when we look at the curves of a bouncing ball. As the ball arrives at the top of its arc, and also the flat tangent of the Y curve, it decelerates evenly before changing direction and accelerating again.

This is not a blanket rule, however! Not every action should slow in and slow out! In the bouncing ball animation, when the ball hits the ground there will be no slow in or slow out. Instead, we animate those tangents with a very sharp direction change as a result of the ball hitting the solid ground and having to change directions instantly. Consider also an animation of a character running. The feet are going to be really pounding the ground, meaning the legs are going to be still accelerating as the foot hits the ground. "Flatting" all of your tangents in the Graph Editor is a common mistake, as is having flat tangents be your default tangent type. True understanding of slow in and slow out means understanding which situations should have nice eased poses, and which ones should have stark direction changes. We are going to take advantage of Maya 2014's Editable Motion Trails to practice when to use slow in and slow out. Also check out the Splines chapter for more details on slow in and slow out.

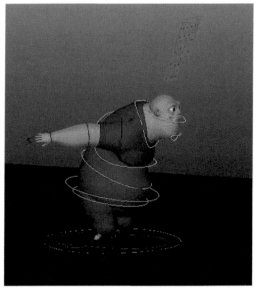

1 Open "slow_In_Start.mb". Groggy is doing a big jump across the scene.

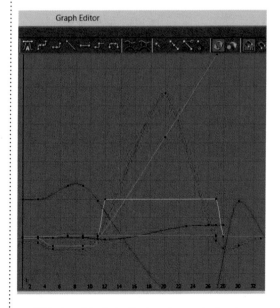

Graph Editor

4 With the pelvis_Ctrl still selected, open the Graph Editor by clicking Windows>Animation Editors>Graph Editor.

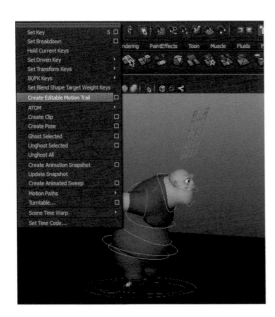

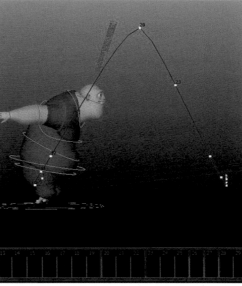

slow_In_Start.mb
slow_In_Finish.mb

2 If you play back the animation, you will see the motion in the air has a problem. Let's investigate. Hit F2 to switch to the Animation Menu set. Select Groggy's pelvis_ Ctrl and click on Animate>Create Editable Motion Trail.

3 Aha! There is the problem. The top of this jump should have a Slow In and Slow Out of the highest keyframe. Let's fix this using the Graph Editor.

HOT TIP

Rather than delete the Editable Motion Trail, just hide it for now. Select the Motion-Trail-Handle in the Outliner and press *ctrl* **H**. You never know if you will need it later.

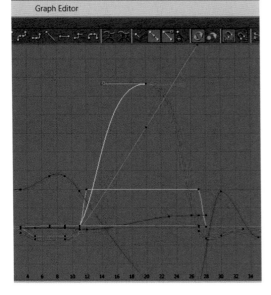

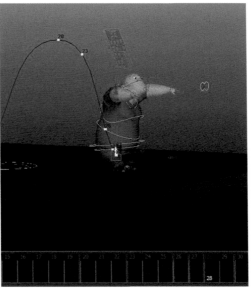

5 The TranslateY curve has an obvious peak in it. Click on the keyframe at the top of the TranslateY curve. The two tangent handles will appear. Select either one, press **W** and MMB drag it outwards to create a nice, smooth plateau at the top of the curve.

6 Check your results in the Persp panel, since the Editable Motion Trail will update in real time. Play it back and see that adding a Slow In to the top of the jump really improved the scene.

19

Arcs

EARLY ANIMATORS OBSERVED the interesting fact that most natural actions follow an arched path. They then practiced applying this trait to their animation to create more appealing movement. This came to be known as the principle of *arcs*. To avoid giving mechanical, robotic performances, check your animation constantly by tracking objects on screen and make sure they do not follow linear paths. Remember to check your arcs from all angles first, but finally and most importantly from your camera view; this is the view the audience will see!

Another very common mistake is to only track arcs on major body controls. As animators, we tend to bias our attention to the controls that give us the gross pose of a character: Root, Hand IK, Foot IK, and Head. All too often, beginning animators will then try to track the arcs of their animation, but because of all the attention and time spent using only four or five main controls, will only look to these areas for smoothing. This can lead to a visual discontinuity within the animation of the body. Instead, you have to look at the entire body, and determine the forces in the body. A fantastic resource for learning how to determine the force in a pose is the book *Force: Dynamic Life Drawing for Animators*, published by Focal Press. Investigate how the entire pose itself has rapidly changing, dynamic shapes, all of which need to move naturally and on arcs.

For our purposes, we are going to adjust the arcs on a full-body turn animation. Our character is looking towards screen left, when he suddenly turns and looks towards screen right. There is no breakdown key in the middle of the turn, meaning there is only a very drab, linear interpolation happening between the left and right poses. To fix this, we are going to add a breakdown and improve the arcs of the turn.

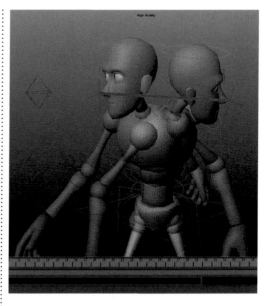

1 Yuck! This body turn is unnatural and mechanical. See how linearly the body and head turns from left to right? We are going to fix this immediately by adding a breakdown in the middle of the turn.

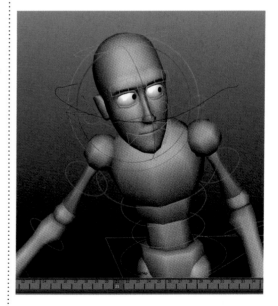

4 Don't forget the head usually leads the body in a turn! I like to have the head rotated slightly in the Z axis so that the chin is tilted on the head turn. This gives the head a little bit of natural motion.

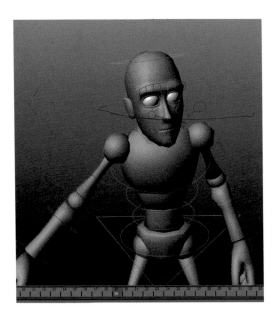

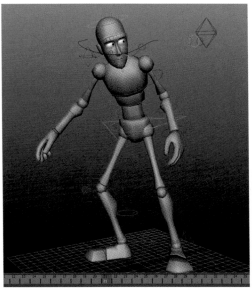

arcs_start.ma
arcs_finish.ma

2 Select the locator on the tip of Goon's nose named noseTrack_Loc. Then go to Animate > Create Editable Motion Trail. We will not be editing the motion trail in this scene, just using it for visual feedback. See how straight the head turn is?

3 Let's add the breakdown. Select the Center_Root_FK_ CTRL, Waist_FK_CTRL, Ribs_FK_CTRL, Chest_FK_CTRL, Neck_FK_CTRL, and Head_FK_CTRL. On f21, create a pose in which Goon is bending a little bit over, making the motion trail bend into an arc.

HOT TIP

If you want to be able to edit the arcs of your arms in panel, try re-animating this shot with IK arms enabled, and by adding an Editable Motion Trail to the controllers after blocking the animation. The visual feedback of motion trails has always been very useful, but now we can use them to actually improve the animation, all in camera!

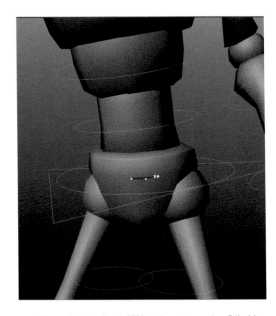

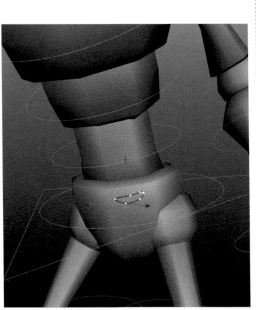

5 Now select the Root_CTRL and create another Editable Motion Trail. The body movement needs some arc smoothing as well!

6 On f21 and 28, create some breakdown keys by translating the Root_CTRL downwards and make a nice, arced motion. Motion trails are powerful tools, included in Maya 2014 and are directly editable in panel. Track the arcs throughout the rest of the body to get nice smooth motion.

Secondary Action

THIS PRINCIPLE REALLY GIVES a scene some deep subtext. Secondary action is any action that is not the primary action in a scene. A character sharpening a pencil as he complains about his boss would be secondary action; the primary action has to do with the poses and body language involved in speaking about the boss. A character running his hand through his hair as he turns away from the mirror, giving himself a wink, would be good secondary. The main action in this example is the turn, but the hand through the hair adds a nice level of meaning to the whole scene.

The wonderful thing about Secondary Action is that there really is no amount that is too much. Especially with humans; we're constantly multitasking, constantly occupying ourselves with more than one thing at a time. The animation can, of course, become too busy. The fact is there is a balance, but for the most part your scenes can always use an extra level of animation and therefore subtext.

The way master animators truly utilize secondary action is by "coloring" the action to suit the subtext of a scene. This means changing the secondary action in pose, timing, spacing, etc. to distinguish it from a normal, "vanilla" performance of the same action. Let's look at an example. Let's imagine a scene where a mother is ironing clothes while looking out a window. Her husband walks into the room and tells her that their son has been killed in war. She is facing away from him, and still continues to iron. But her body language changes. Her hands start shaking. She looks like she's about to faint as her eyes well up with tears. The adjustments to the action of ironing clothes (the secondary action in this scene) is what we call coloring the action. Now imagine the same set up, with the wife looking out the window and the husband entering the room. This time, he enters and simply asks her how her day was, but this time, she found out that morning that she is pregnant. She answers him "Fine," and smiles. How would you "color" the secondary action in this scene? When she hears the husband enter the room, would she excitedly speed up her action? Maybe she got some baby clothes out of a box and that's why she's ironing. She'd then pause and look at the clothes as she describes her day to her husband. Suddenly, through secondary action, animators have access to an enormous amount of subtlety in a scene. I like to call Secondary Action the "Window to Subtext".

We are going to do a simple trick with Animation Layers to practice using secondary action to show subtlety in a scene. In our scene, Goon is sitting at the library, tapping his finger, very bored. Then someone who he really likes walks by, and his eyes follow them. By animating the weight of the animation layer with the finger on it, we are going to "color" that action; basically, he forgets to tap his finger while he is captivated by this person walking by. Secondary action can be so subtle, that sometimes just STOPPING a secondary action is enough to completely color it!

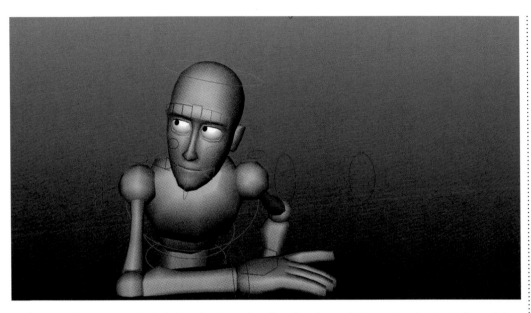

secondary_start.ma
secondary_finish.ma

1 Open secondary_start.ma. Playback the animation, and you'll see Goon is completely bored and tapping his finger at the desk. Then a person who he likes walks by and he is captivated.

HOT TIP

Check out Chapter 12 for an in-depth look at Animation Layers and how to use them.

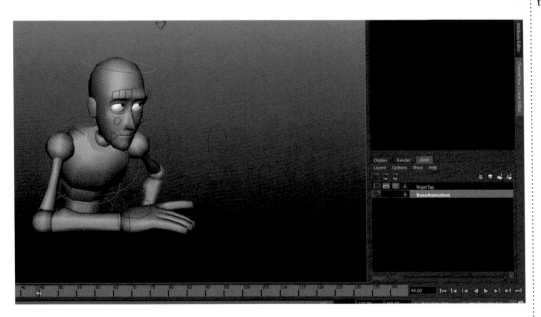

2 In the bottom half of the Channel Box your Layers tabs are all visible. When you select the layer tab labeled "Anim", you'll see that there is a "BaseAnimation" (with the entire body pose animated inside) and a "fingerTap" layer.

Secondary Action (cont'd)

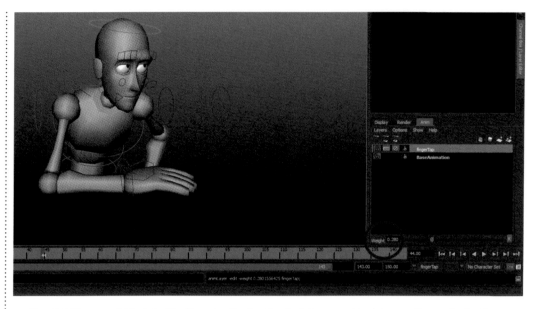

3 Maya 2014 has powerful tools for blending animation together. In fact, you can blend dozens of layers of animation together if you please; the only limit is what you can keep track of. Slide the Weight slider up and down and see how the finger tapping is affected.

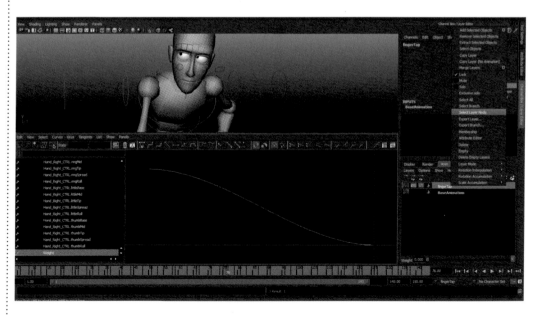

5 Advance 10-20 frames in the animation and slide the weight of the fingerTap anim layer down to 0. Goon is now so transfixed on this person that he's completely dropped his secondary action, a very powerful way of "coloring" it! To see your weight curve in the Graph Editor, right click on the anim layer and click on "Select Layer Node".

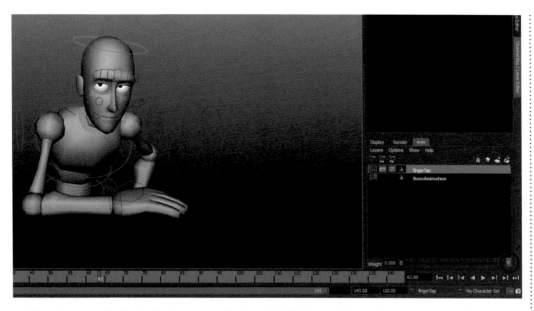

4 Not only can you blend animation, but you can key the weight! Find a good frame when you are sure that Goon has recognized the person walking by. Set a key on the weight of anim layer "fingerTap" by hitting the **K** (set key) button next to the weight slider.

HOT TIP

If you are unsure about a secondary action, sometimes it can be better to key the main action on the master animation layer, and only when it is looking solid, key the secondary action on a new anim layer. You can always turn off the layer if the secondary doesn't work out, without fear of destroying your main action.

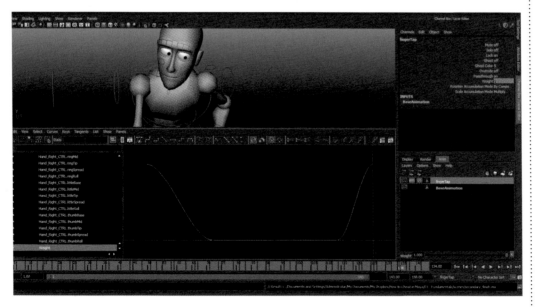

6 Experiment! Play around with the secondary action and see if you can tell different stories by animating the weight of the layer around. Maybe bring it back to 1 at the end of the scene and observe the resulting change in the subtext of the scene!

Timing

TIMING IS LESS A FUNDAMENTAL than it is the very foundation of the art of animation. Animation is, of course, just a series of still images that flash by fast enough to create the illusion of motion. Our task is to use timing not just to accurately portray motion in realistic scenes, but also as a method to convey meaning in a scene.

In character animation, the main goal is to get your audience to emote with a character. As they succeed, the audience celebrates; when they fail, the audience feels their loss. As animators we can get so caught up in the physics and mechanics of the motions that we create that sometimes we forget that the timing of a scene can be improved to tell a deeper story. The pauses in between actions can have more powerful messages than the actions themselves.

In the last section, we adjusted the secondary action of the character to show that he is so captivated in that moment that his hand just naturally stops moving. It has a subtle, but powerful effect on the performance of the character. Although a full animation curriculum on timing is outside the purview of this book, we can definitely experiment with this scene to give ourselves some insight into the powerful effect subtle timing changes can have on a performance. We'll use the keyframe editing tools in the timeline and Graph Editor to make these adjustments.

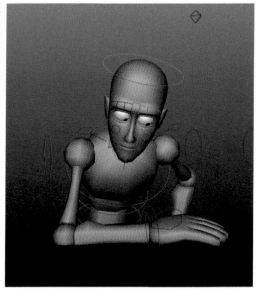

1 Open timing_start.ma. The timeline of our secondary action exercise has been extended on the end to allow us to make some adjustments here. Pay particularly close attention to the performance at the end, where Goon looks back towards the desk.

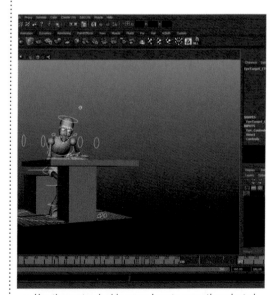

4 Use the center double arrow icon to move the selected keys forward 30 or so frames. We aren't going to choose a specific timing, because we want to observe the subtle differences that timing change. What does this new timing tell you? To me, the longer he pauses in this in-between pose, the more it looks like he's THINKING about what he saw.

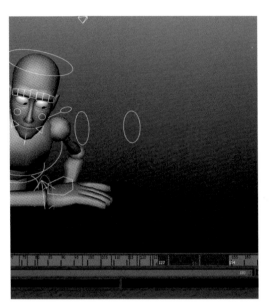

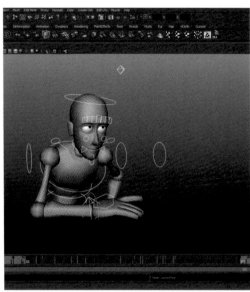

timing_start.ma
timing_finish.ma

Novice animators often struggle with the difference between timing and spacing. While they are connected to each other, they're NOT the same. A movement over 10 frames can look completely different depending on how you change the spacing, even though the actual time in which it moves (10 frames) stays consistent.

2 Let's extend the time that Goon spends looking towards the desk halfway between his gaze towards screen left and the final pose back towards screen right. Select all of Goon's controls. Don't forget to select Goon's eyeTarget_CTRL too. Position the cursor over f127 on the timeline, then *Shift* LMB and drag the cursor all the way past f150.

3 This red box is your selection on the timeline. The left and right arrows scale your keys in either direction. The middle double arrow icon moves the selection through the timeline. Drag each one of the arrows around and get familiar with their use, then Undo so that you are back to the original timing.

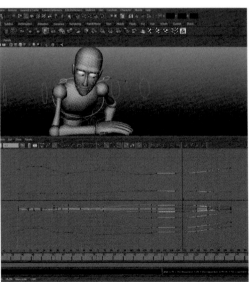

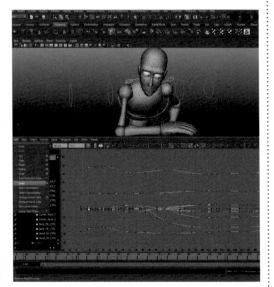

5 Let's play with the end too. Experimenting is fun! Select all of Goon's controls again and open the Graph Editor. Select the last two poses by dragging a selection box around all of the keys. Now scale the last two poses' keys by hitting *R* and then *Shift* MMB Drag to the right with the cursor placed near f150. Release the mouse button when the last key is near f180.

6 Play the animation and it not only looks like he's thinking more, this slower transition to the end pose feels like he's a little melancholy. However, whenever you scale keys in the Graph Editor, your keys usually end up placed in between frames. Select all of the keys in the Graph Editor and click on Edit>Snap. Now the keys are back on integer frames.

27

Exaggeration

EXAGGERATION IS ONE OF THE SIMPLEST, yet most misunderstood principles of animation. Why? For decades novice animators have tried to blindly exaggerate their animation to try to recreate the amazing cartoony styles of the animators of yore. However, exaggeration doesn't necessarily mean better animation, or even more cartoony. Exaggeration must be used with a keen eye for the effect you are trying to achieve.

Find the core idea in your scene and figure out the best way to exaggerate the message. If you are animating a character getting pricked on the butt with a pin, then you are going to exaggerate the timing and spacing of him shooting into the air. If you are animating a character that gets scared by a spider, you might exaggerate the squash and stretch in his body by having his legs run away from his torso, stretching out his spine! In both of these cases, we choose the main idea and exaggerate only where we need to in order to strengthen the message. Both scenes would look way over-complicated if we had exaggerated the posing, timing, spacing, composition, weight, anticipation, etc.

Your animation scenes in Maya should be as lean as possible. To illustrate how easy it can be to exaggerate a fundamental, we're going to take a finished walk cycle and adjust the overlap in the spine using the Graph Editor. Your workflow must create animation that has minimal keys, therefore making it easy to change the animation later on. For our purposes, the overlap in the spine on a walk cycle is a great fundamental to experiment with, because it has such a large impact on the performance.

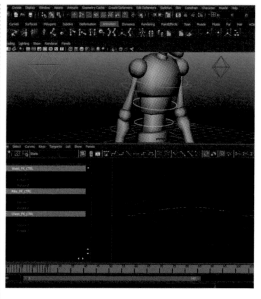

1 Open exaggeration_start.ma. Goon is walking a straight-ahead, "vanilla" walk with little performance to it. Select the controls in the spine and open the Graph Editor.

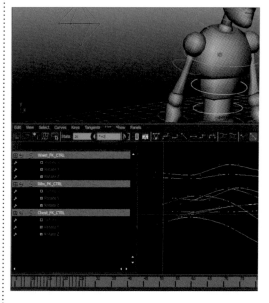

4 You can also perform the scale by using some of the math functionality in Maya. Select the controls in the spine and then in the Graph Editor value box (the right box of the two) type in "*-2". The ✱ symbol means to multiply the values and the "=2" tells Maya how much to multiply by.

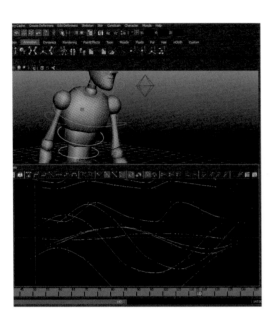

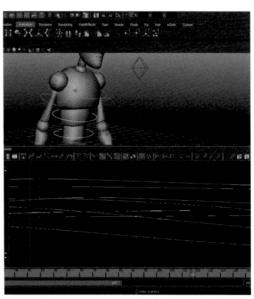

exaggeration_start.ma
exaggeration_finish.
ma

HOT TIP

To make
reselecting the
same channels
easier, select a
channel (Rotate
X for example)
and in the
Graph Editor,
go to the menu
and click Show
> Show Selected
Type(s). You'll
see that only
the selected
channel shows
on the left side
of the Graph
Editor now for
all selected
objects. This is
a good cheat
to use when
adjusting
a single
fundamental
like we did
on the spine.
Restore the
other channels
by clicking Show
> Show All. The
Graph Editor is
covered in depth
in Chapter 3.

2 As you can see, as of right now these curves are not exaggerated at all. Hit **R** to use the Scale Tool in the Graph Editor. Now select the curves in the spine and MMB drag up and down to scale these keys. Notice that the point on the graph where your mouse starts the dragging motion is considered the center of the scale.

3 Scaling keys up and down in the Graph Editor scales their values, whereas scaling left and right scales timing. Without the rest of the body's controls selected, scaling the timing of the spine won't produce good results.

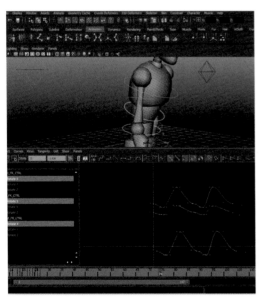

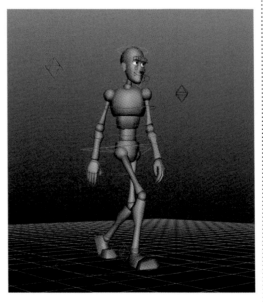

5 Playing back the animation now shows more exaggeration in his spine, but it needs some tweaking. Select just the Rotate X curves in the Graph Editor and then hit **W** to use the move tool. MMB drag them upwards to get the spine to overlap more forward over his center of gravity.

6 Experiment! The best thing you can do to grow your list of cheats is to find some more on your own. Use the Graph Editor to exaggerate other aspects of the walk, like the arms, or the Translate Y in the Center_Root_FK_CTRL to get some more extreme up and down motion as Goon steps.

29

Solid Drawing

A T FIRST GLANCE, *solid drawing* has little to do with CG animation in Maya. What does drawing have to do with animating on the computer? On the contrary, this is an extremely important fundamental to remember when creating animation on the computer. Why? As CG animators, it is very easy to relax our artistic sensibilities and let Maya do all of the work. However, the moment you forget the art of pose, perspective, form, volume, and force, you will quickly see your animation dissolve into unappealing mush. Solid drawing is a fundamental that persists from the hand-drawn days of cel animation. What it basically imparts is a dedication to the figure-drawing principles that the master animators all adhered to. When you started your drawing, you always had to begin with the same simple construction of the character: simple shapes combined with clean, meaningful lines, taking into consideration the line of action, the force of the pose, and the weight of the character. Perhaps most of all, perspective and a sense of the character's volume had to be extremely consistent. In other words, all 24 drawings per second of animation had to look like the same character.

In CG, we have a lot of help from Maya to achieve solid drawing, but we should pay close attention to make sure we aren't being lazy. Since we are working with 3D models, for the most part Maya takes care of staying "on model". Even still, you have to be careful not to pose your character in such a way that the body or face is distorted so much that it doesn't look like the same character. Most of the time this happens when an animator hasn't thoroughly tested the rig, and is using controls to create movement that were not intended for that purpose. In CG we can indeed go off model, and it is your job to avoid this.

We are going to fix a piece of animation that has some very bad counter-animated controls, and is also experiencing some skin-weight issues. Speaking strictly as an animator, you don't have to be as concerned with technical issues, but remember that CG animation is often a team effort, and solid drawing is the result of everyone working together.

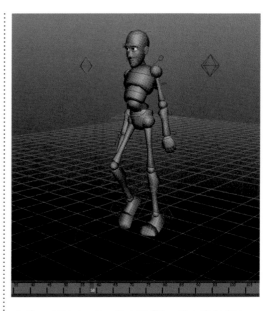

1 Open solid_drawing_start.ma. This walk cycle looks a little off. The spine controls have been animated against each other. As a general guide, body sections that work together should move in harmony with each other. Going against the natural design of how something moves, even if intentional, can create off-model looking poses.

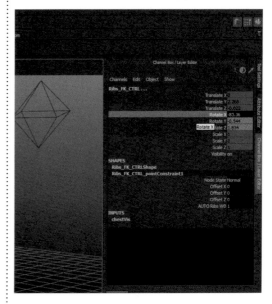

4 Delete the Rotate X curves. Notice that there are still values in Rotate X when you switch to the Channel Box. This is because Maya leaves a channel's value at the current frame whenever you delete ALL animation on a channel. Select the Rotate X channel and type in **0** and hit **Enter**.

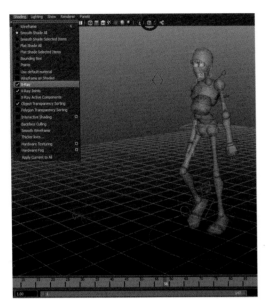

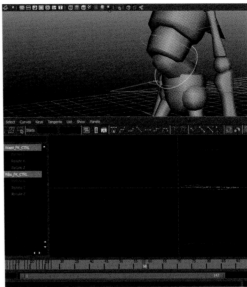

2 A good way to see your controls is to use the X-Ray rendering in panel, either in the Shading menu or with the X-Ray button. This mode makes all of the geometry semi-transparent so you can see joints, edges, and curves very easily.

3 Select "Waist_FK_CTRL" and "Ribs_FK_CTRL" and open up the Graph Editor. As you can see, they have been posed in such a way that they are rotated against each other.

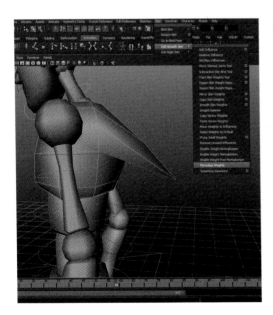

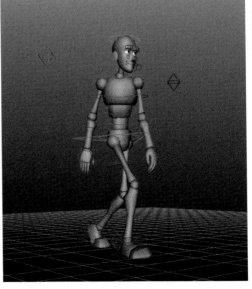

5 Now that the controls have been zeroed and the counter-animation removed, Goon is still leaving some vertices behind as he walks away. Select his chest geometry and switch to the Animation menu set. Click on Skin > Edit Smooth Skin > Normalize Weights.

6 Now the model should be behaving! Don't worry what that did, as it's a rigging issue that most animators won't have to deal with. The point is, with CG animation, artistic choices, like posing, and some technical choices, like skin weights, can have an impact on solid drawing.

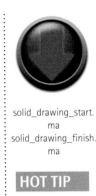

solid_drawing_start.
ma
solid_drawing_finish.
ma

HOT TIP

Instead of deleting the curves themselves in the Graph Editor, we can delete animation from a channel by right clicking on that channel in the Channel Box, and clicking "Delete Selected". This will delete the animation on the channel, not the channel or attribute itself. Remember, the channel's value will remain at the current frame value whenever you delete all animation.

31

Appeal

I T COULD BE SAID that all of the fundamentals combine to make *appeal*. Beautiful, organic timing is appealing to the eye. Interesting, dynamic posing is also appealing. Character designs, contrasting shapes, and rhythm are all fine tuned, worked, and re-worked to get the most appeal. Does appeal mean "good"? Not at all; the evil villains in our most beloved animations all have appeal. From their striking silhouettes to vibrant colors, even the bad guys must be appealing. Appeal is the pinnacle of our task as animators, it is the goal. Above all else we should strive to always put images in front of our audiences that are worthy of their time.

Let's focus on posing for our discussion of appeal. As animators our work takes place far after the characters have been designed, modeled, textured, and rigged. But even with appealing characters, bad posing can ruin the entire show. For instance, an arm pointed directly at camera loses all of its good posing from foreshortening; the animation must work well with the chosen composition. Take the camera into consideration and be sure that your staging is well thought out. The silhouette of your pose should be strong, without limbs lost within the silhouette of the body. And "maxed-out", or hyperextended arms and legs never look very good.

Twinning is another major issue in posing. In nature, nothing is ever perfectly symmetrical. Without being careful to avoid twinning, it sneaks its way into our animation. It saves time, for instance, to set channels on both sides of a character at the same time. If this is a cheat you use, then you must remember to go back through the scene and un-twin your poses. Arms, legs, hands, even facial poses can fall victim to twinning.

We must be mindful of the appeal of our animation by constantly critiquing our work and showing it to others.

To practice, we are going to take a look at a customizable character called Morpheus, and try to build an appealing variation using his controls.

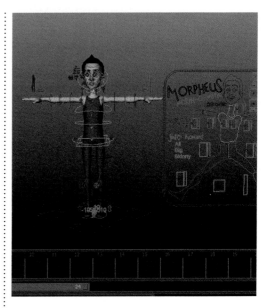

1 Open "appeal_Start.ma". Morpheus is a free downloadable rig, and he comes with controls to change his body and head shape. We're going to practice appeal by making an appealing variation on him.

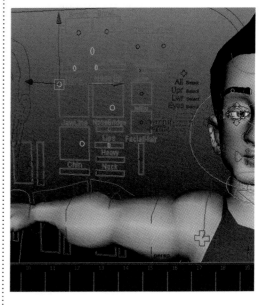

4 Use the facial deforms to give him a large chin and cheek bones.

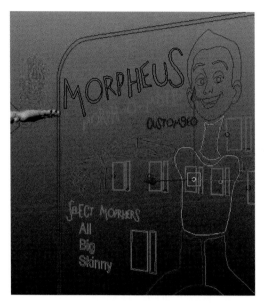

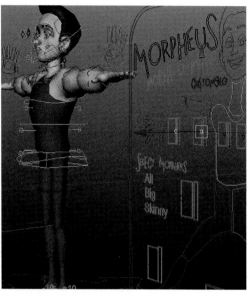

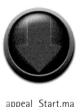

appeal_Start.ma
appeal_Finish.ma

2 Let's make Morpheus look like a superhero, with appealing superhero features; big chin, broad chest, and skinny waist. Start with the torso deforms (located in the middle of the chest in the controller object).

3 Select the arm deform controls as well, and move them to the right to dial them up.

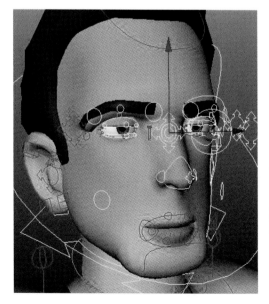

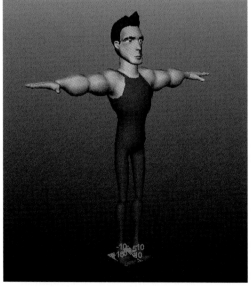

5 When you are done using the face deforms, adjust the actual controls and positioners on the face itself. Moving them around changes the position of the facial parts.

6 Check out our cool character. I like his wide-set eyes and how his arms are super buff but his legs are skinny. Play around with the customization options for this character and come up with your own appealing variations.

What Is "Workflow"?

by Kenny Roy

IT WAS YEARS into my teaching career, with hundreds of classes and thousands of hours of animation critiques under my belt, before a student suddenly asked me, "You keep on saying the word 'Workflow', but what does it mean?" I was stunned, because after all of my harping on the subject, it never occurred to me that the very concept of "Workflow" itself might be unclear to beginner animators.

Simply put, a workflow is the *step-by-step* process you employ to create a shot from start to finish. It adapts to the project, it grows and changes slowly over time, but on a shot-to-shot basis your workflow always stays the same.

This may sound like a no-brainer, but the reality is most new animators pay little to no attention to the actual *process* as they learn. Instead, they animate "by the seat of their pants", and judge the unpredictable results on screen for indication of improvement. Let's take a related example in another area of art to illustrate this point.

Back in school, I had a figure painting teacher who was very strict. His name was Yu Ji. In his class, students were subjected to a constant barrage of commands regarding how and when to do each step of a painting. First, you wipe the canvas with some highly thinned burnt umber or raw umber paint until the entire canvas is a nice, fleshy brown. Then do a quick sketch in pencil to define the form. Immediately go over that with a thin brush with umber paint, completely filling in all of the shadow areas. THEN, and ONLY THEN, do you start mixing paint to try to match the colors you see. And even when it came to finally painting with color, Yu Ji sounded like a broken record as he walked through the class to correct the color choices of his students. "Is the color warmer or cooler than the color next to it?" "Is it lighter or darker?" "What is the color tendency?" (Within warm colors, was it more red, or yellow, e.g.) These same three questions were repeated at least a hundred times over the course of a three-hour class.

It would be years before I realized that what Yu Ji was doing was teaching us good workflow, above all else. Everything we were forced to do helped us avoid the major struggles that befall young painters. Most importantly, these were tried-and-true methods that produced better results. For instance, making the entire canvas brown made it so that we did not mix our colors too light just because they were competing with a blinding white canvas. Filling in shadow areas early on and foregoing minor details made the students focus on the large shapes in the form. Finally, his three questions made it so that we were mixing our colors based on the color *relationships* that we saw, barring preconceived notions from influencing our color choices. When I think back on it now, I cherish the amazing workflow that Yu Ji gifted his class, and I feel bad for thinking he was so strict!

Back to animation.

In animation, students typically start with a workflow that roughly resembles the order in which they learned the fundamentals. Pose the character with some rough timing and spacing, add some squash and stretch here, some anticipation and follow-through there. This is a messy way to work, and until you learn how to really let the fundamentals work in concert, your animation will lack the fluidity and beauty that the legends are capable of. There are just as many pitfalls awaiting novice animators as figure painters. In Yu Ji's class, we were forced to make our canvas brown so as to not wrongly exaggerate the colors; perhaps the first step in your workflow should be to thumbnail some REALLY pushed poses and try to hit them with the model. You would be doing this because you know that as you move forward with the shot and get into polish, many of the pose choices will become watered down to accommodate timing, spacing, and compositional constraints. Yu Ji made us fill in all of the shadow areas with brown before adding any details. Sounds a bit like getting body movement looking really good before adding facial animation, doesn't it? And finally, those three questions we asked ourselves reminded us to constantly critique our choices within the painting, and with the live model. Before you move into your polishing phase, it would be a good idea to establish a workflow step in which you look at the animation one more time and ask yourself some questions. "Are my poses as dynamic as I originally planned?" "Is there still contrast in the animation in pose, timing, and composition?" "Does this resemble the reference and observation I've gathered?"

Your questions might be different, but the main point is, both in figure painting and animation workflow, that you *do it every time*. Instead of leaping at a shot with no plan in mind, just begin at step 1 of your workflow. Stop animating feverishly for huge lengths of time only to step back and realize the shot has not progressed at all.

If at any time in the middle of animating a shot you catch yourself asking the question "OK, now what's my next step?" you know you've crossed into the world of workflow. Welcome! You are on your way to becoming a great animator.

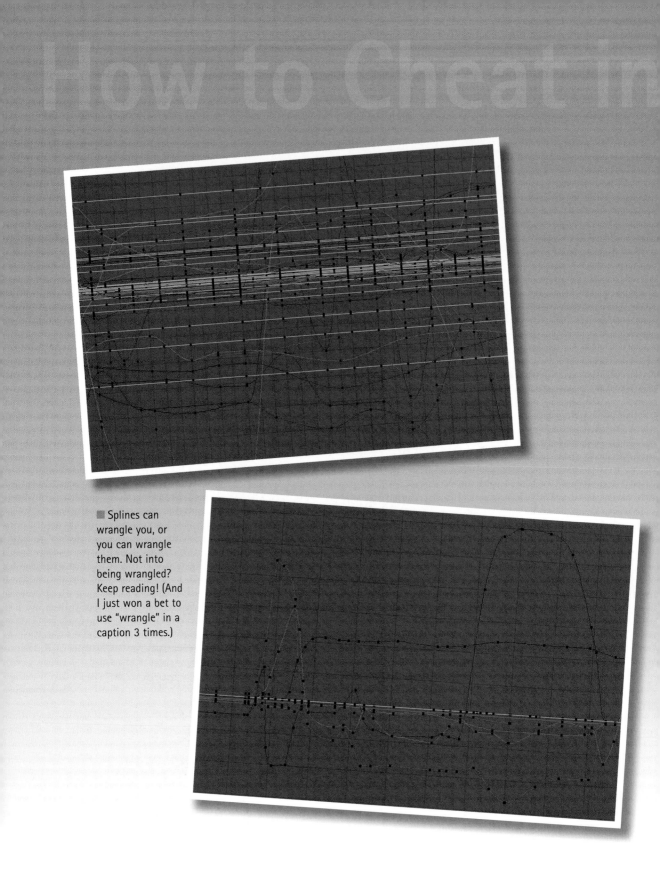

Splines can wrangle you, or you can wrangle them. Not into being wrangled? Keep reading! (And I just won a bet to use "wrangle" in a caption 3 times.)

2
Splines

SPLINE CURVES, or just "splines" (or even just "curves"), are the lifeblood of computer animation. They're a surprisingly efficient and comprehensive method of representing motion. Much of your time animating will be spent perusing these little red, blue, and green intertwined curves, so it makes sense to get comfortable with them. This chapter is all about facilitating your comfort.

Opening the Graph Editor to what looks like a spaghetti dinner gone bad can be intimidating, but we'll make understanding splines a quick study. We'll go through the simple concepts that make reading them easy and powerful. Then we'll try out some cheats on editing splines that will have you wrangling them under control in no time. Get ready to meet your new best friends in animation!

How Splines Work

UNDERSTANDING HOW SPLINES display their information is the key to making them work for you. Some beginner animators are intimidated when they see all those intertwined curves, but the concepts behind them are really quite straightforward. It takes a little practice to make it second nature, but only a few moments to really grasp the concepts we'll go over in this cheat. In no time, you will find that they are a surprisingly elegant way of working with your animation, and understanding them thoroughly will quickly create a noticeable improvement in your work. The main idea with splines is that they represent changes in value over time. As the curve travels to the right, frames are ticking by. As the curve raises and lowers, it's an increase (traveling up) or decrease (traveling down) in the value of the attribute. If the curve changes direction, as it does at the middle key in the following diagram, the object it represents will change direction. The thing to remember, and where it's easy to get confused, is that up and down do not

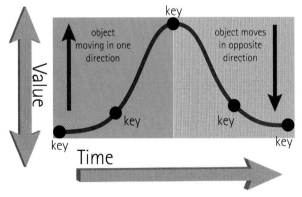

necessarily correspond to up and down for what you are seeing in the viewport. That may seem counterintuitive at first, but it has to do with how the character rig is set up and there are many possible scenarios with that. For some attributes, like Translate Y, the curve will actually look like what the body part is doing, but most don't. The thing to take from this cheat is that up and down are simply changes in value, not a direct visual correlation to what you see in the viewport.

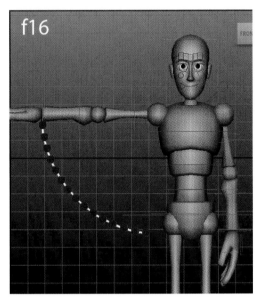

1 Open HowSplinesWork.ma. From f01-f16 the character is raising his arm. Take note of how even the movement is. Every frame, the arm moves the same amount.

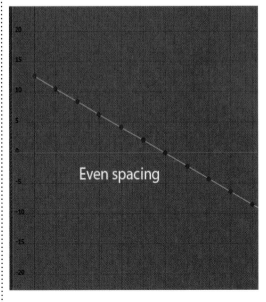

3 If I plot each frame along the curve, we see that they are all equidistant, just like the spacing tracked in the viewport. (Some curve colors in this chapter were changed in Photoshop for better clarity on the page.)

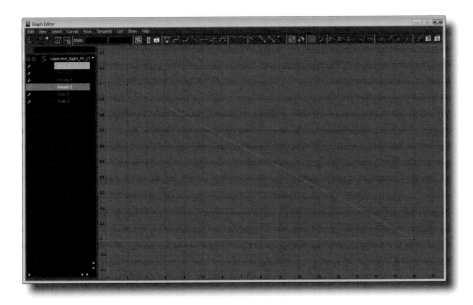

2 Open the Graph Editor and look at the upper arm's Rotate Z curve. Notice that it's a perfectly straight line. This corresponds to the even spacing of the motion we see in the viewport.

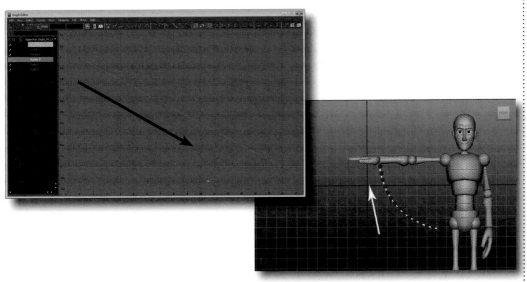

HowSplinesWork.
ma

4 Also notice that the curve is traveling downward while his arm is raising. Remember that we said the up/down in curve direction is simply a change in value, not a direct representation of the viewport.

How Splines Work (cont'd)

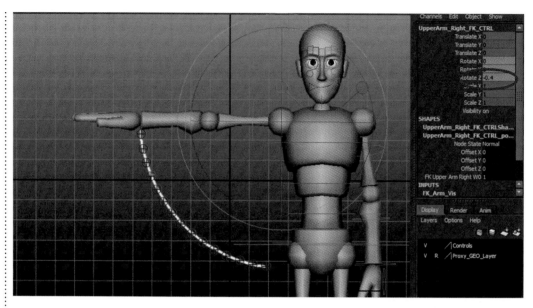

5 Select the upper arm control and rotate it in Z while watching the channel box value. Notice that rotating the arm up makes Rotate Z increase in negative value. This has to do with how this particular character was rigged and is why the curve travels down, since down is an increase in negative value in this case.

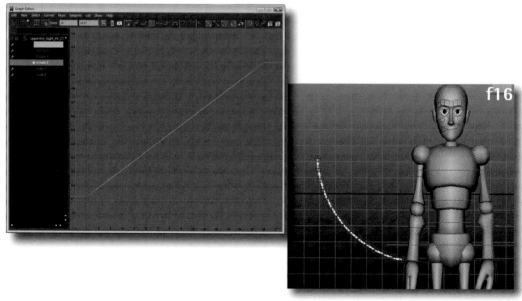

8 Continue making adjustments to the keys in the curve and watching the animation until you're comfortable with the concepts. Here I switched the positions of the keys and now he does the opposite motion.

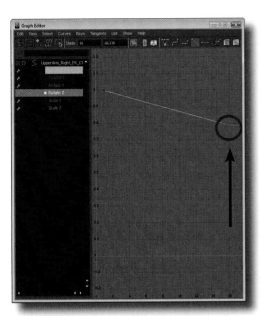

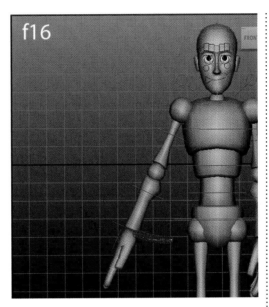

f16

6 In the Graph Editor, select the key at f16. Use the move tool **W** and **Shift** MMB drag it up. **Shift**-dragging with the move tool will constrain movement to either horizontal or vertical motion, whichever you do first.

7 Since the curve travels downward a much shorter distance, therefore increasing negative value only a little, his arm now moves up only a short distance. Tracking the motion shows us how much tighter the spacing is.

HOT TIP

Every character can be rigged differently. While rotating this one's arm up in Z increases the negative value of the attribute, another could increase the positive. That's why it's important to get a grasp on up/down simply representing value, not direction.

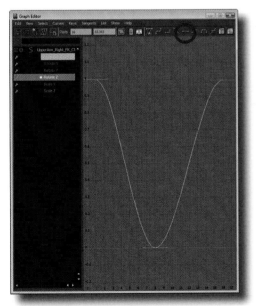

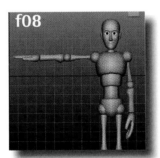

f08

f16

9 Hold **I** and MMB click the curve at f08 to insert a key. Select the entire curve and press the flat tangents button. Then use the move tool to MMB drag f08's key down and f16's up to look like above.

10 From f01-f08 the arm travels up. When the curve changes direction, the arm travels back down.

41

Splines and Spacing

L ET'S TAKE A MORE IN-DEPTH look at how changes in our
spline curves affect the spacing of a motion. If the curve's
direction over a given range of frames is mainly horizontal,
the value is not changing much. Therefore the attribute will be
moving very little in the viewport.

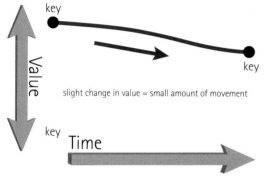

slight change in value = small amount of movement

If the direction over the frame range is predominantly
vertical, a larger change in value is happening and the
movement will be large.

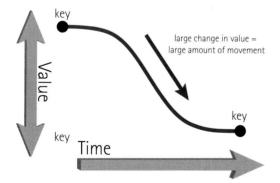

large change in value =
large amount of movement

Finally, if the curve is perfectly horizontal for a frame
range, that curve's attribute will hold perfectly still, as there is
no change in value. We'll try some things in this cheat that will
make these ideas perfectly clear.

Throughout this cheat, we'll make some pretty stark
changes in the speed of the movement while never changing the
number of frames (timing) it happens over. Timing and spacing
are intertwined, but problems in spacing tend to be less forgiving
than the number of frames you're using.

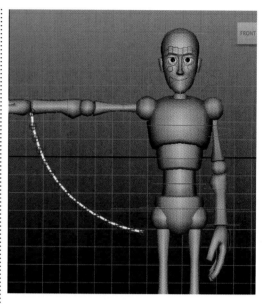

1 Open TimingSpacing.ma. We'll start with the upper arm
moving up with linear, even spacing. Open the Graph
Editor and select the R upper arm's Rotate Z curve.

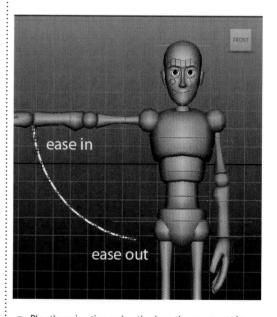

ease in

ease out

3 Play the animation and notice how the movement is
much smoother. There is an ease-out when the arm
starts moving, and an ease-in to where it stops.

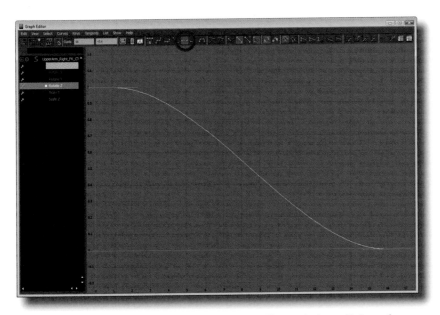

2 Select the entire curve and press the flat tangents button. The curve's shape will change from a straight line to a smooth "S" shape.

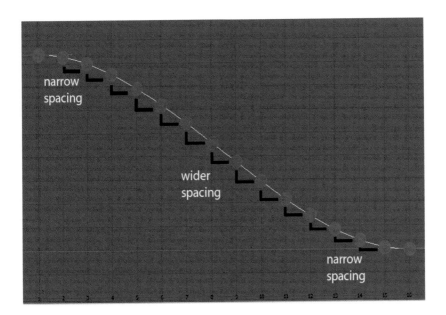

narrow
spacing

wider
spacing

narrow
spacing

4 Plotting the spacing on the Rotate Z curve shows how the curve's spacing corresponds to what we see in the viewport. The arm moves shorter distances in the beginning and end, and wider in the middle.

TimingSpacing.ma

HOT TIP

To track the spacing of a movement, many animators use dry erase markers right on their monitor. If your monitor is an LCD, put clear plastic over it to protect the screen, and press very gently. CRT monitors should be fine as is since they have glass screens.

43

Splines and Spacing (cont'd)

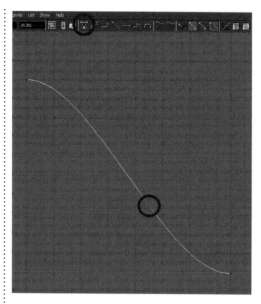

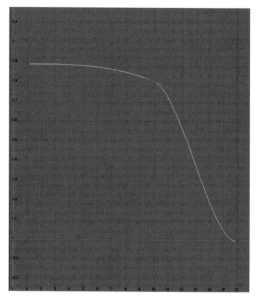

5 Go to f10 and set a key on the R upper arm. Select the key you just set in the Graph Editor and click the auto tangent button if the curve is not smooth. This will keep that key's tangents smooth no matter where you move it.

6 Use the move tool **W** and **Shift** MMB drag the key up so it's a little under the value of the first key.

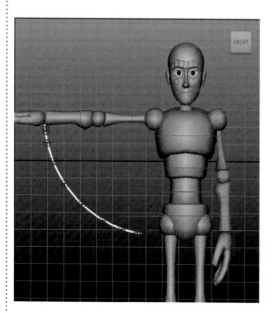

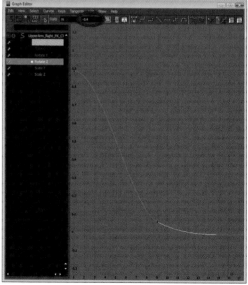

9 Now the opposite happens, where the arm moves quickly at the beginning, and eases in to the end pose more gradually.

10 Select the last key at f16 and look at the value field. In my case it's -0.4.

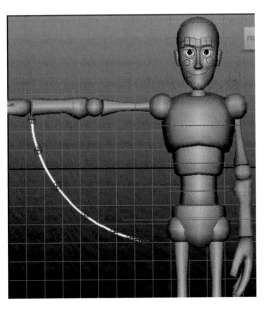

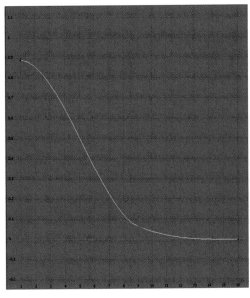

7 Play the animation and notice how much we've affected it. The arm moves very little during the first 10 frames since the spacing is so close. The value changes very little until f11, where the wide change makes it move quickly.

8 Edit the key at f10 so it's close to the value of the end key.

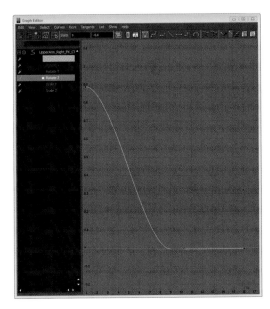

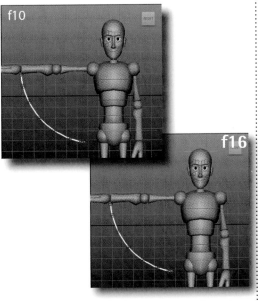

11 Select the key at f10 and enter the value of f16's key into the field to make it the same. Since we set this key to AutoTangent, it will automatically become flat. This will ensure that the curve holds at the same value through those frames.

12 Now the arm travels with an ease-out and ease-in from f01-f10, but holds still until f16. Since there is no change in the up or down of the curve while the frames tick by, the arm holds still.

Tangent Types

T ANGENTS AND THE STYLES AVAILABLE in Maya are the other side of understanding splines. If you've used graphics programs like Illustrator, tangents will be familiar to you. They're the handles that exist around a keyframe and are used to adjust the curve's angle and direction before and after the key. As we've just seen in the previous cheats, the curve's slopes have a profound effect on the animation's spacing, so having a solid grasp on how tangents work is invaluable.

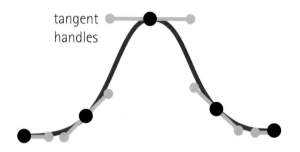

tangent handles

Maya has several different tangent types, which are really just preset angles for the handles (albeit useful ones). The handles are completely customizable, and Maya's tangent types are mostly a starting point. Using only the "out of the box" tangent types tends to make the motion look very "CG" and uninteresting. However, knowing which ones will bring you most of the way to your desired result will go a long way towards speeding up your workflow.

Here we'll take a look at Maya's tangent types and what sort of situations they're best for. The icon with the "A" over it is the AutoTangent function, which is a great time saver. This isn't a tangent type per se, it's a setting that will adjust your keys' tangents automatically depending on their location. Keys at the extremes (wherever a change in curve direction happens) will be flat, while transitional keys (keys where the curve is the same direction on both sides) will be smooth. As you edit the keys, the tangents will automatically orient to whatever situation they're in. Awesome!

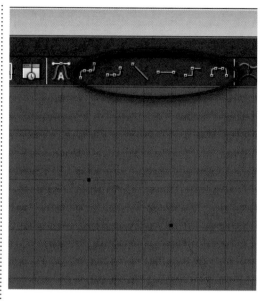

1 The tangent type icons are along the top of the Graph Editor. Simply select any or all keys and click whichever type you need. The first icon (with the "A") will enable the AutoTangent functionality for the selected keys and/or curves.

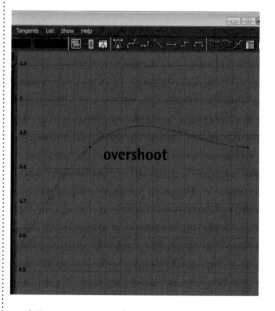

overshoot

4 Spline tangents will make a smooth transition between keys and don't flatten out. They're great for keys that are transitional (going the same direction each side of the key), but with extremes (keys at which the curve changes direction) they can overshoot, which is difficult to control.

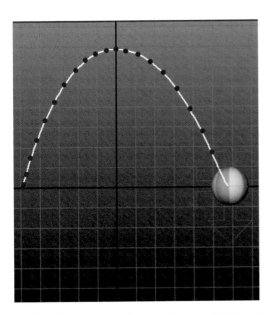

2 Open TangentTypes.ma. In the front view we have a very basic animation of a ball going in an arc.

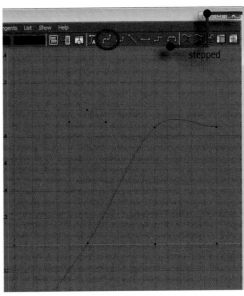

stepped

3 Select the ball control (Show > Nurbs Curves in the viewport menu if you don't see it) and open the Graph Editor. Select all the curves and click the spline tangents button. Notice how the ends of the curves become straight.

TangentTypes.ma

HOT TIP

Once you're refining an animation, you usually won't use one tangent type for all keys, but rather the appropriate type for the particular keys and situation you're working on.

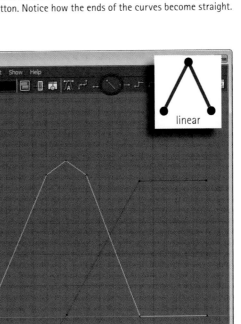

clamped

flattened

linear

5 Select all the curves and press the clamped tangents button. Clamped are almost the same as spline tangents, except they will not overshoot on adjacent keys that are the same value or very close in value. Notice that the overshoots from before are now flat.

6 Next press the linear tangents button. Linear tangents simply make a straight line from key to key and therefore make very sharp angles and transitions.

Tangent Types (cont'd)

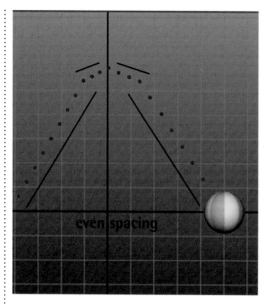

even spacing

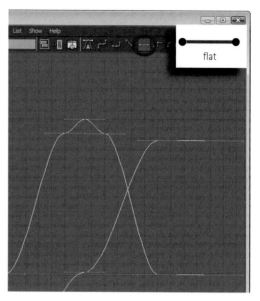

flat

7 Notice the spacing in the path of the ball is even between each key. Linear tangents are good for times when an object is traveling and then impacts another object at full momentum, such as when a ball hits the ground.

8 Next are flat tangents, which make a plateau at each key. They're common at the extreme keys, where a curve is changing direction, easing in and out of the key. In transitional keys, they will make the object slow down in mid path.

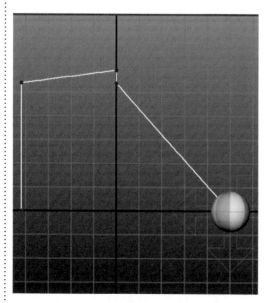

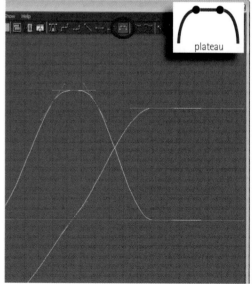

plateau

11 We see here that the ball pops to each position when it gets to that frame. Stepped keys are most commonly used for blocking in full animations, and for attributes that need to change over a single frame, like IK/FK switching or visibility.

12 Finally we have plateau tangents, which are almost identical to clamped in that they won't overshoot, and will flatten out extreme keys. The main difference is that they also flatten the start and end of the curve as well.

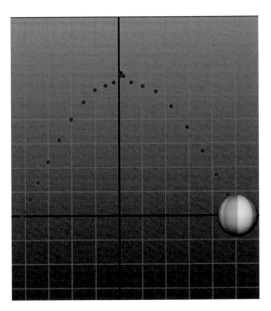

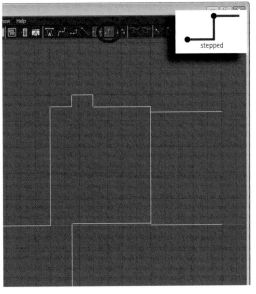

9 Notice the spacing on the ball easing out and in to each key. Flat tangents are a good starting point for keys you want ease-outs and ease-ins on. They will also hold flat through keys of the same value and never overshoot.

10 Next are stepped keys, which do not interpolate at all. They will hold still until the next keyframe. Because of this they create these stair-like keys.

HOT TIP

Plateau, clamped, or auto tangents are the best all-around choice when you're moving out of stepped blocking into splined curves. They're a great starting point since you don't have to worry about cleaning up overshoots, and manually making transitional keys spline and extreme keys flat.

	spline	Smooth interpolation, good on transitional keys where the curve is the same direction on both sides, tends to create overshoots in the curve
	clamped	Smooth interpolation, doesn't overshoot keys with close or identical values, first and last keys in the curve are splined, good for moving to spline mode from stepped keys
	linear	Direct line from key to key, makes spacing between two keys perfectly even, sharp angles in curves, works well for keys where an object is meeting another at full momentum, some use for blocking to avoid any computer-created eases
	flat	Creates plateaus at keys that are perfectly flat, automatically puts an ease-out and ease-in on a key, never overshoots, good for keys at extremes (where the curve changes direction) and keys where a value needs to hold through frames
	stepped	No interpolation between keys, simply holds until the next keyframe, commonly used for pose-to-pose blocking, attributes that you want to switch over 1 frame such as constraints, IK/FK, creating camera cuts, etc.
	plateau	Same as clamped, except first and last keys in the curve are flat

13 To recap, here's a chart of some common uses for different tangent types. To reiterate, these are just starting points that may be helpful, and not rules by any means. AutoTangent isn't a tangent type, but rather an automation function. It basically sets keys to spline or flat tangents dynamically as you edit keyframes, depending on the situation. Keys at extremes (where the curve changes direction) are made flat, while transitional keys (where the curve continues in the same direction) are smoothed to a spline tangent.

Tangent Handles

NOW THAT WE HAVE A GOOD UNDERSTANDING of Maya's tangent types, we can look at customizing the handles to create any type of curve we want. Maya's tangent handles offer the ultimate flexibility of any animation/graphics programs, so we should obviously take advantage of this power. Keep thinking about the spacing you want for your animation, then how a spline should look when it has that spacing, and use the handles to make it happen.

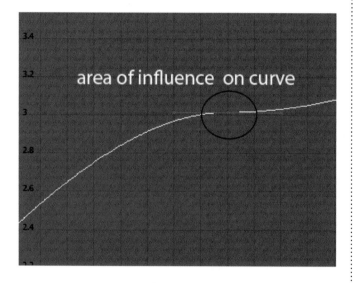

There are two types of tangent handles, weighted, and non-weighted. We'll go over them in this cheat, but they're really just styles of working and all up to preference in the end. Everything we talk about here is simply a way to get differing levels of control using the tangent handles. Note that I didn't say *more* control! Any curve shape you can get using handles you can also get by using more keyframes. At the end of the day, it's up to you and how you like working, so experiment with everything. My philosophy is it's best to get a handle (ahem) on all of the tools available, and then pick the best one for the job at hand.

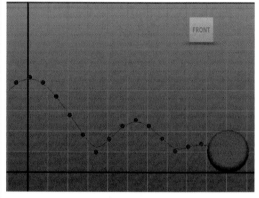

1 Open TangentHandles.ma and you'll find a simple bouncing ball animation. Select the ball control and open the Graph Editor.

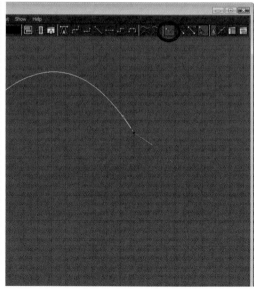

4 Select a handle and press the break tangents button. The left handle will turn blue, indicating they are now independent and you can drag select and then move them individually to get any curve shape you want.

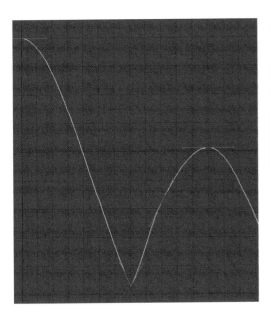

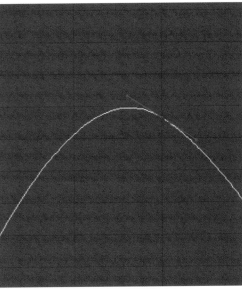

TangentHandles.ma

2 Select the translate Y curve and examine the tangent handles. They are currently non-weighted handles, which means they are all the same length relatively and have the same amount of influence on a curve.

3 Select the move tool **W** and select any handle. MM drag it to rotate it. These handles are unified, which means they are attached and act as a single piece when moving either of them.

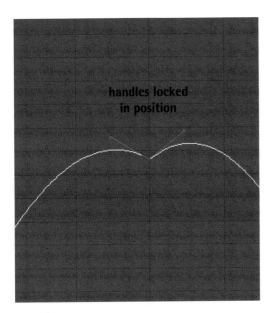

handles locked
in position

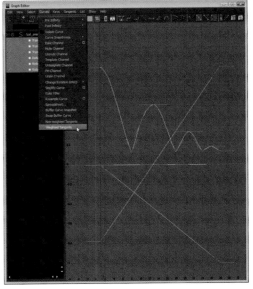

5 You can break tangents, position them, and then press the unify tangents button to lock them in that shape. They will then rotate as a single unit again. You may get erratic curve behavior if you do this with a very sharp angle, however.

6 Undo all your edits and select the entire translate Y curve. In the Graph Editor, go to Curves > Weighted Tangents and the handles will change.

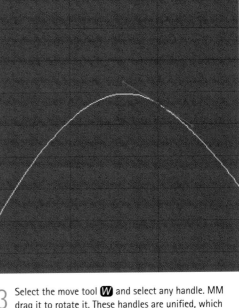

HOT TIP

As powerful as tangent handles can be, they do add another layer of complexity to your spline editing. Don't break handles or free their weights needlessly. Using the simplest solution is always the best.

51

Tangent Handles (cont'd)

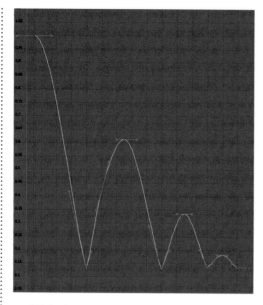

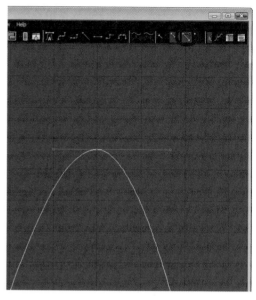

7 Weighted tangents have differing lengths which depend on the distance in value between the keyframes. The longer the distance, the longer the handle, and the more influence it will have along the curve.

8 You can break and manipulate the handles just like with non-weighted, but you have an additional option with weighted tangents. Select a key and click the free tangent weight button.

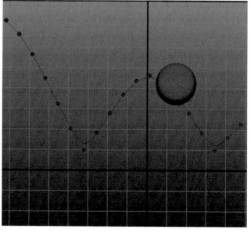

10 You can even break the tangent handles as we did before to create any shape of curve possible.

11 Continue to experiment with the tangent handles and learn how to create the spacing you want using them.

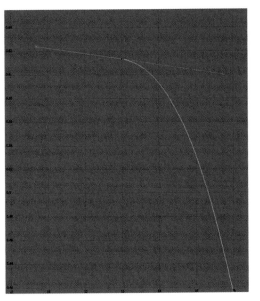
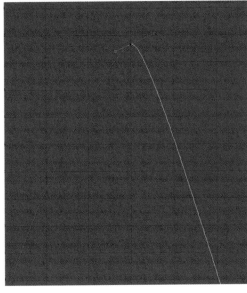

9 The ends will turn into open squares indicating free weights. You can now use the move tool and make the tangents any length you wish, increasing or decreasing the amount of influence they have on the curve.

HOT TIP

If you're new to animation, it may be a good idea to hold off on a lot of tangent handle weighting and breaking. Once you learn to control the animation using only keys, it will be much easier to understand what the handles are doing to the spacing.

Handles Pros
- Keeps curves less cluttered with fewer keys
- Powerful curve-shaping options
- Curves scale in time more accurately
- Good for subtle spacing adjustments without adding density
- Create sharp angles with fewer keys

Handles Cons
- Adjusting adjacent keys can affect spacing
- Some shapes not possible without keys
- Too few keys tends to feel floaty
- Can be more difficult for other animators to edit if necessary
- Less control over larger spacing areas

Keys Pros
- Exact, value isn't affected by adjacent keys
- Complete control, any shape possible
- Clearly readable in Graph Editor
- Simple to work with, not complex
- Easy to edit by other animators

Keys Cons
- Curves can get very dense and more difficult to make changes to
- Scaling time can be less accurate if you need to snap keys to frames
- More control usually translates into needing more keys

12 Remember that using handles is just another way to approach animating, not something you need to do or should never do (depending on who you talk to). Some animators never use tangents and only set keys, others use broken weighted handles all the time, but many use both methods when necessary. It's up to you in the end, but here are some factors to consider with the various methods. Ultimately, choosing the best approach for the task at hand will ensure that everything stays as simple as possible.

Spline Technique

YOU NOW HAVE a good grasp on the capabilities splines have and how you can approach using them, so let's go over some things that can tighten up your spline workflow. We're all about making things easier here, and there are a few tendencies splines have which can sabotage that. Having good spline technique means you have control, and that means you're making the animation look the way you want, not the way the computer happens to do it.

As I've said before, none of these things are really rules and there will be situations where actually doing them may be the best approach. But those are the exceptions and for general guidelines, especially if you're still becoming acclimated with splines, this cheat will go a long way towards helping you get ahead.

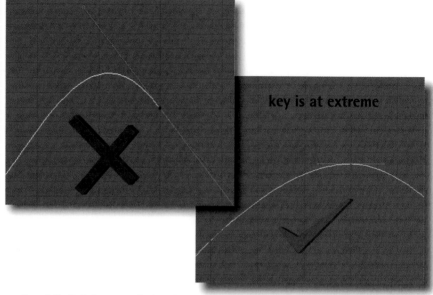

key is at extreme

1 Open SplineTechnique.ma and select the ball's move control. Look at the Translate Y curve at f12. F13 is the extreme key, but the tangents are making f12 a higher value, also known as an overshoot. Use flat or linear tangents at extremes and adjust the eases to what you need.

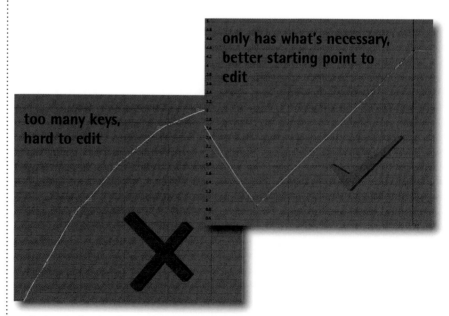

only has what's necessary, better starting point to edit

too many keys, hard to edit

3 Look at the Translate X curve. Often when setting keys on all controls, we can get a lot of redundant keys. Splining can turn these curves into a wobbly mess. Only use the number of keys you need and make sure the tangents are the way you want them. Too many keys makes changes very difficult. Since this curve should be a smooth translation, we can delete almost all of these keys.

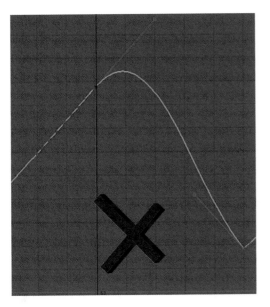

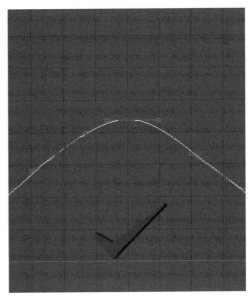

SplineTechnique.ma

HOT TIP

As awesome as the AutoTangent functionality is, don't let it make you lazy! In the end it's still spacing and slow ins/ outs generated by a computer algorithm. It will get your curves closer to what you want with less work, but you still need to maintain control of what the computer is doing. Finely calibrated curves are the mark of a great animator.

2 At f21, there's another type of overshoot, where the curve was shaped this way purposely with tangent handles. While this may look fine in the viewport, it's definitely not the best way. When the extremes have keys representing them, it makes things clear, easy to edit, and the values can't be changed without us knowing. With any kind of overshoot, moving an adjacent keyframe or handle can change where your extreme is. As much as we all love Maya, we don't want it making these kinds of decisions for us!

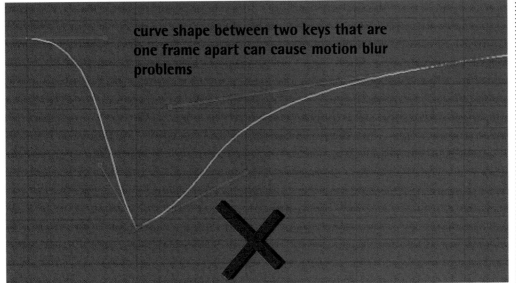

curve shape between two keys that are one frame apart can cause motion blur problems

4 Look at f24-f28 on the Rotate Z curve. Extreme angles are sometimes necessary, but if you need sharp angles, you're better off using keys rather than handles. Handles change when you shift keys around, but keys will always hold their value. It's good to avoid even 1 frame glitches like f27-f28 that aren't seen in the viewport. Some studios use motion blur that look in between the frames and will give strange results at render time with curves like this. This can actually be used to make motion blur look the way the animator wants, but unless this is intentional, don't do it!

Spline Reference

W E'VE SEEN THAT SPLINES are simple tools, yet capable of describing any movement to pinpoint accuracy. It takes some practice to make looking at them second nature, and as you keep animating, you'll get better at reading them. One thing many beginning animators don't realize at first is that reading splines is just recognizing common shapes. An ease-in will always look pretty much the same as far as the general spline shape goes. The size and angle of the shape will simply determine how big (or small) of an ease-in it is. You know when a circle is a circle regardless of how large or small it is. It's really the same idea.

The file for this cheat, SplineReference.ma, contains six spline shape examples that you can use as a reference for common animation spacings. Every 50 frames has a separate animation and description. Move the time range slider to start at frames 1, 50, 100, 150, 200, and 250 to see each one. The upper arm's Rotate Z curve has the animation. Memorizing these shapes will make looking at the Graph Editor an enlightening experience, rather than a puzzling one. Happy wrangling!

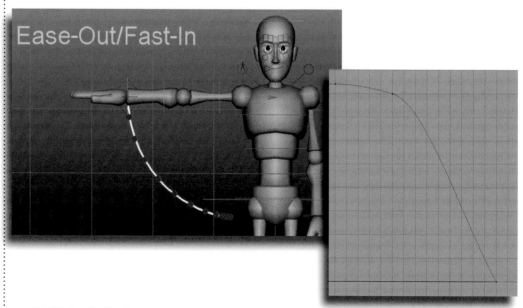

Ease-Out/Fast-In

2 f50–f99: Ease Out/Fast In

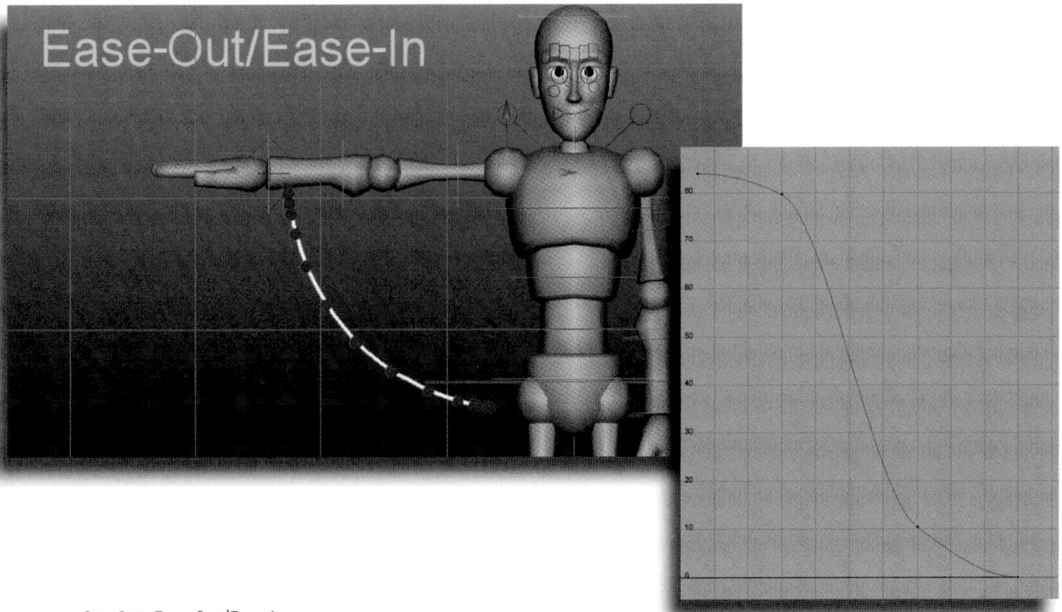

1 f01-f49: Ease Out/Ease In

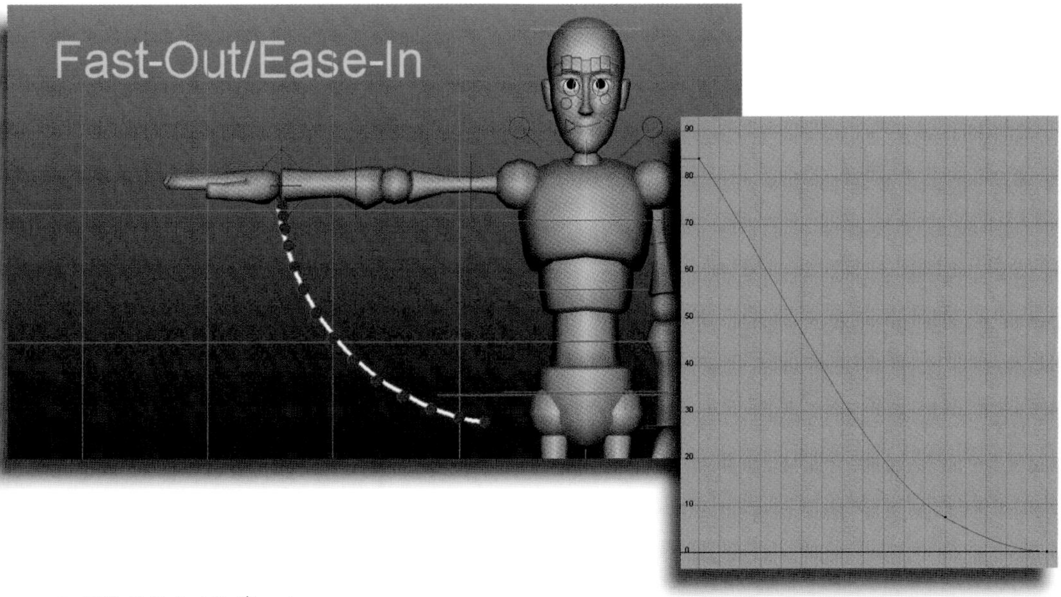

3 f100-f149: Fast Out/Ease In

SplineReference.ma

HOT TIP

Adding an extra key to shape your ease-outs and ease-ins will really help make them better. Maya's default eases are always the same ratio and tend to feel a bit flat timing-wise.

Spline Reference (cont'd)

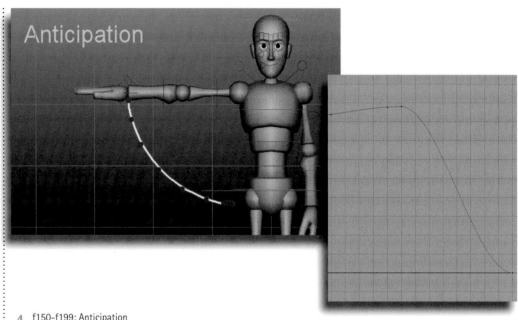

4   f150–f199: Anticipation

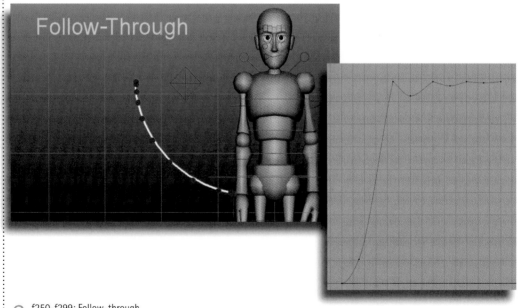

6   f250–f299: Follow-through

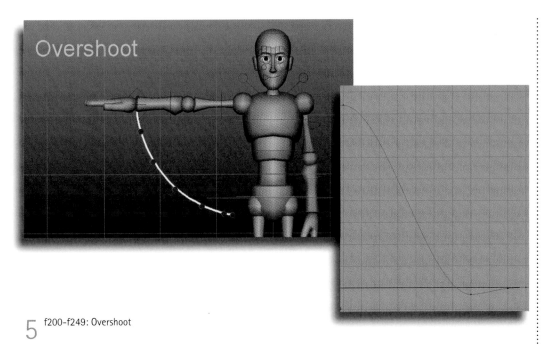

Overshoot

5 f200-f249: Overshoot

HOT TIP

Linear tangents are a great starting point for any key where an object is hitting another and ricocheting off it, such as when a bouncing ball hits the ground.

If I Had to Start Over

by Kenny Roy

I WAS ASKED ONCE BY A STUDENT OF MINE, "If you had to start over learning animation, what would you do differently?" My answer? "Everything!" Well, of course I would love to have known everything I know now back when I was learning, but where's the fun in that? I would probably try to develop a few more of my outside hobbies and draw more, but there is a single thing that I would change for sure. I thusly changed the question to "If I had to start over learning animation, and you could only change ONE thing about how you learned, what would it be?" The answer is so simple, it might surprise you.

I would do a whole lot LESS animation.

Alright, now that doesn't seem right. What the heck does that mean? It means that I, like nearly all animators that came before and who have come after, always took on WAY too much when I was in the middle of learning. If I saw a new tool or learned of a new technique, I would try it out in 300 frame multi-character dialog sequence with multiple camera cuts, and with some special FX and crazy lighting thrown in for good measure. Since I took on EPIC shots while I was still learning, it meant that nearly all of the mini projects I started were never finished. This cycle fosters a dangerous attribute of most young animators; fast blocking but no polishing skills. By year three of my almost five-year self-taught animation training, I could block a scene like lightning, but could not even see the problems that kept my work from achieving a level of finish that I saw in my head. It was frustrating. More importantly, it was avoidable, so this is my advice:

If you are in school, and you get an assignment that has a range of options for you to choose from, DO THE SIMPLEST ONE YOU CAN. For instance, if you are given an assignment that you can animate one or two characters in a simple scene, and the frame range for this assignment is 150-250 frames, then do one character in a 150 frame shot. Seriously. Can you guess why the animator that does LESS will actually learn faster? Simply put, the more practice you give your workflow from start to finish, the faster you will become at all stages of a scene's lifespan. Giving yourself assignments that are bite sized means that you will finish everything you start as well, which is a huge motivational boost right when you need it. You'll need plenty of those learning animation.

The students of mine who took on less work would demonstrate a deeper understanding of the concepts, and a greater ease of applying the concepts in their work. Although it may seem like animation is much more subjective than this, it is almost as if it is not the quality of the shots you do as you are learning, but the quantity. One of my illustration teachers used to say that everyone has 10,000 bad drawings "in them". And the sooner you just get those 10,000 bad drawings out of you, the sooner you will get to the good drawings that are waiting behind the bad ones. In fact, he would just encourage us to draw, even mindlessly. Literally, you don't have to even think about what you are drawing because all that is important is getting that bad drawing "out of you". It was funny sometimes when he'd pick up a student's artwork, and sometimes say "Oh my god look how bad this is. That is fantastic. It is such good news that now you've gotten that one out of you. Think of how good a drawing there must be waiting behind that one!" We all had a good laugh thinking about the stacks of drawings waiting to just come out...

Here is a list of some good animation tests that are the perfect complexity to tackle in your short tests:

A ball bouncing.

A rolling ball.

An obstacle course for your ball.

Adding anticipation and overlap to a ball with a tail.

A flour sack test.

The sack standing and stretching.

The sack trying to jump over a wall.

The sack pulling on a stuck door.

The sack doing a weight shift from one foot to the other.

The sack waking up from sleep.

A person taking out their phone.

A person answering their phone.

A person sneezing.

A person coughing into a hanky.

A person jumping straight up.

A person jumping forward.

A person ducking a swinging object.

A person with a sword swinging it wildly.

A person with a sword stabbing a dummy.

Someone jumping on a trampoline.

A person doing any simple action from any sport.

> Kicking a soccer ball.

> Shooting a basketball.

> Swinging a golf club, etc.

Character interacting with any heavy object (crate, box, barbells, etc.)

A character sitting down/standing up.

Someone doing a simple acrobatic (somersault, roll, flip).

Someone checking the time.

Someone being scared by a loud noise.

Someone smelling something awful.

Eating an apple.

Climbing up on a ledge.

Climbing down from a ledge.

Walking on thin ice.

Winning the lottery.

A run cycle.

A walk cycle with character.

Getting hit in various places in the body with a bullet.

Putting on clothes.

Putting away dishes.

Cooking a meal.

Picking up a baby.

Having an uncontrollable itch.

Fending off an attacking bee.

Taking off wet clothes.

Getting into a car.

Brushing your hair.

Brushing your teeth.

Tying your shoes.

Turning a large valve.

Opening the refrigerator.

Passing out.

So to put it simply, if I had to learn animation all over again, I would do a lot more, of a LOT LESS. Instead of the crazy, 300-frame dialog sequences with three or four characters, I would do 48-96 tests. A simple turn. A character picking up a ball. A character chuckling to himself. A character pulling out a chair and sitting down. Another shot of a character pushing away his plate, then standing up. All the practice I could get, in huge quantities. I'm confident that I would be able to shave at least HALF of my learning time off if I followed that one simple piece of advice.

Plus, I'd be a lot closer than I am now to getting out those 10,000 bad animations.

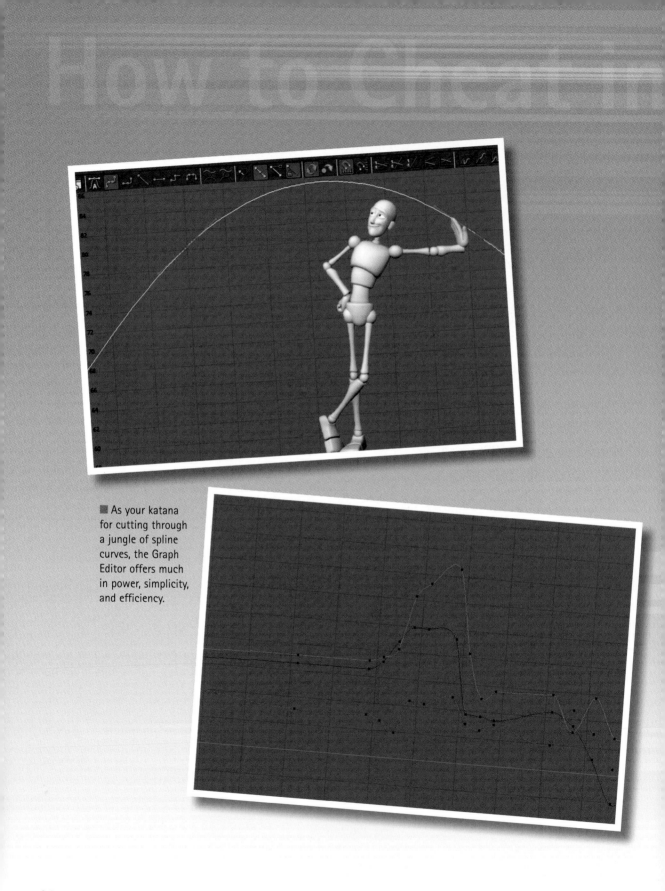

As your katana for cutting through a jungle of spline curves, the Graph Editor offers much in power, simplicity, and efficiency.

3

Graph Editor

MAYA'S GRAPH EDITOR is easily its most powerful
and most used tool for animating. It's likely that you
will spend much of your time working with it, so it's
a no-brainer that we learn all the ins and outs of this
fantastic editor. Maya 2014 introduces several new
features to the Graph Editor that make it even more
powerful and easy to use.

We spent the last chapter understanding splines, and now
we'll learn how to use the Graph Editor to interact with,
edit, and manipulate them.

Graph Editor Windup

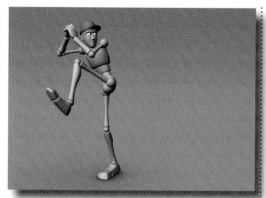

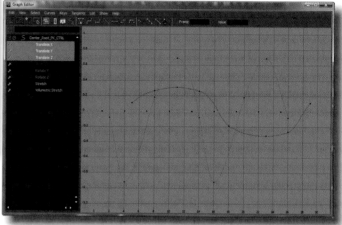

BㅤEFORE WE LAUNCH INTO all the cool stuff the Graph Editor has in store for you, let's go over the basics of using it! One of the best features about Maya 2014 is the unified Graph Editor. This means that the curve editors in other Autodesk products like 3DS Max and MotionBuilder are exactly the same as what's here in Maya. We'll be using this unified editor throughout this chapter, as it's simpler and more streamlined, but you can always go back to the old editor by choosing View > Classic Toolbar.

1 Selecting a control initially displays all curves. Selecting attributes in the left panel displays only those curves. You can drag select or **Shift** select for sequential attributes, or **ctrl** select for multiple, non-sequential ones.

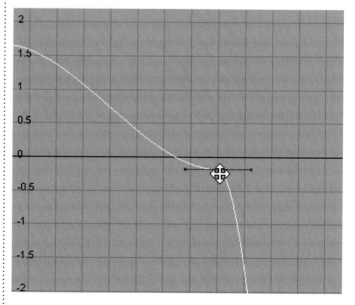

3 The move **W** and scale **R** tools work in the Graph Editor. Once selected, the MMB will drag or edit the curves or keys selected.

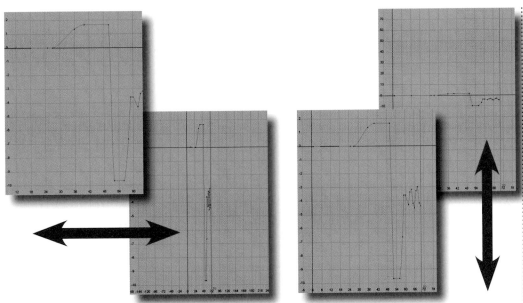

2 **Shift alt** and RMB-dragging horizontally expands or contracts the frame range of the graph in view, while dragging vertically contracts/expands the value range.

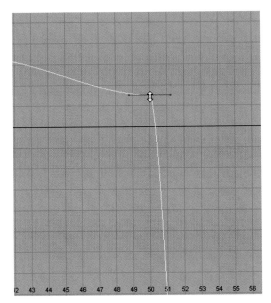

4 **Shift**-MMB-dragging will constrain the movement horizontally or vertically, depending on which way you initially move the mouse.

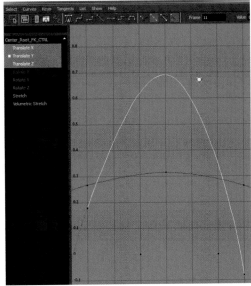

5 If you get a circle when trying to edit, it just means you have the Select tool **Q** active and need to select an edit tool such as the move or scale tool to do an edit.

Visual Tools

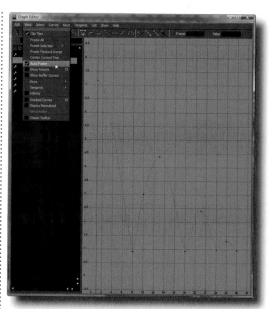

T HE GRAPH EDITOR IS FULL of goodies, and some of the most important ones let you view the curves in the most efficient way for what you're doing. Whether you need to type exact values, search for keys that may be amiss, compare drastically different curves, or want to isolate specific attributes, the Graph Editor can accommodate you. In this cheat we'll use a simple bouncing ball animation to test out the options the Graph Editor gives us for oggling curves. Make sure you are using the streamlined Graph Editor, by going to View > Classic Toolbar and making sure it's unchecked.

1 Open visualTools.ma, switch to the front camera, and open the Graph Editor. Select the ball's move control and its curves appear. Clicking on the attributes in the left panel isolates them, but some of the curves are difficult to see. Enabling View > Auto Frame will automatically focus on any attribute(s) you select.

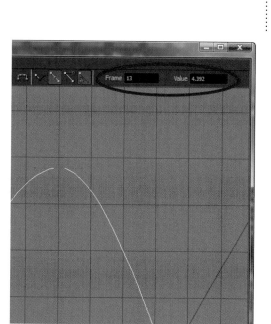

4 The stats fields show the frame and value of the selected key (or the frame length of a selected curve), which is useful for typing in precise frame numbers or values. You can also use **ctrl**+**C** to copy and **ctrl**+**V** to paste values of one key to the fields for another key or curve.

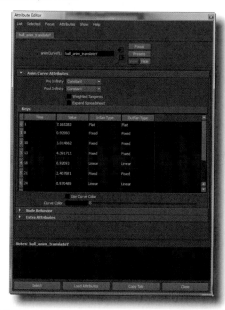

5 If you need to do precise entering of values for multiple keys, you can select curves and choose Curves > Spreadsheet. This gives you values for every key on the curve. You can use copy and paste here, and even change tangent types.

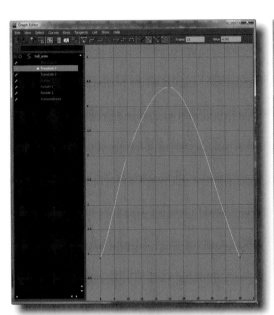

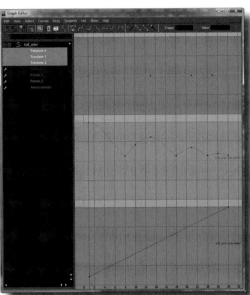

visualTools.ma

2 Select a few keys and press **F** to focus on them.

3 Maya 2014 comes with a way to visualize multiple curves. Select multiple channels and go to View > Stacked Curves. Now all of your channels are displayed in their own stacked panes.

HOT TIP

In addition to using the Graph Editor, you can also mute and unmute channels in the channel box by right clicking the attribute and selecting "Mute/Unmute Channel".

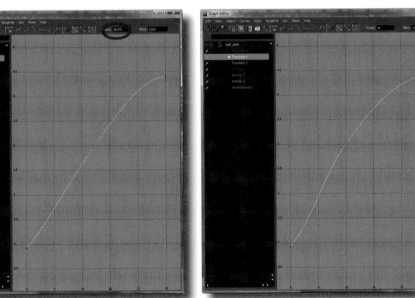

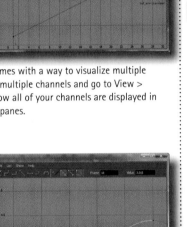

6 On the Translate Y curve, select the key at f10. You'll see in the stat field that the current frame is 10.472. In the course of scaling keys or editing them, we can end up with keys that are between frames.

7 Select the Translate Y attribute and go to Edit > Select Unsnapped. All the keys that are not on exact frames will be selected. You can select multiple or all attributes as well. Go to Edit > Snap and the selected keys will be moved onto the nearest frame.

Visual Tools (cont'd)

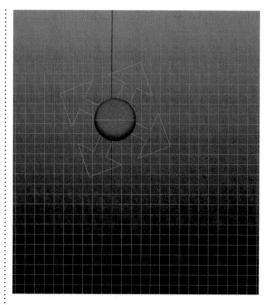

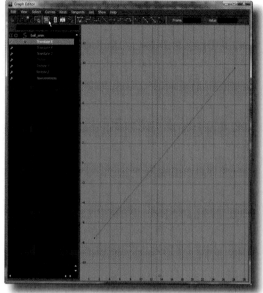

8 The ball is travelling in X as it bounces, but sometimes it's helpful to watch an animation without one of the attributes playing. Select the Translate X channel in the Graph Editor and go to Curves > Mute Channel.

9 You may have to pan the camera to see it, but now the ball no longer moves in X and simply bounces in place. In the Graph Editor, mute channels have an X next to them. Muting will use the current value as its hold point.

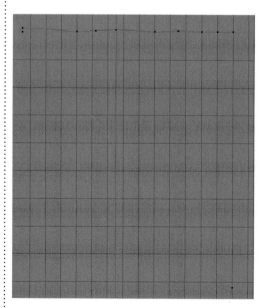

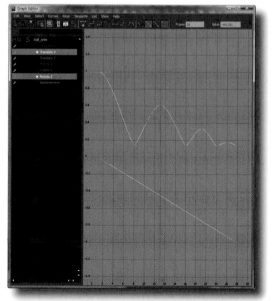

12 Select the Translate Y and Rotate Z channels. Sometimes you'll want to edit curves while comparing to others, but it's difficult because they are in completely different value ranges. Here, we can't see any of the shapes in the Translate Y curve.

13 Select the curves and go View > Display Normalized. Now they are both displayed relatively within a -1 to 1 range and easily comparable and editable. To go back to normal, uncheck View > Display Normalized.

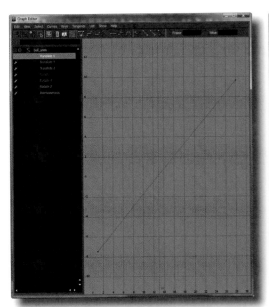

10 To unmute, select the channel, and go to Curves > Unmute Channel. Everything will go back to normal.

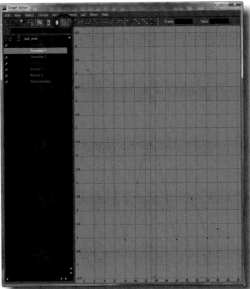

11 To quickly isolate the curves of select attributes, select them in the Channel Box and press the Isolate Curve Display button in the Graph Editor. This is great for quickly showing certain attributes when you have multiple controls selected.

HOT TIP

Go to the Select menu and enable Pre-Select Highlight and Maya will light up selectable objects when you hover over them. Very handy when selecting keys amongst overlapping curves!

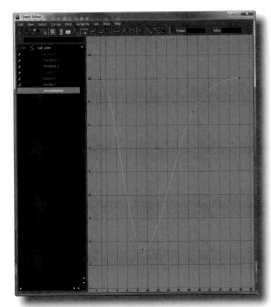

14 Extra attributes beyond the standard Rotate, Translate, etc. are colored gray, but you can change that so they stand out better. On the ball is an attribute called "Awesomeness", which doesn't do anything and is just for example's sake. Select the Awesomeness curve!

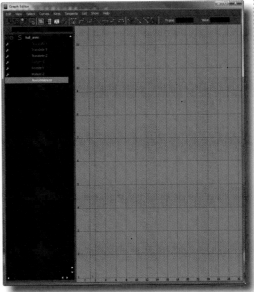

15 Edit > Change Curve Color lets you pick any color you like for the curve. Now it will stand out when looking at multiple curves simultaneously. To remove it, just select and choose Edit > Remove Curve Color.

Working with Keys

I N ADDITION TO its visual advantages, the Graph Editor offers some methods of working with keys that you can't get in the timeline or Dope Sheet. There are often times when we know the general shape of the curve we want to create, but setting keys and then dragging them to create that shape is time consuming. The Add Keys tool allows us to simply click keys where we need them and very quickly create a curve that can be tweaked for the results we want.

There will also be times where you want to add a key into a curve. Simply setting a key works, but the key is created with whatever Maya's default tangent is set to, which can alter the curve more than you want. Setting a key and editing the tangent is a lot of unnecessary work so Maya offers the Insert Keys tool, which can be called upon instantly at any time.

Maya 2014 offers a Retime tool, an even simpler and more powerful way to retime animation, over the Lattice Deform and Region Tools. By double clicking on a spot in the Graph Editor, you create a retime handle that can be moved back and forth in time, scaling the keys as you do so. This is an incredibly intuitive way to retime animation because the handles basically define "beats" of your scene. The Lattice Deform keys and Region tools are still present, but the Retime tool has far more potential to become a part of your regular workflow, so we'll show you how to use it here.

We'll be using the streamlined Graph Editor which you can enable by going to View Classic Toolbar and making sure it's unchecked.

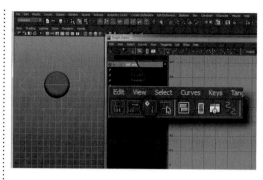

1 Open workingWithKeys.ma for the start of a bouncing ball animation. Currently we have it translating in X, but no up and down. Select the Add Keys tool in the Graph Editor, then select the Translate Y attribute and select the first key.

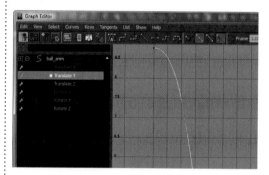

4 Without messing up our Translate Y curve, we need some extra keys at the peaks for a little extra hang time. Select the curve and hold down the **I** key. The pointer will become a crosshair indicating the Insert Keys tool is active.

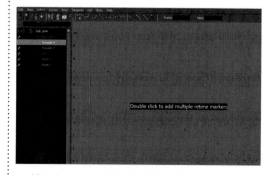

7 Maya has a powerful tool called the Retime tool. This powerful tool allows you to scale the timing of keys in multiple user defined regions. Select the Retime tool and double click anywhere in the Graph Editor to create retime handles.

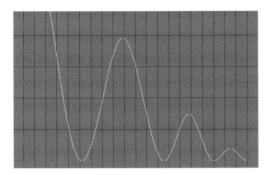

2 Middle click in the graph to add keys. In about 10 seconds I have the general shape of the curve and am ready to refine it.

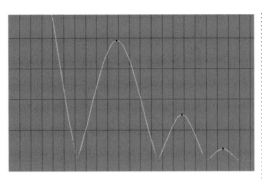

3 Converting the bottom keys to linear tangents gets us most of the way to a bouncing ball.

workingWithKeys.
ma

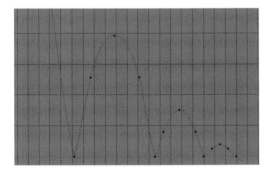

5 Middle clicking on the curve inserts a key without messing up the shape.

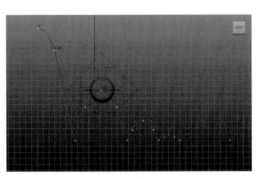

6 A few more tweaks and we have all the translation for a bouncing ball in about a minute.

HOT TIP

Maya has a type of keyframe called Breakdown keys, but they're not breakdowns as animators traditionally understand them. They're simply keys that maintain an exact ratio between the previous and following key. This can put them between frames if the other keys get moved. Generally speaking, most animators just use Maya's regular keyframes for everything.

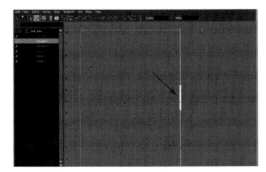

8 Now grab a retime handle and move it back and forth. Notice how the keys scale in time? You can add as many handles as you like, whenever you like!

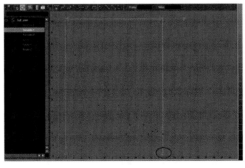

9 To remove a handle, hit the circular "X" at the bottom. It disappears, but your retimed keys stay put. Very nice.

Value Operators

THERE ARE OFTEN TIMES when we need to make specific changes in value to many keys at once. For instance, we might want to see what a walk looks like if we increase the spine's Rotate X by 20%. Or we need to quickly scale down a curve's frame range to 33% of its current value. Though you wouldn't know it by looking at them, Maya's stat fields can do calculations that you can use to quickly make precise mass edits on multiple keys. By using a set of value operators, we can get results fast, without clicking on and manipulating tools. Sounds like a great addition to the cheating portfolio, eh?

The value operators are as follows:

+=value Add

-=value Subtract

*=value Multiply

/=value Divide

So if we wanted to add five units in value to the selected keys, in the stat value field, we would type +=5 and hit **Enter**. To increase them by 20% type *=1.2 and so on. This cheat will walk you through using value operators in several different situations.

We'll be using the streamlined Graph Editor, which you can enable by going to View > Classic Toolbar and making sure it's unchecked.

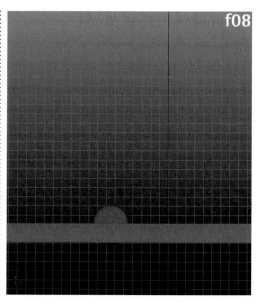

1 Open valueOperators.ma for our familiar bouncing ball animation. There's a ground, but the ball is bouncing too low, about 1 unit or so, and intersecting it.

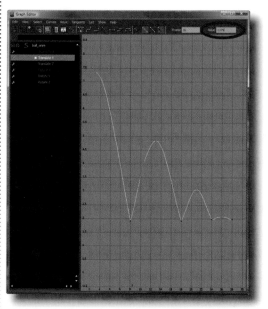

4 Let's bring the peaks of the Translate Y down 10%. Select the keys when the ball is in the air, and type *=.9 to reduce the value by 10%.

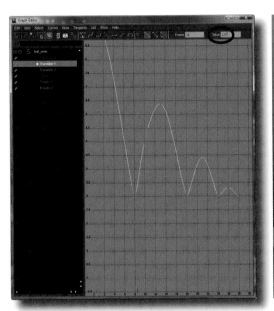

2 Select the Translate Y curve in the Graph Editor, and in the value field type +=1 and hit *Enter*. This adds 1 to every key selected.

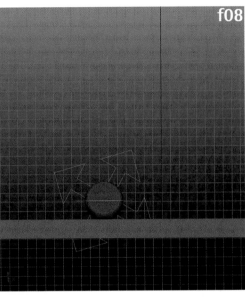

f08

3 Now every key is 1 unit higher and the ball lines up with the ground.

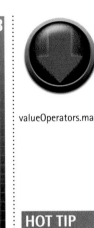

valueOperators.ma

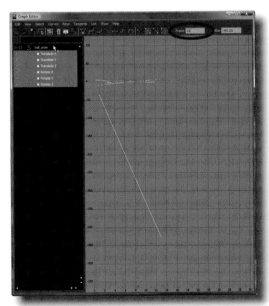

5 We can scale the time for keys as well. Select all the curves for the ball and in the frame stat field, enter /=2 to divide by 2 and cut the frame numbers the keys happen on in half. The animation plays twice as fast now.

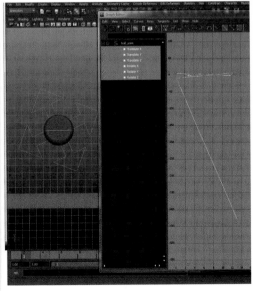

6 You can also use -=value to subtract. Remember that all the operators work for both frame and value stat fields.

75

Buffer Curves

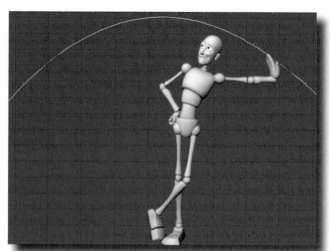

A NIMATION IS RARELY a linear process, and often times we need to compare different ideas to see what works best. Looking at variations saved in different files is a hassle and inefficient, so Maya offers buffer curves in its Graph Editor functionality. We can have two different versions of any curve and switch back and forth between them instantly. For times when we're not sure if we like a certain movement over another, this allows us to experiment without having to redo or lose work.

Buffer curves are best for trying out variations on one or a few attributes. While it's possible to use them on a whole character, there's not a definitive interface for working with them. Switching between many attributes can make it easy to lose track of what you're looking at. Animation Layers are a much better approach for working with variations on a bigger scale, and they're covered in Chapter 12. But when it comes to comparing an attribute or two, buffer curves have a nice efficiency.

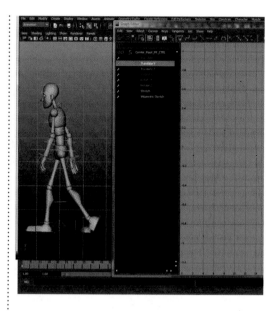

1 Open bufferCurves.ma, which has the Goon doing the walk from Chapter 9. Select the body control's Translate Y curve.

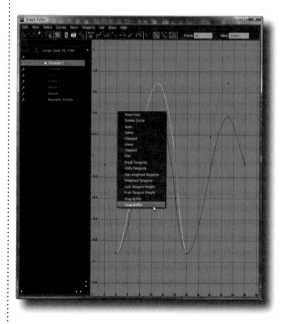

4 Hold the right mouse button and in the pop-up menu choose Swap Buffer to make the buffer curve active. The version you were working on goes into the buffer and you can edit the previous version.

bufferCurves.ma

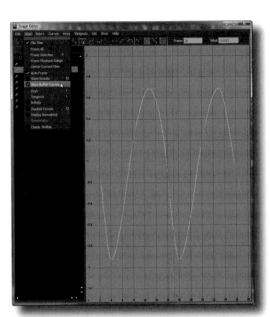

2 Buffer curves are not visible by default, so go to View >
Show Buffer Curves. You won't see anything change yet,
as both versions of the curve are currently the same.

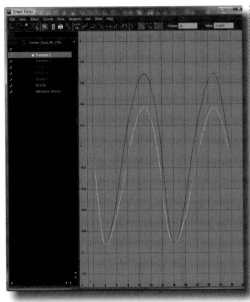

3 Move some of the keys around and you will see a gray
curve in the background with the shape you locked into
the buffer. Now you can edit the curve as normal, keeping
the buffer version intact and referencing it if necessary.

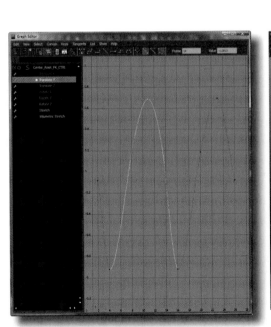

5 In the right click menu, choosing Snap Buffer will snap
the buffer to the current version of the curve. This is
good for quickly saving the current state of the curve, and
then moving on to further experimentation.

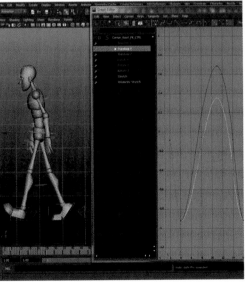

6 Use the different curves to compare varying amounts of
up/down in the body. If the buffer curves get distracting,
or you're finished working with them, just go back to View >
Show Buffer Curves to toggle them off.

HOT TIP

If you want to
make a curve
visible but
uneditable or
unselectable
(for instance,
if you're
referencing
it to another
curve and keep
selecting it
accidentally),
select the
channel and
go to Curves
> Template
Channel.
To unlock
it, choose
Untemplate
Channel.

77

3

Speed Cheats

YOU WILL NOTICE as you progress in animation that you are doing a lot of the same operations in the Graph Editor. Maya 2014's Graph Editor adds some great tools that allow you to remove some of the unnecessary tasks and clutter as you work. Specifically, we're going to take a look at setting bookmarks for our commonly used curves, and isolating our view to specific attributes (very common when doing cycles).

It will become increasingly important as you move on in your animation training to develop ways to quickly access the controller or information you need. Professionals know that time spent hunting around a scene or a UI is time wasted. The following cheats will give you a few quick ways to sidestep the clutter when your scene starts getting complex.

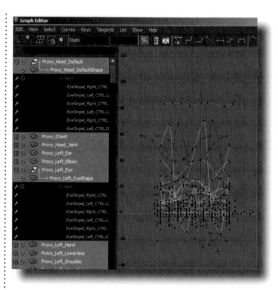

1 Open SpeedCheats.ma. In the Persp panel, drag a selection over the entire goon rig and open the Graph Editor. It should look like this – spaghetti anyone?

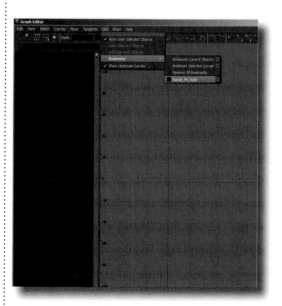

4 Now deselect everything in the panel and notice how the Graph Editor also clears out. Click on List>Bookmarks and find the "hands_FK_RotX" bookmark we just created and click on it.

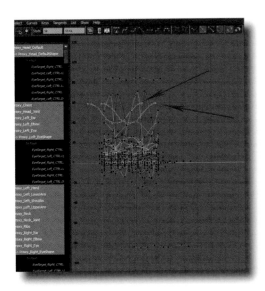

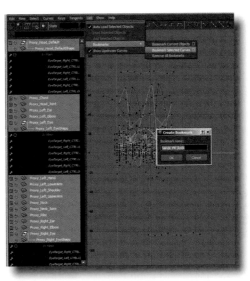

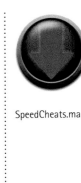

SpeedCheats.ma

2 We're going to pretend that we want to work on the hand_IK Rotate X curves over and over. Select them carefully by clicking on the first and *Shift*-click the second one as shown.

3 That's a pain! We don't want to have to do that again. Click on List>Bookmarks>Bookmark Selected Curves □. Call the bookmark "hands_FK_RotX" and hit *Enter*.

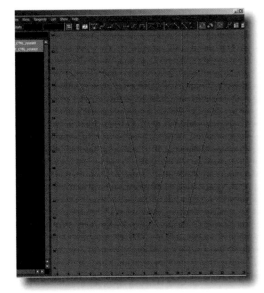

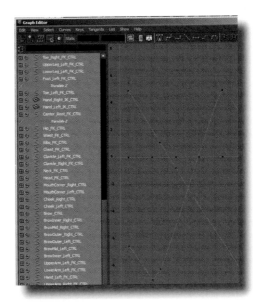

5 Now just the two curves we want to see are loaded in the Graph Editor. We can use this bookmark any time. But what if we want to just look at a certain curve type? This is very easy to do.

6 Select all of the controls in panel again, then select any Translate Z channel in the Graph Editor. Go to Show>Selected Type(s). If you select all of the channels on the left, you'll see only the Translate Z channels are in the Graph Editor!

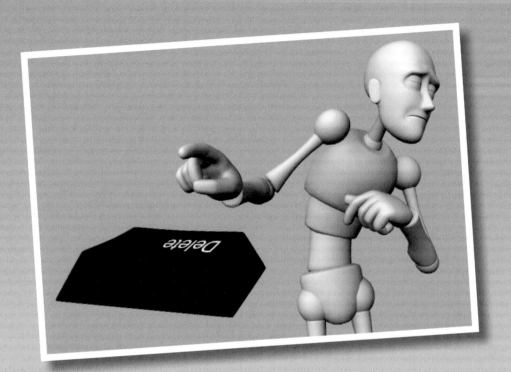

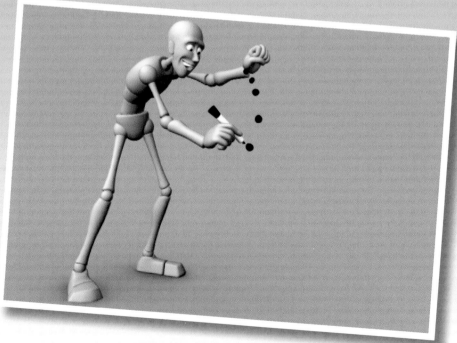

Making changes, tracking arcs, working with multiple pivots, using the timeline, and much more are discussed in depth in this chapter.

4
Techniques

FOR EVERY ANIMATOR there are a variety of techniques that are used throughout the animation process. As you develop your skills, a portfolio of mantras that you call upon regularly will also develop: your kung fu, so to speak.

This chapter contains a wide selection of very useful tools and techniques for animating. While creating a piece of animation, you may call upon some of these techniques dozens of times, others only once, but all of them will make a regular appearance in any animator's workflow. Prepare, grasshopper, for efficiency lies within...

Auto Key

HAVING TO PRESS THE **S** KEY incessantly while animating does two things: gets tedious, and wears out your **S** key. So in the interest of preventing tedium and extending your keyboard's life, let's look at the different ways we can use Maya's Auto Key. This feature eliminates most of your manual keying, and while it's pretty straightforward, it works great with the Hold Current Keys option, which is easy to overlook.

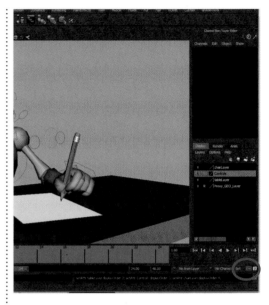

1 Open AutoKey.ma. The quickest way to turn Auto Key on or off is the button in the bottom right corner. Make sure it's red to indicate Auto Key is on.

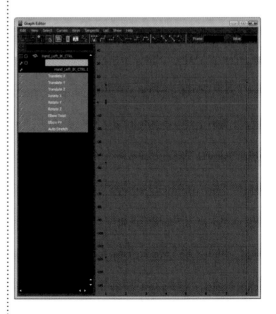

4 Looking at the Graph Editor, we see that there are keys on all the hand attributes at f01, but only on Translate Y at f08.

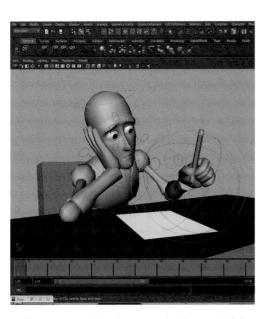

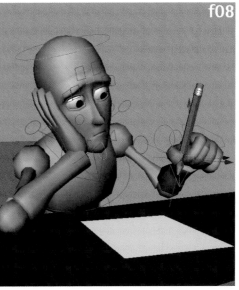

f08

AutoKey.ma

2 There are currently no keys set on the character, he's just posed. Grab the L hand and move it, and you'll notice no key is set. Auto Key only sets keys on controls when you've manually set a key on it first. Undo the move and set a key on it by pressing **S**.

3 Go to f08 and move the hand in Translate Y. Now a key will be set, but only on Translate Y. By default Auto Key only sets a key on the attributes that are changed, not the entire control.

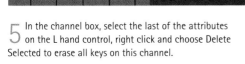

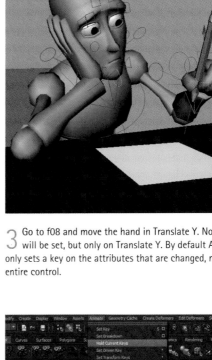

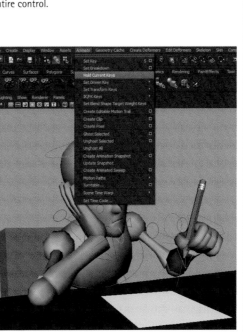

5 In the channel box, select the last of the attributes on the L hand control, right click and choose Delete Selected to erase all keys on this channel.

6 Move to f14 and go to Animate > Hold Current Keys. When using Auto Key, you may want to keep some attributes unkeyed, yet still set a key on all keyed attributes. Using this menu option will set a key on all keyed attributes of a control, but not on unkeyed ones.

HOT TIP

You can manually key just the Translate, Rotate, or Scale attributes by pressing *Shift*+*W*, *Shift*+*E*, or *Shift*+*R*, respectively.

Timeline Techniques

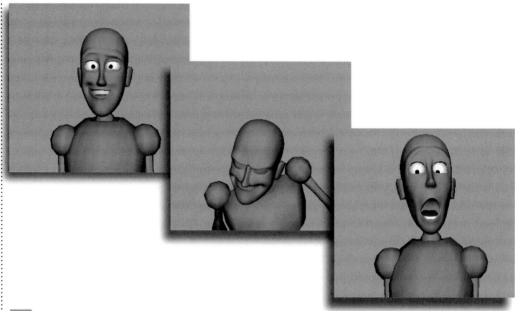

THE TIMELINE is the interface element you will use more than any other when animating in Maya. It has a lot of functionality beyond scrubbing, but its simple appearance can hide how powerful it is. There are lots of edits you can do without ever leaving it, from copy and pasting keys, to reordering them or setting tangent types. Even playblasting is readily available. After working through this cheat, you'll have some timeline chops that will serve you as long as you animate.

We're going to use a simple animation of the Goon doing a take. We have three basic poses and right now that's all they are: poses that interpolate to each other. Let's use some fancy timeline editing to make it less poses and more animation.

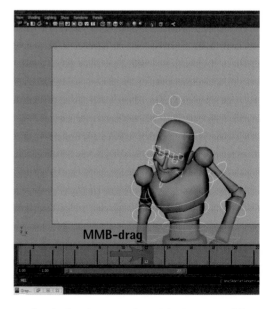

MMB-drag

3 Now he doesn't move to the anticipation pose until f05, but he needs to hold there also. MMB-drag from f09 to f12 and set a key to copy that pose also.

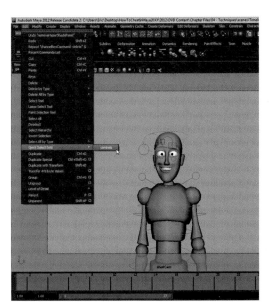

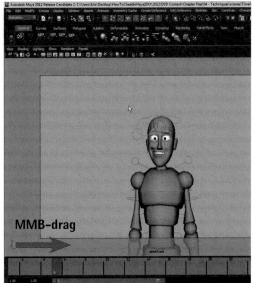

Timeline.ma
Timeline_end.ma

1 Open Timeline.ma. The first pose needs to hold a few frames longer before the anticipation pose. Go to Edit > Quick Select Sets > controls to use a predefined set to select all of the Goon's controls.

2 In the timeline MMB-drag from f01 to f05. The animation doesn't change like when you scrub. MM dragging holds the frame on wherever you started, so it's a quick way to copy poses. Make sure the tangents are set to Auto, and set a key at f05.

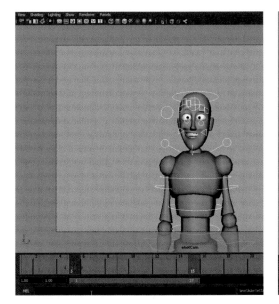

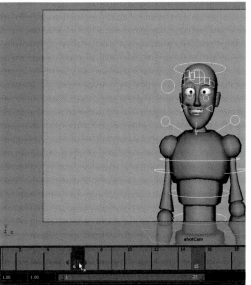

4 It's looking better, but let's make the transition into the anticipation a little snappier. *Shift*-click f05 and it will turn red.

5 Click and drag on the two center arrows to move the key to f06. Now the transition is only three frames, which feels better.

Timeline Techniques (cont'd)

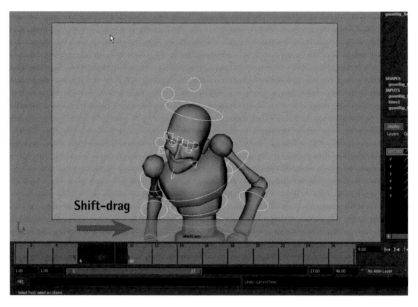

Shift-drag

6 He hits the anticipation pose very hard, so let's cushion him hitting that pose. Shift drag from f06 through f09 to highlight them red.

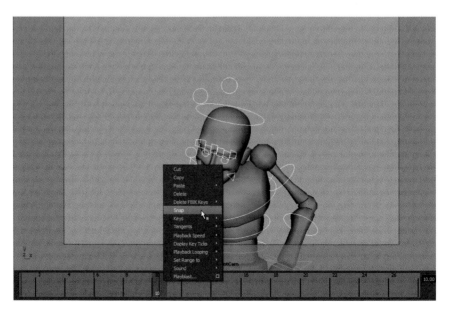

8 That feels much better, but the scaling has put the key between f11 and f12, which can make refining more unpredictable and cause motion blur problems. Right click on f11 and choose Snap to snap the key to the closest frame, which puts it back on f11.

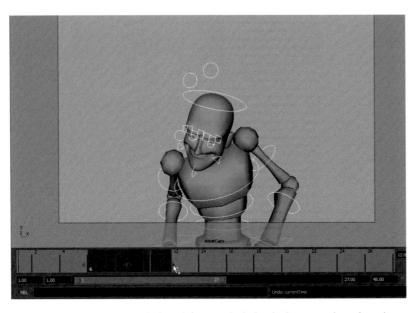

7 Grab the end arrow and drag it through f12 to scale the keys' values out and ease in to the anticipation pose.

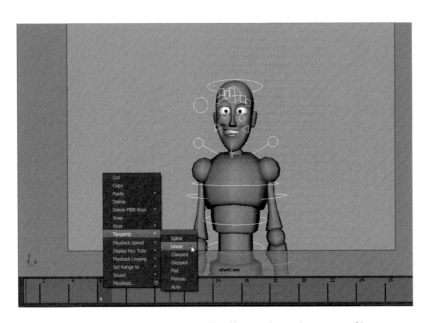

9 The timeline right click menu has many options. You can change the tangents of keys without the Graph Editor, playblast, adjust speed and display options, and more. Use these for speeding up your workflow considerably.

HOT TIP

The timeline is where you can activate sound for dialog animations. Import the sound file through the File menu, then right-click on the timeline and select the sound to activate it during scrubbing and playback.

87

Cartoony Motion

CARTOONY STYLE IS A VERY DIFFICULT style to attain. Most novices make the mistake of trying to push all of the fundamentals. By exaggerating EVERYTHING, they feel like the animation will automatically become cartoony. This could not be further from the case.

To create cartoony movement, we need to create the IMPRESSION of an exaggerated movement by picking a visual simile. What does that mean? Choose a motion that is realistic, and can be observed in everyday life, and put that motion into your character.

You've seen it all before – a character's head rings LIKE A BELL after he gets punched. A character falls to the ground LIKE A SHEET OF PAPER after he gets flattened. A character's arm wobbles LIKE SPAGHETTI after he gets a shot of Novocain in his arm. All of these examples reference REALISTIC motions that when we put them into the body of our character, become cartoony. You will notice none of these examples mention anything about exaggerating. We're going to be creating the last example of the numb arm in this cheat, using some reference geometry Using reference geometry, we do not have to guess the motion we're trying to get out of the wobbly arm, it's right there in front of us to copy. Use this cheat whenever you need to closely reference any motion for cartoony styled animation.

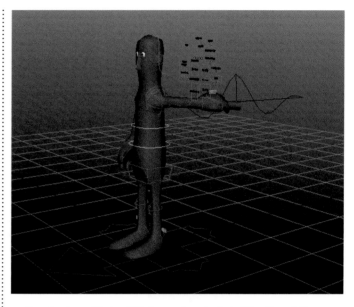

1 Open "cartoony_Start.ma". We have a character just gliding through the scene. We can imagine they are running away. We want to give the impression his arm is totally numb, and flopping around like spaghetti. Let's get started.

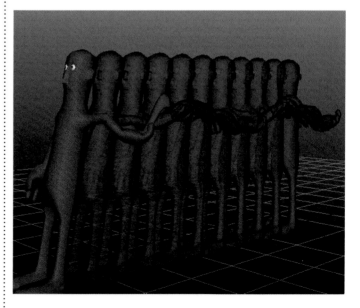

4 Continue going through the animation on 2's, and then back again on 1's, until the arm matches the movement of the cylinder in the entire shot.

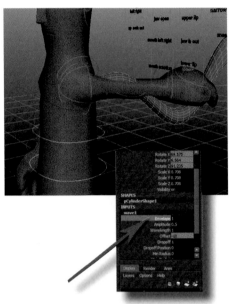

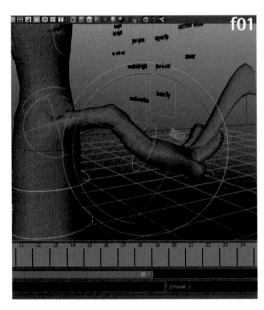

f01

cartoony_Start.ma
cartoony_End.ma

2 There is a cylinder attached to Bloke's arm. That is the piece of geometry we are going to use to apply the wobbly motion for reference. Select the cylinder geometry and in the channel box, go down to the wave1 input and turn the "Envelope" parameter up to 1.

3 Now that the cylinder is wobbling very Spaghetti-like, let's key our arm to follow it. Grab all of the arm controls and set a key matching the pose on f01.

We used a wave deformer to get this wave action, but there are many different ways to get some awesome cartoony movements, including deformers, dynamics, and even hair and cloth. Think about the IMPRESSION you want to give, and then create some reference geometry that is as easy as copying into your character's body.

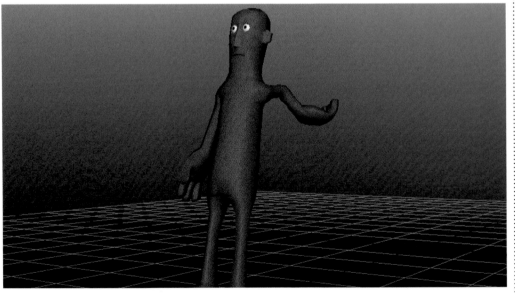

5 Done! Hide the cylinder and play your animation back and watch the awesome wobbly motion come to life. Remember, we didn't just exaggerate, we used motion inspired by real life. This is how true cartoony action comes to life.

Trax Editor

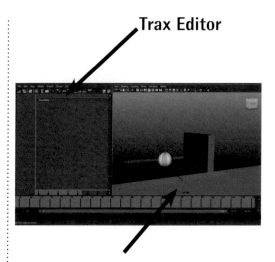

Trax Editor

Perspective Viewport

T HE TRAX EDITOR, apart from being the best place to import and manipulate audio, was actually built to load animation "clips" onto character sets. This can be very fun and intuitive.

Manipulating clips is kind of like "mixing" animation. You can create a library of clips and mix and match the animation to create entire performances, or perhaps more applicable, multiple permutations of background animation. Imagine how easy it would be to animate a small crowd if you can just drag and drop animation clips onto the characters, mixing in movement into cycles and blending between clips. The Trax Editor does just that.

Some things to know about using clips is that the character sets normally have to be identical, so working with a finished rig is highly recommended. Also, you want to make sure your animation is created to be mixed and matched. Meaning you should be thinking about creating actions that are modular, and/or layered to be used in a non-linear fashion.

1 Open "trax_Start.ma" and set up your panels like mine are arranged, with the Trax Editor on the left and persp camera on the right. Just go to Panels> Panel> Trax Editor.

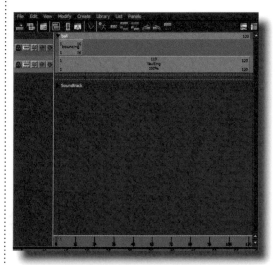

4 Import another clip by going to File>Import Animation Clip to Characters. Choose "Vaulting_Clip.ma" and it will load into a new track.

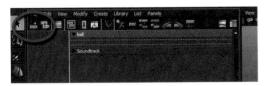

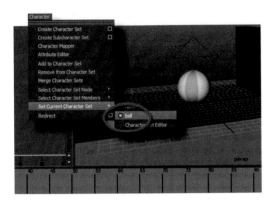

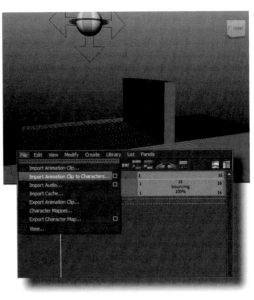

trax_Start.ma
trax_End.ma

2 Set the current character set by hitting F2 to switch to the animation menu set and then going to Character> Set Current Character Set> ball. Then create a track in the Trax Editor by clicking the button in the top left corner.

3 Import the first animation clip, (the ball bouncing) by going (in the Trax Editor) to File>Import Animation Clip to Characters. Choose "Bouncing_Clip.ma" It will load into the Trax Editor and you can find it using the normal camera tools or by hitting **A** to frame it.

HOT TIP

These clips were exported with the animation taking place in "relative" space. This setting means that the position of the controls will start from the end position of the last clip. So, you can have a clip where a character starting at 0 walks forward 5 units, and then in the next clip he'll automatically walk from 5 to 10.

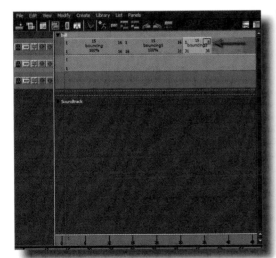

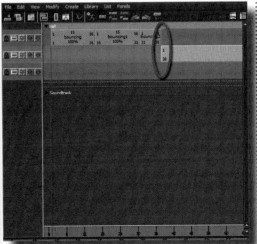

5 Now copy the bouncing clip by selecting it and hitting **ctrl**+**C**. Paste it twice by hitting **ctrl**+**V**, and arrange them one after another on the same track. Drag the clip range of the last clip to end on f08 of the clip, by grabbing the top right corner and dragging it left to "8".

6 Finally, drag the "Vaulting_Clip" so that f01 lines up with f08 of the third "Bouncing_Clip". Play back the animation, and you'll see the ball bounces twice, then lands, and vaults over the wall.

Copying Curves

COPYING DATA GOES BACK to the earliest functionality of computers, and it is alive and well in computer animation. Maya's curve-copying abilities are rather extensive, and it offers many options for shuffling animation data around to save time and effort. We're going to build on the previous exercise and apply the curves on the character's head to his neck and body to make him much more, well, animated.

As we'll see in this cheat, copying isn't only for putting the same curve on another control. Any attribute's curve can be copied to any other attribute. This is great for taking a curve that is similar in shape to what we want on another control (even if it's a rotate going to a translate, for example) and using it as a starting point. Tweaking a curve can be much faster than positioning the control and setting keys. Faster = good.

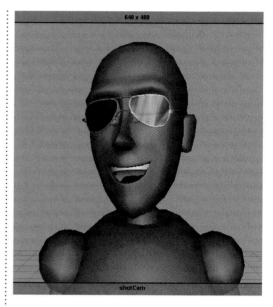

1 Open CopyingCurves_start.ma for the completed exercise found in the previous cheat.

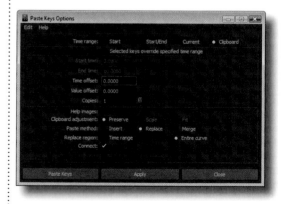

4 Select the neck control. Before we paste these curves, go to Edit > Paste > options box. Set the Time range to "Clipboard" (to use the curves we just copied) and Paste method to "Replace" and Replace region to "Entire curve". Then press Paste Keys.

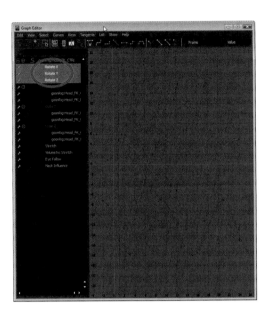

2 In the Graph Editor, select the Rotate X, Y, and Z
   attributes for the head control. Be sure to select the
attributes in the left panel, not the curves themselves.

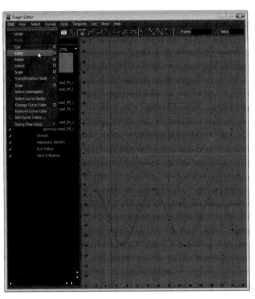

3 Go to Edit > Copy in the Graph Editor menu to copy the
   curves.

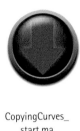

CopyingCurves_
start.ma
CopyingCurves_
end.ma

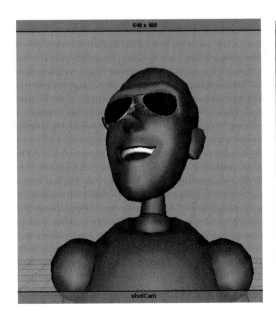

5 The curves will automatically be placed on the same
   attributes they were copied from if nothing is selected in
the Graph Editor. They've been copied to the neck, but now
his head is back a bit too far.

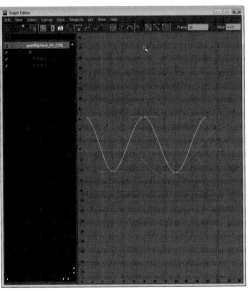

6 I moved up the entire Rotate X curve to bring his head
   forward, then scaled the whole curve down. Now his
movement is bigger, but not too much.

Copying Curves (cont'd)

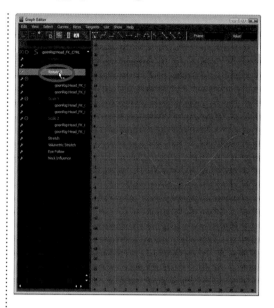

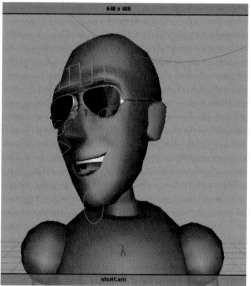

7 Let's use some of these curves to add side-to-side movement on the chest. The head's rotate Z curve has a similar contour to what we can start with, so select the attribute in the Graph Editor and Edit > Copy.

8 Select the chest control and set a key at f01. Since we'll be putting the head's Rotate Z on the chest's Rotate Z and Rotate Y, we need to be able to select those attributes in the Graph Editor. Without a key they won't appear.

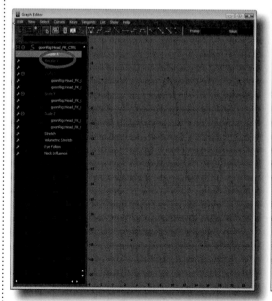

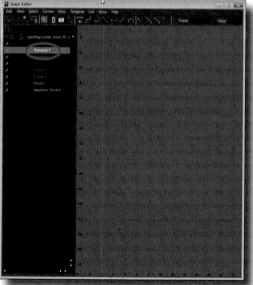

11 Finally, let's add some bounce on his body. The curve most similar to what we want is the head's Rotate X, so select that attribute on the head and copy the curve.

12 Select the main body control and set a key at f01. Select its Translate Y attribute and paste the curve onto it. He'll move out of frame because of the values, so let's quickly tweak this curve.

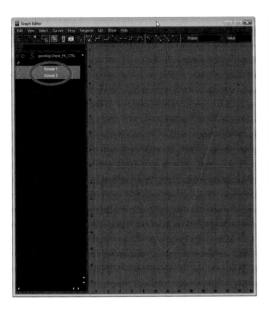

9 In the Graph Editor, select the chest's Rotate Y and Z attributes and go to Edit > Paste. The curve will be put on both attributes.

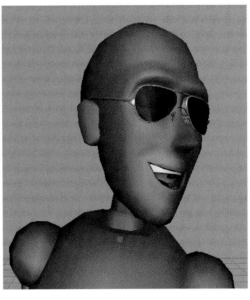

10 I shifted both curves one frame earlier for a little offset, and scaled them up. Now his movement is much more energetic.

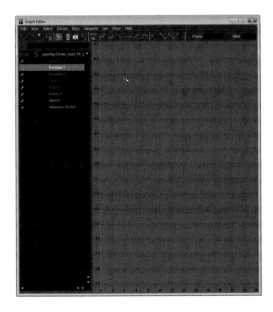

13 I edited the curve so it starts on f01 and his bounces stay in frame. There are also some differences in the values so everything doesn't feel exactly the same.

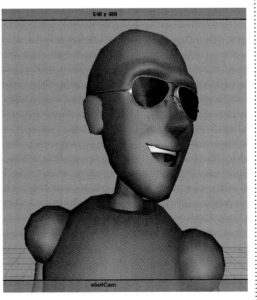

14 The animation can be refined a lot from here, including adding some bounce in the shoulders, but now you see how we can quickly get a smooth starting point simply by copying curves and not doing any character positioning.

HOT TIP

Copying curves is a great technique, but it's almost always best for quickly giving you a curve to start refining, rather than a finished result. It can also work well for starting overlapping action on things like tails and floppy ears.

95

Editable Motion Trails

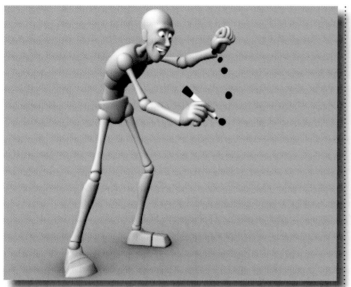

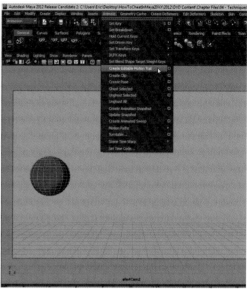

I N ORDER TO GET APPEALING, polished animation, it's a good idea for the motion to travel in pleasing arcs. After all, it is one of the 12 animation principles! There have been plenty of tools made for Maya to track arcs, but what about fixing them directly in the viewport? Wouldn't that be nice? Or even adjusting your spacing without having to go into the Graph Editor? If only there was a way...

There is. One of the best features in Maya 2014 for tracking and editing arcs (and other things) is the Editable Motion Trail. Not only does it show you the path an object is taking through 3D space, but it also allows you to edit that path directly in the viewport. Needless to say, this has been a feature animators have desired for quite some time, and Maya 2014 makes it a reality.

Editable Motion Trails give you lots of power. They work in conjunction with the other keyframe tools (Graph Editor, Dope Sheet) so anything you edit on them will be reflected everywhere else. You can adjust the path of action, timing, and spacing, as well as add, delete, and move keyframes right on the path. This cheat will give you all the ins and outs of this most welcome addition to Maya's animation toolset.

1 In the project file EditableMotionTrail.ma, double check that your tangents are weighted, and that the tangent type is set to Auto. (See Chapter 2 for more info.) The motion trail's behavior is dictated by what tangent settings are present on the curves. Select the ball and go to Animate > Create Editable Motion Trail.

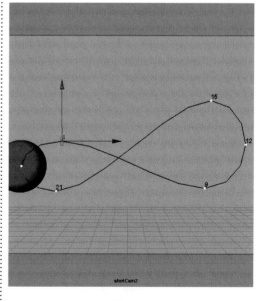

4 Select the move tool **W** and select the key at f04. Just like moving an animation control, you can move the key in 3D space and adjust the path instantly.

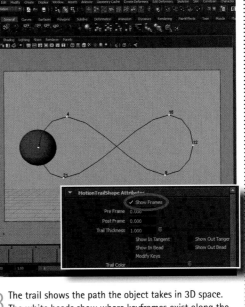

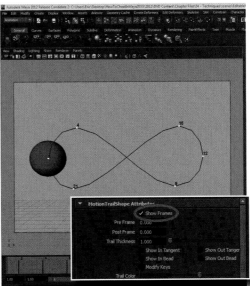

EditableMotionTrail.
ma

2 Open the Attribute Editor if it isn't already and click on the motion trail to bring up its options. You can also right click directly on the trail to quickly access the settings most commonly toggled on/off.

3 The trail shows the path the object takes in 3D space. The white beads show where keyframes exist along the trail. Click the Show Frames box in the Attribute Editor to display the frame number for each key.

HOT TIP

The Trail Color slider is very handy for when you have multiple motion trails happening. Keeping the colors different makes it easier to remember what is what.

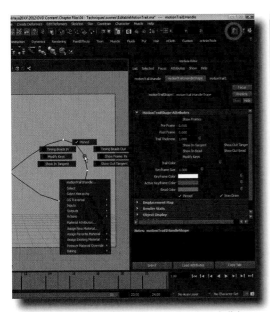

After

Before

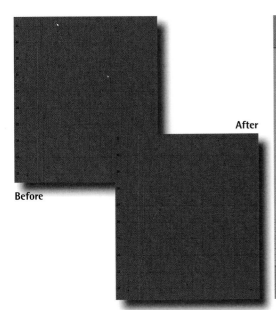

5 Notice the Translate Y curve before and after the change I made in the previous step. Adjusting keys in the motion trail is really just another more visual and natural way of editing the curves.

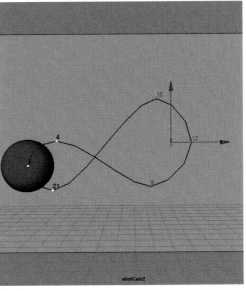

6 You can select multiple keys and move them just as easily. *ctrl* -dragging will move the selected keys perpendicular to the viewport (i.e., backwards/forwards), which is great for not having to change cameras to make an edit.

Editable Motion Trails (cont'd)

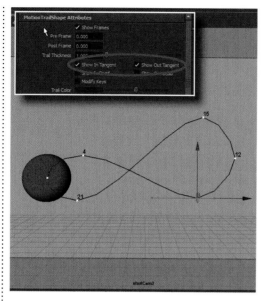

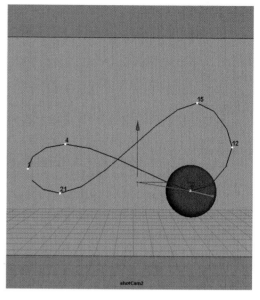

7 Select the key at f09 and in the Attribute Editor (or right click menu) turn on Show In Tangent and Show Out Tangent to show handles for the key. Remember that the way these handles will behave depends on the settings for the curves they are found on.

8 Marquee select the handle and you can use it to edit the spacing in the motion path, just like in the Graph Editor. Editing handles is easiest when you only use one axis on the manipulator at a time, rather than grabbing them in the middle and dragging all axes freely.

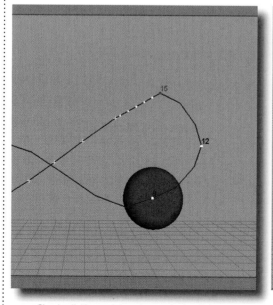

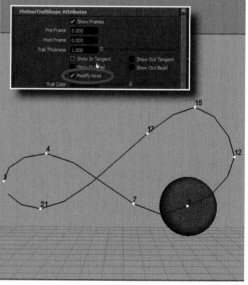

11 Simply clicking and dragging on the beads lets you adjust the spacing. Remember, if you don't see any beads, it's because your tangents on this key are not weighted.

12 Click the Modify Keys box in the Attribute Editor or right click menu. When this is turned on, simply clicking on the trail will add keys, which will use whatever tangents are currently set to default.

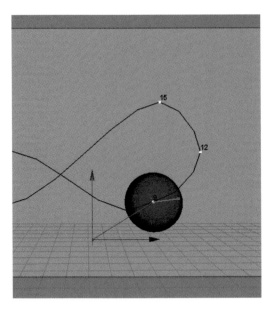

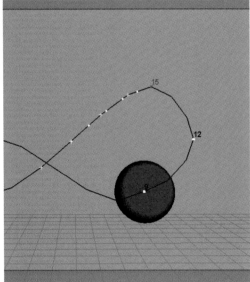

9 If you break the tangent handles (select the curves/keys in the Graph Editor and click the break tangents button), you can edit them independently in the viewport as well.

10 Select the key at f15 and click Show Out Bead in the Attribute Editor or right click menu. Beads representing the in-between keys appear on the trail. Notice that you cannot show both tangents and beads at the same time, as they're really just different representations of the same thing - spacing of the in-betweens.

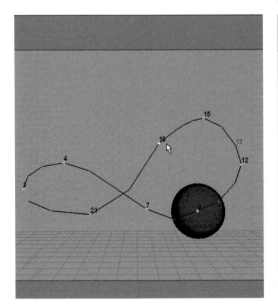

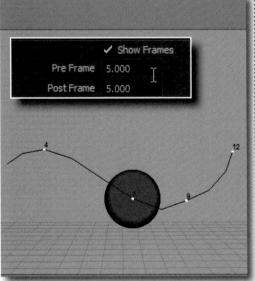

13 For making quick timing changes with Modify Keys, simply hold S and MM drag keys. You'll see the frame number adjust, as well as marks indicating the current position of the in-between frames. Very nice!

14 In the Attributes, you can enter Pre and Post Frame values. This controls how many frames before and after the current frame to display. This helps if the path crosses over itself multiple times in a small space, which makes the trail hard to read. Setting 0 shows all frames.

HOT TIP

The "Pinned" option means that the trail will stay present all the time. If you turn it off, it will only appear when the object with the trail is selected.

99

IK and FK

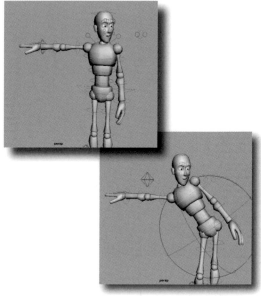

1 Open IK_FK.ma. The left arm is currently in FK. Rotating any of the body controls brings the arm along with it.

ALMOST ANY RIG that is intended for character animation will have the arms and legs available in two modes, IK (inverse kinematics) and FK (forward kinematics). Many animators have a mode they prefer to use when either is viable, but there will often be times when you have to use a specific mode, at least for part of the animation. If your character is going to plant his hand on something to support his weight or push or pull it, you will have no choice but to use IK arms if you want acceptable results. Switching between the modes can seem tedious at first, but when you understand how switching works, it's really quite simple.

For a quick refresher, FK (forward kinematics) means that the position of the hand (or foot) is dependent upon the joints leading up to it. This is how our bodies work in the real world. To reach up and grab something with your hand, your shoulder must rotate, taking your upper arm with it, which takes your forearm with that, which takes your hand up to the object. You can't raise your hand without at least raising your elbow, and so on. With FK, if you move the character's body, it will move the arm as well. This works well for things like walks and gesturing, but not for pulling or pushing things.

IK (inverse kinematics) is the opposite. The hand is positioned on its own, and Maya figures out where the rest of the arm would be angled based on that. You can think of the hand almost as a separate object that's tethered to the body. If you move the body the hand will stay where it is, making it ideal for pushing or pulling. This way we can work on the body animation without losing the positioning of the hand.

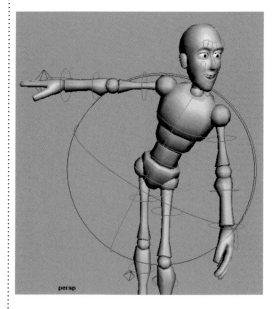

4 When Chest Influence is 0, the FK arm will follow with translation of the body, but not rotation. Some animators prefer this because you need to do much less correction on the arms if you change the body.

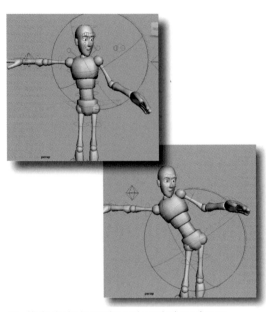

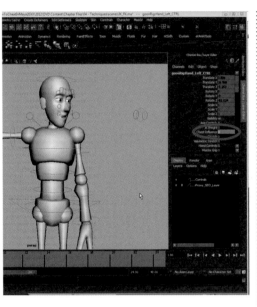

IK_FK.ma

2 Undo the body rotation and put the L arm in any
   pose you wish. Again, the arm will follow along with
anything we move in the body and spine.

3 Undo everything and select the hand control. In the
   channel box is the chest influence attribute. Change it
to 0. The arm may jump slightly when you do this, which is
normal.

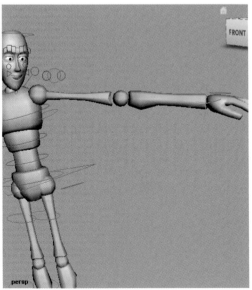

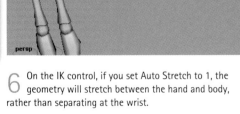

5 Undo everything. Select the hand control and set the IK
   weight to 1 (100%). The arm will move to the IK control
and is now an IK arm. Move the body and the hand will stay
in place no matter what you do.

6 On the IK control, if you set Auto Stretch to 1, the
   geometry will stretch between the hand and body,
rather than separating at the wrist.

IK/FK Switching

W HEN PLANNING AN ANIMATION, an important step is determining if it's best to use IK, FK, or both at different times. When we need to use both, switching between them in a way that's smooth and seamless is the key to quality work. While some animators may dread this element of animating, when you keep in mind how switching works under the hood, it's very straightforward.

The thing to realize is that there are actually two different arms as far as the joints underneath the geometry are concerned. One arm isn't switching between IK and FK modes, we're actually moving the geometry to another joint skeleton. So when you switch from, say, FK to IK, keep in mind that in the frame where IK takes over, the FK arm is still in its last position, following along (albeit invisibly). Remembering that there are two arms at work will make switching more clear in your mind.

While it's possible to blend into the other arm over several frames, I believe it's almost always best to do the switch over a single frame. When you blend, there are frames where the geometry is partially attached to both arms, so both controls affect the geometry to varying degrees. This makes it difficult to be precise in both posing and timing. It can work, of course, but I always prefer complete control at every frame.

Some rigs do have IK/FK snapping, which makes life much easier by automatically lining either arm to the other. Many rigs don't, however, and you just have to pose the switching frame manually, which is how we'll do it here.

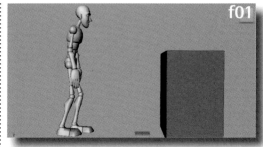

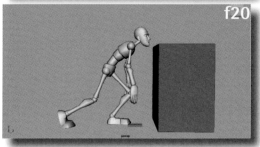

1 Open IKFKswitching_start.ma. There's a simple blocking animation of the character standing, then stepping to push the box. The arms aren't animated yet and they start in FK.

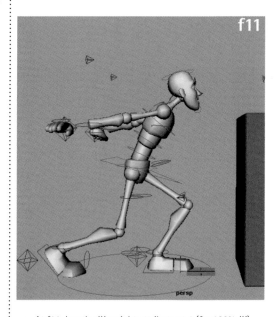

4 At f11, key the IK weight attribute at 1 (for 100% IK). The arms will snap back to where the IK arm skeletons are located.

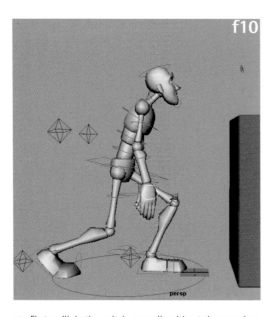

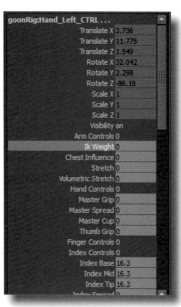

IKFKswitching_
start.ma
IKFKswitching_end.
ma

2 First we'll do the switch manually without the snapping tool. F11 is where the switch to IK will happen, so select the hand controls and move to f10.

3 At f10, in the channel box right click and choose Key Selected on the IK weight attribute. This keys it again at 0 so we hold in FK up to f10.

HOT TIP

For any kind of
IK/FK switching,
don't sweat the
small stuff until
the transition
is working.
Focus on just
the hands and
hide or ignore
the fingers until
the foundation
is set.

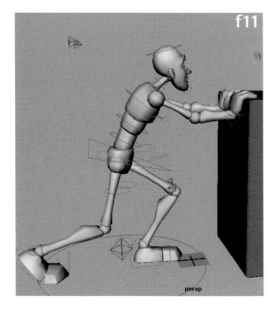

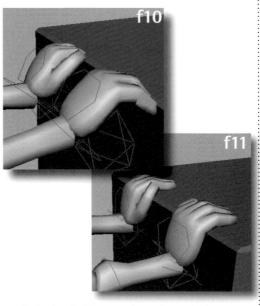

5 At f11, pose the IK hands and fingers on the box. Use the shoulders to help you get a good pose. When doing a switch, it's helpful to first establish the pose you're switching to, rather than basing it off the transition into the pose.

6 At f10, key the FK arms and pose them going into the IK pose. Try to ignore the fingers and just focus on the palm since we'll need to edit them again anyway. It won't be perfect yet, since we'll also have to adjust the IK pose again in a moment, so just get it in the ballpark.

IK/FK Switching (cont'd)

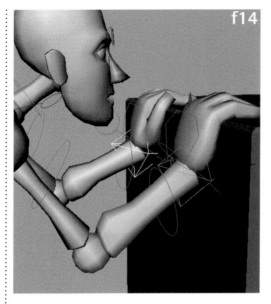

f14

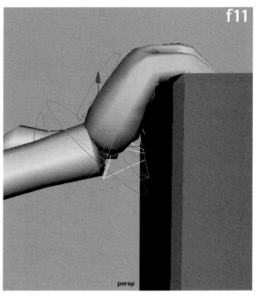

f11

7 Now that the transition is better, we can improve the contact point. Right now his hand just kind of sticks to the box and we don't feel it compress into it. Select the IK controls and set a key at f14 to set the same pose a little later.

8 Go back to f11 and pull the IK controls away a bit and rotate them down slightly. Again, focus only on the palm and don't worry about the fingers yet. Make the palms ease in nicely to f14 to give a feeling of the palms pressing.

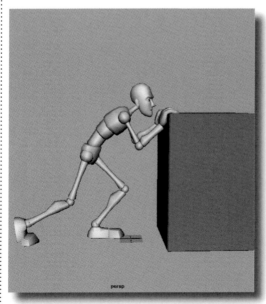

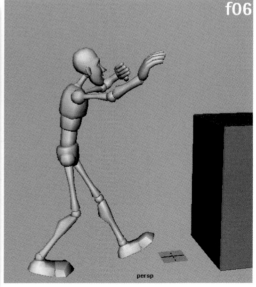

f06

10 You probably noticed that once you get the switch frame, the rest is just normal animating except you're switching between two different types of controls.

11 You may or may not have the problem of his arms going crazy during the transition. If so, it's because of gimbal lock, which can happen from time to time.

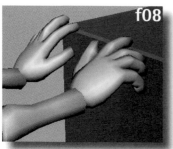

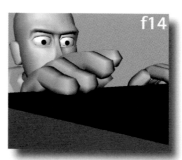

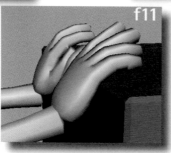

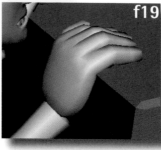

9 With the press working better, now is a good time to rough in some finger poses and have them trail the palms pressing for some overlap.

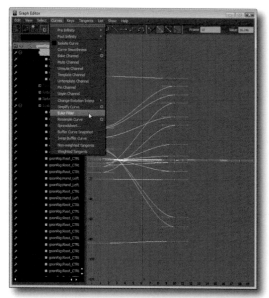

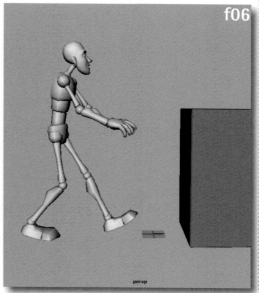

12 To fix it, select all the FK arm curves in the Graph Editor and use Curves > Euler Filter.

13 Now his arms interpolate to the push pose the way we'd expect and we can continue to refine the animation from there.

105

Character Sets

URING PART OR ALL of their animation process, some animators like to use Character Sets, which are basically selection sets you don't need to select to key. They're kind of a legacy feature, as they've been around since the earlier versions of Maya, but a number of animators still find them useful. Personally, I think they work best in situations where you have to do a lot of keyframing on specific channels of a control, such as the fingers, and for that they can be handy. In this cheat we'll look at how to create and edit character sets.

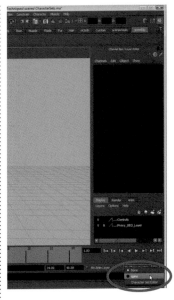

1 Open CharacterSets.ma. The Character Set selection menu is at the bottom right, next to the Auto Key button. Click the arrow next to it and select "spine".

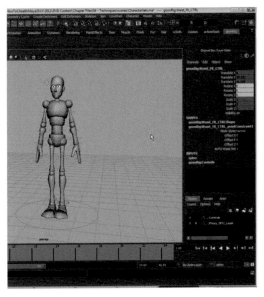

2 Without selecting anything, press **S** to set a key. This set contains all the spine controls, so they will automatically be keyed with any key. Notice their channels are yellow, indicating they are connected to a set.

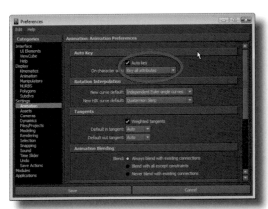

5 With the arms set selected, setting a key will now key all the controls. Open the Animation Preferences and turn on Auto Key if it isn't already. On character sets, set to Key all attributes.

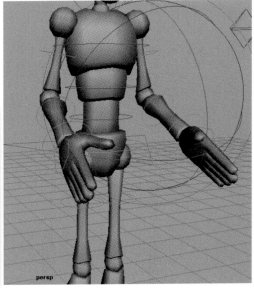

6 Now adjusting any of the arm controls will set a key on all the other arm controls automatically. This can be handy for blocking if you make a set for all controls.

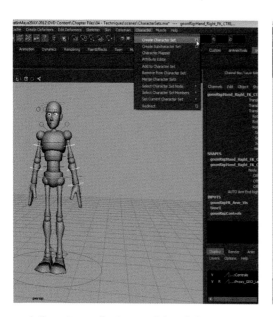

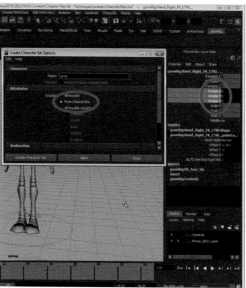

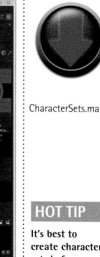

CharacterSets.ma

3 Let's create a set for the arms. Select all the arm controls and in the animation menu set f2 go to Character > Create Character Set > Options box.

4 In the options, name the set "arms" and select "From Channel Box". Highlight the rotate XYZ channels in the channel box, and click Create Character Set.

HOT TIP

It's best to create character sets before you start animating. If you need to create a set with controls that are already animated, create a new set with nothing selected. Then add the controls/ attributes to the set using Add to Character Set.

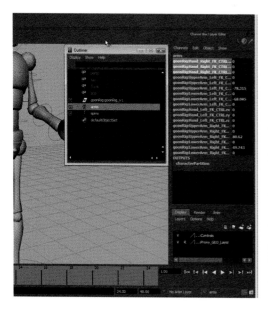

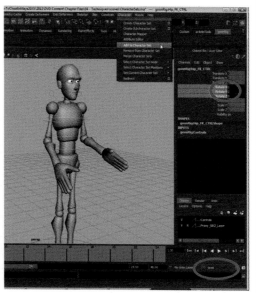

7 To remove attributes, go to Window > Outliner and select the set you want to edit. The attributes will appear in the channel box. Select the attributes you want to remove and go to Character > Remove From Character Set.

8 To add to a character set, have it selected in the list at the bottom, select the objects/attributes you wish to add, and go to Character > Add to Character Set.

Grease Pencil Tool

ONE OF THE MOST VALUABLE and long-sought updates to Maya 2014 is the Grease Pencil tool. In traditional animation, a grease pencil was simply that; a pencil that leaves a greasy or waxy mark on cels or glass. You could make marks on a drawing and rub the mark off easily. Nowadays, CG animators clamor for tools that allow us to more easily access our creativity. Tools like the Grease Pencil that allow our imagination, our off-the-cuff ideas, and our gestures to infiltrate Maya's otherwise stoic UI.

Many Grease Pencil or Blue Pencil (as it is otherwise known) scripts have existed in Maya for years, but none have the ease of use, functionality, or the advantage of being built in.

It should be noted that you will get very little benefit from the Grease Pencil tool without the use of a pen tablet, tablet PC, tablet monitor like a Wacom Cintiq, or a touchscreen monitor. It is nearly impossible to get any useful gestural strokes from a mouse. I have been a longtime proponent of the use of a pen tablet for general mousing for ergonomics reasons. If you have not made the change yet, perhaps it is time you considered it.

We will be starting very slowly with the Grease Pencil tool by creating some simple poses for a bouncing ball animation using the Grease Pencil. You will see that it is much quicker and easier to draw the frames you want before going into a rig and posing the model or character. Your workflow will improve immensely by having a multi-discipline approach to your animation. Let's get started.

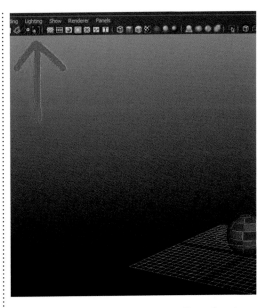

1 Open "grease_Pencil_Start.ma". You will see there is a bouncing ball rig waiting for you to animate it. Turn on the Grease Pencil tool by clicking the button at the top of the Persp Panel.

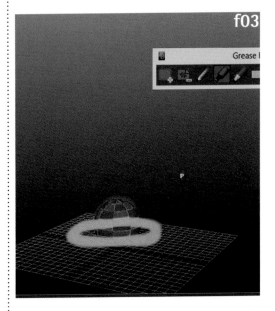

4 Advance the timeline to f03 and click Add Frame again on the Grease Pencil tool. On f03, draw the sphere squashed down in anticipation.

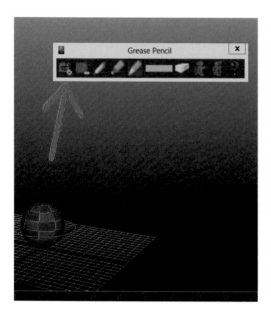

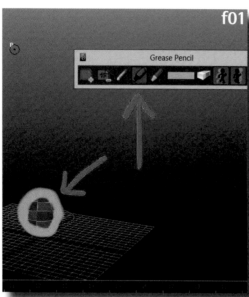

grease_Pencil_
Start.ma
grease_Pencil_End.
ma

2 In Persp1, click on the Add Frame button on the Grease
Pencil tool. Frames act like stepped keys, meaning they
will stay on screen until a new frame is created.

3 Switch to the Soft Pencil tool by clicking on it. This
style is good for rough drawings. On f01, draw the
sphere as it sits on the grid.

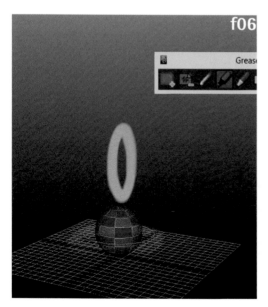

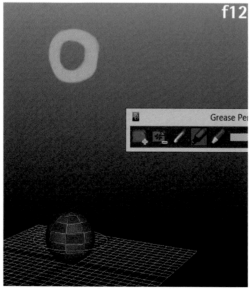

5 On f06, add another frame and draw the sphere
stretched out, flying up into the air.

6 On f12, add another Grease Pencil frame and draw the
sphere at the top of its arc in the air with no squash and
stretch.

Grease Pencil Tool (cont'd)

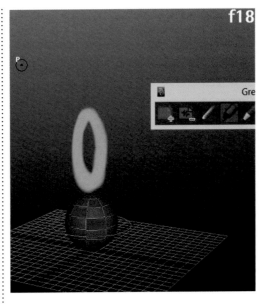

7 On f18, add another Grease Pencil frame and draw the sphere returning to the ground, and stretching out again.

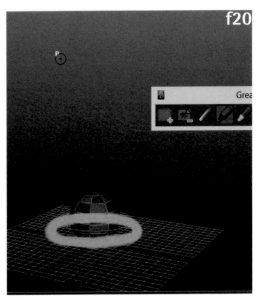

8 On f20, add another frame and draw the sphere flattened on the ground.

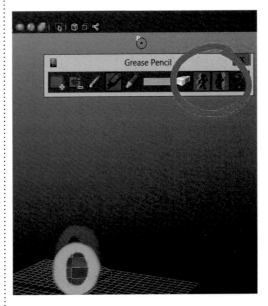

11 You can add in-betweens by looking at where the drawings are using ghosting. Turn on the preframe ghosting and the post frame ghosting by clicking their buttons in the Grease Pencil tool.

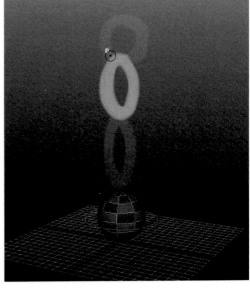

12 Add a few in-betweens by moving the timeline to a frame, adding a Grease Pencil frame, and making a drawing that is in-between the two ghost frames that you can see.

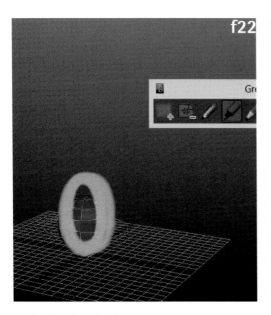

f22

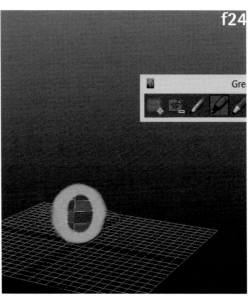

f24

9 On f22, add another frame and draw the sphere stretched slightly as it overshoots.

10 Finally, on f24, add another frame and draw the sphere in its resting position. If you make a mistake, you can always use the eraser.

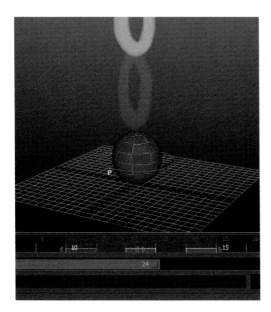

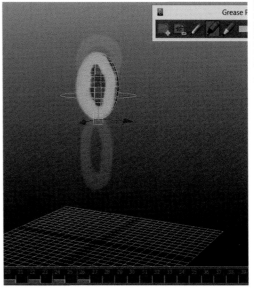

13 Now that you have the hang of it, adjust the timing of this bounce by moving the Grease Pencil keys on the timeline the same way you would with object keyframes. Shift_LMB selects a frame or a frame range, MMB a selected key moves it.

14 Once you are done, simply use the controller on the sphere to 'match' what you have created with the Grease Pencil tool. See how much easier it is to quickly thumbnail the animation than it is to pose the character?

111

Grease Pencil & Trails

As you saw in the last section, the Grease Pencil is great for coming up with pose and timing choices, but it can also be used to determine and refine the arcs in your scene. We are going to use the new Grease Pencil tool in conjunction with Maya's powerful Editable Motion Trails to really hone in on a perfect arc.

Used together, the Grease Pencil and Editable Motion Trails offer you real-time and in-panel feedback on your work. Best of all, your planning stages can seamlessly be integrated into your blocking stage. This creates a much more coherent workflow going from planning to animating.

We are always looking for ways for our planning to help us make decisions deep into the animation process. In other words, we are trying to squeeze as much information out of thumbnails, reference, etc., all in a bid to let these planning materials improve our final animation. By marrying the Grease Pencil and Editable Motion Trails, we are doing just that.

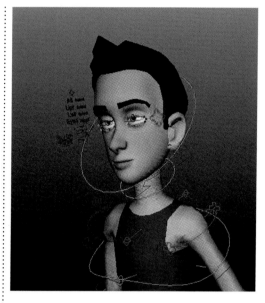

1 Open "grease_Trail_Start.mb". You will notice a camera framed with a character in a start position.

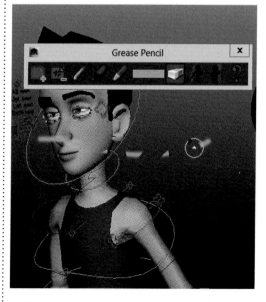

4 If you don't get it at first, erase and redraw. You can undo (**Z** key), use the Erase tool, or even delete the frame and add a new frame again. Any method will work.

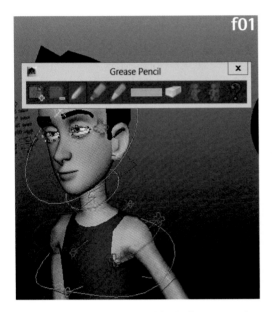

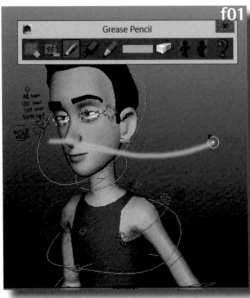

grease_Trail_
Start.mb
grease_Trail_End.
mb

2 Click on the Grease Pencil tool in the Camera1 panel and click on the plus sign in the Grease Pencil tool settings to add a frame on f01.

3 In f01, draw a nice arc, starting on Morpheus's nose and tracing a smooth arc to the right.

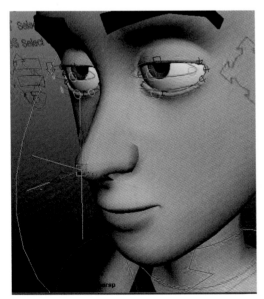

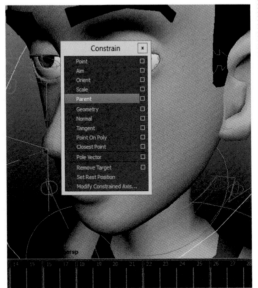

5 Now create a locator and snap it to Morpheus's nose by holding down the **V** key as you move it.

6 Select Morpheus's head control, *Shift* select this new locator, and in the Animation menu set (press F2) click on Constrain>Parent.

113

Grease Pencil & Trails (cont'd)

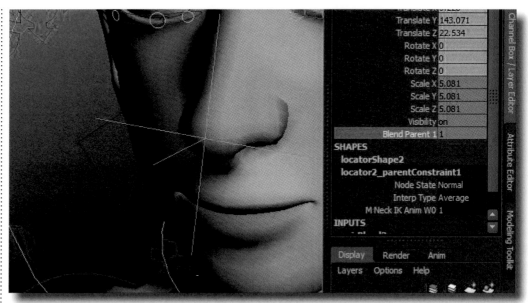

7 Select the locator, and hit **S** to set key. Then go into the channel box and make sure Blend Parent is at 1.

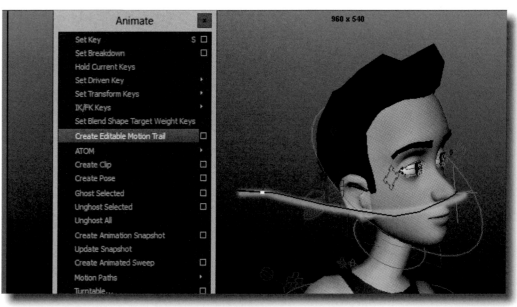

9 Select the locator on the nose and click on Animate>Create Editable Motion Trail.

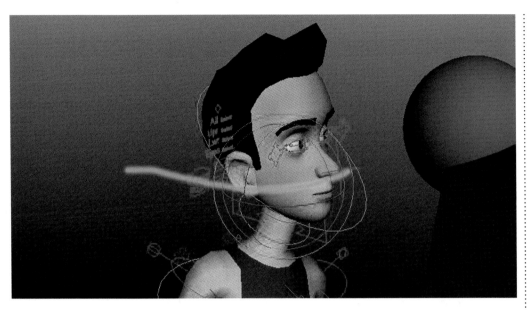

8 Now create a simple head turn by keying the head rotating from left to right across 24 frames or so, trying to do your best to keep the nose on the arc you drew.

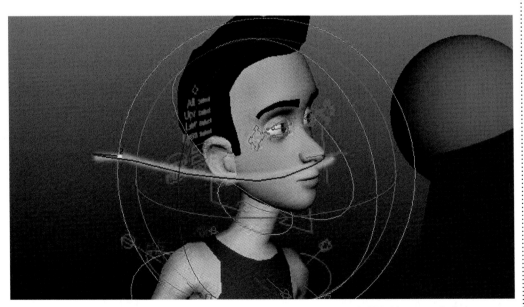

10 Now adjust the head turn even further to match the arc that you drew in panel. With this new method of arc tracking, your planning will help you LONG into the life of your shot!

All in the Hips
Do They Always Lead the Action?
by Kenny Roy

SIMPLY PUT, YES! But there's more to this story.

This was a question asked of me by a student on my website www.kennyroy.com. When I answered the question I only succeeded in confusing the student even further. In short, I said that when you are planning a character from the very beginning, it can be fun to choose a part of the body that the character "leads" with. This obviously contradicts the edict that the hips lead all actions. I will try to dispel the confusion here.

Let's start at the very beginning with the concept of the hips leading each action. All characters will constantly find balance in their poses and their movements. That is, if they are standing still, their weight is over their hips so that they don't fall over. And if they are in motion, they are extending their legs to catch the 'controlled fall', again to keep from face-planting. It just so happens that the biggest weight that we can move to achieve this equilibrium is our entire torso, controlled in major part by our hips. If we are standing still, and want to lift our left leg, we automatically use the muscles in our legs, hips, back, stomach and all stabilizers to shift our weight over the right leg. As the weight comes off the left leg, we are able to lift it. Similarly, if we are starting to walk from a standstill, the muscles of the legs and torso allow the body to lean forward and build momentum. We say that the hips lead the action because, in addition to the muscles making the weight shift prior to a leg being lifted, the hips move to take on the new weight. They are our "gauge" as animators to see where the weight is distributed.

So in short, the answer is yes, the hips always lead the action because we have to change our balance to change our pose or motion; and the hips are constantly shifting to take on the new weight.

However! It is also true what I said to the student before: choosing a part of the body to "lead" the action is a fun way to come up with an interesting character. This is an exercise we would do all the time in Improv class to come up with interesting characters. In fact, why don't you try it right now:

Stand up and take a moment to breathe and relax. Now think of a really nasty villian. Take on a little bit of the physicality of this character, but now choose any part of your body that will "lead" the action. It can be anything. Your elbows, knees, chin, top of your head, even your butt. Now spend a little more time thinking about how this body part is really pulling you through space. Imagine a string is tied to this body part and you are being tugged around by the string. Start pacing around the room with this "body lead" and feel the villian's character take shape. Why does this character move this way? What is the back-story, why did this person become a villian? As you continue to pace around as this villian, with a strong body lead, you may notice that you take on an even deeper physicality to your gait. If you chose the chin as the leading body part, then you might actually feel your neck craning to push the chin out further. Your back may become bent and you may take long steps and thrust your chin forward with each step. It's amazing how much physicality can come from a simple body lead. As you continue to explore this character, you will also find that the deeper physical choices are calling for some very strong character choices as well. Test out an action other than walking for this character. Maybe pick up a pencil, look around and make sure nobody is watching, and steal it. Now before we get too carried away, do the action you chose one more time, but slower and paying very close attention to where your weight is. Notice how even though you have a very strong body lead, the weight is always seeking balance. Your hips are also still telegraphing the placement of the weight on your legs.

Alright, we're getting a little carried away. Shake out your arms and legs and relax. Try this exercise with many different body leads. Better yet, try this exercise in front of a full-length mirror, and perform some actions while watching the weight shifts in your body. Watch how the hips are where the "idea" of all the movements in the body really start, but you can still have a strong body lead elsewhere. Record some reference of this new villian character you've invented. And when you are totally comfortable and sure that you've fully explored this new physicality, animate this character!

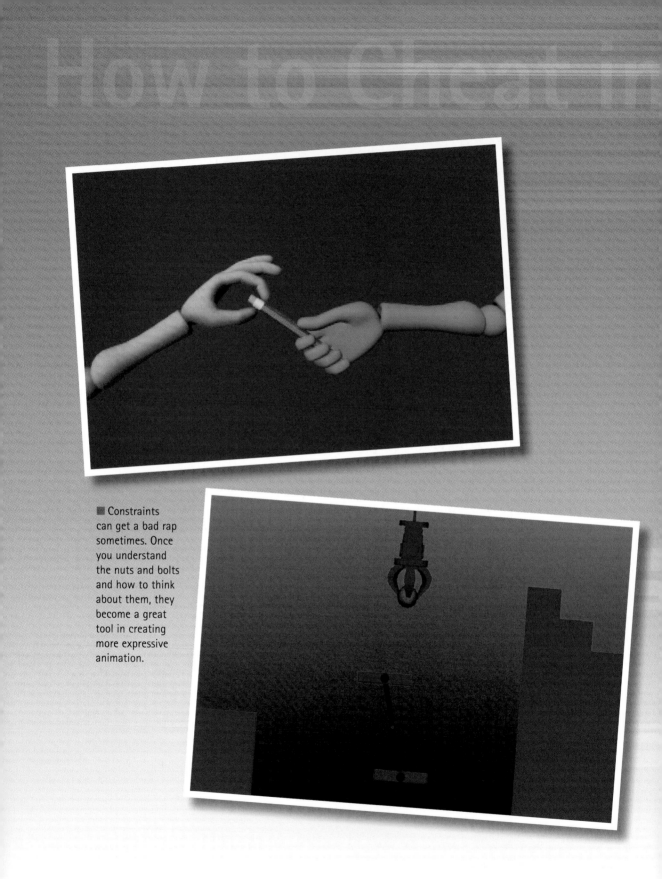

■ Constraints can get a bad rap sometimes. Once you understand the nuts and bolts and how to think about them, they become a great tool in creating more expressive animation.

5
Constraints

SOONER OR LATER every animator must have a character interact with a prop, and that means we need to work with constraints. They can seem a tad complicated at first, but once you understand how they work, you can design a constraint system that is simple and flexible. The next few cheats will tell you what you need to know about constraints as an animator. Then we'll look at some tools that will make constraining a breeze.

Parenting

NOVICE ANIMATORS SOMETIMES confuse parenting and constraining. These two processes behave somewhat similarly, but are quite different under the hood. First let's look at how parenting works.

Parenting is essentially indicating the center of an object's universe. By default, an object created in Maya exists in 3D space, and the infinite area inside the viewport is its central universe.

When we parent an object to another object (referred to as the child and parent), we are making the child object's central universe the parent object, instead of the 3D space. The child can still be moved independently, but its location is defined by where it is in relation to its parent, not where it is in space.

Think of it like this: you are currently parented to the earth. If you are sitting at your computer reading this book, as far as you're concerned, you're not moving. If you get up to get a soda from the fridge, you would say you've moved to a new location. Now think beyond earth and consider your position in the galaxy. When you're at your computer thinking you're not moving, you actually are moving through space (at 65,000 mph!) because the earth is moving through space and you are on it. It's your own perspective that you're not moving, but in relation to the entire universe, you are. This relationship of you to the earth to the galaxy is respectively the same as a child parented to its object in Maya's 3D space. Let's observe this in Maya.

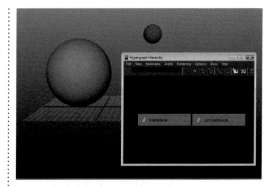

1 Open parenting.ma. Here I've created two spheres, and right now they're independent of each other. We can see in the hypergraph (Window > Hypergraph: Hierarchy) that they're side by side, indicating two separate objects.

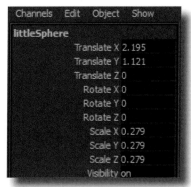

4 This is also indicated in the channel box, where we see that, although nothing has changed in the viewport, the little sphere coordinates are different to reflect the new relationship.

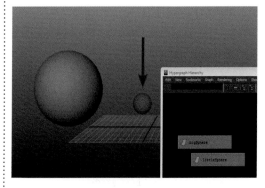

7 Use the move tool again to translate the little sphere.

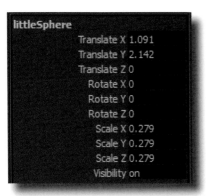

2 Notice the coordinates for the little sphere in the channel box, indicating its position in world space. Move the little sphere and you will see these coordinates update accordingly.

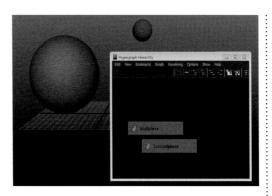

3 First select the little sphere (the child), then shift select the big sphere (the parent) and press **P** to parent them. We can see in the hypergraph that they are now connected. We've created a hierarchy. The little sphere now uses the big sphere as its reference point.

parenting.ma

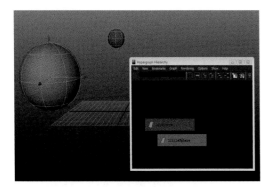

5 Move the big sphere using the move tool **W**, and the little sphere follows accordingly, maintaining its position.

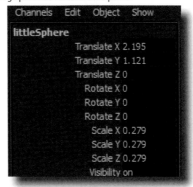

6 If we look at the little sphere's coordinates in the channel box they're still the same. Its reference point of moving is only in relation to the big sphere, just like our intro example: our perception of moving is related to the earth, rather than the universe.

HOT TIP

When parenting, the order you select the objects in determines what is parented to what. Think "child runs to the parent" to help you remember to select the child first. To unparent, use *Shift*+**P** with the child selected.

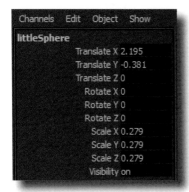

8 Now the translate channels for the little sphere change, because it's in a different position relative to the parent.

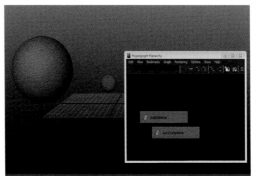

9 What's this have to do with animating? Knowing the difference between parenting and constraining will help you make a flexible system when using props with your characters. Next we'll look at how constraints work, and then how to use these methods together.

Parent Constraints

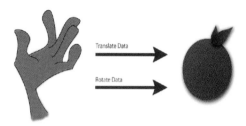

Parent Constraint

Translate Data →

Rotate Data →

Character's Hand   Prop

CONSTRAINED OBJECTS are fundamentally different from parented ones in that they still ultimately reference their position from the origin. They simply get their translate, rotate, and/or scale information told to them by their master object. Think of it as a direct line from the master object's attributes into whichever attributes are constrained (which can be any or all of them) into the target object. When we have constrained a prop to a character's hand, it isn't actually "stuck" there; it just receives the same location information which makes it follow along.

Because of this direct line, we can't move constrained objects because they're "hardwired" to the master object. We can turn the constraint off (using what's called the weight), but if it's on, the constrained attributes cannot be altered independently of the master object.

We can see that there is sort of a yin/yang balance with parenting and constraints. Parenting cannot be turned off or on over the course of an animation, but you can move the child object independently. Constraints can be turned on or off yet are locked to their master object while on. In setting up effective constraint systems, we can use the strengths of each to get the results we need.

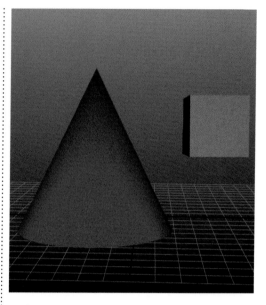

1 Open parentConstraint.ma. There are many types of constraints, but as an animator, you'll probably use parent constraints most of the time. Parent constraints connect the translate and rotate attributes, and the constrained object behaves as if it were parented, except for not being able to move it independently.

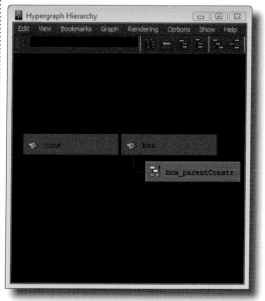

4 In the hypergraph, notice that the objects stay disconnected, and we see a constraint node appear. This is connected to the box, because it looks at the translate and rotate data of the cone, and "tells" the box to do the same.

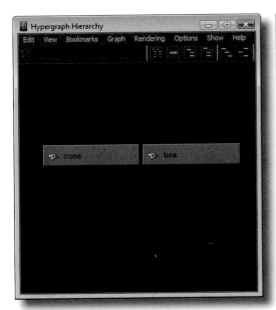

2 In this scene we have two independent objects, a cone and a box. Go to Window > Hypergraph: Hierarchy. Notice how they are not connected like in the previous parenting example.

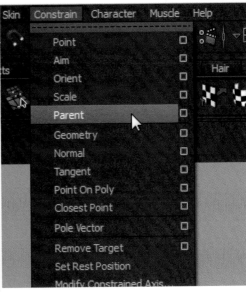

3 Constraint selection order is the opposite of parenting, where the master object is selected first. Select the cone, then shift select the box, and in the Animation menu set go to Constrain > Parent. The names can make things confusing, but keep in mind this is a constraint, so you are not actually parenting these objects.

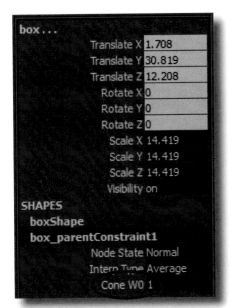

5 In the channel box the box's translate and rotate channels are blue, indicating they're constrained to something. If you click on the box_parentConstraint1 node, you'll see "Cone W0". This is the weight, or how much the constraint is affecting the object. 1 = 100% influence.

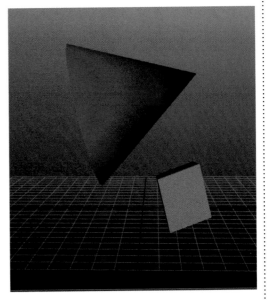

6 Translate and rotate the cone and the box follows. Notice how it maintains its position relative to the cone. This is why it's a parent constraint, because it assumes the pivot point of its master object, just like in a parent-child relationship.

parentConstraint. ma

HOT TIP

Constraint weights are used when we need to have an object constrained to different objects at different times in an animation. For instance, if we had a character throw a ball to another character who catches it, the ball would need to be constrained to their hands at separate times. We set keys on the weights to tell Maya which constraint to use at a given time. It's also possible (but not common) to have multiple weights on. Two objects at 100% influence would keep the object halfway between both of them. We'll look at weights in the next cheat.

Constraining a Prop

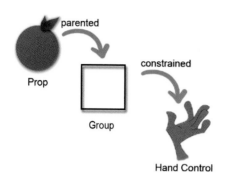

parented

Prop

constrained

Group

Hand Control

I N THE NEXT CHAPTER I WILL SHOW you how to create a simple prop rig. In this cheat, we will walk through the process of how to constrain that prop to a character's hand like you would if you were working on a shot with the prop.

You want to avoid constraining the prop geometry to a control. Why? Remember we learned that the difference between parenting and constraining is that as a child of a parent, an object can move around, but it is locked into the constrained position when it is constrained. This prevents you from making adjustments to the position of the prop after it is constrained.

You will see when you take a look at the prop rig in our scene that we instead use a combination of parenting AND constraining when it comes to props. This provides an extra layer of control so that we can adjust the prop within the constrained group.

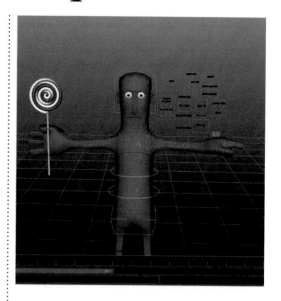

1 Open "prop_Constrain_Start.ma". Bloke is standing in the scene and he has a prop in his hand. The prop will not move with the hand yet because we haven't constrained it.

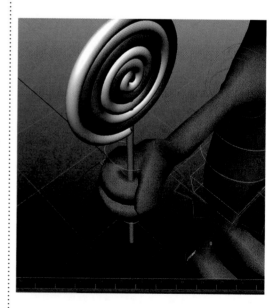

4 Now select Bloke's finger controls, and adjust the pose to make Bloke grip the lollipop.

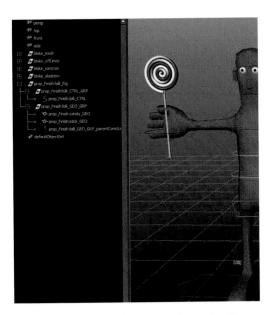

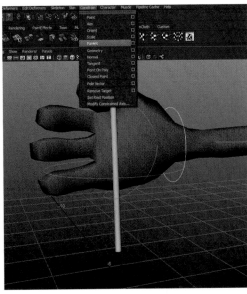

prop_Constrain_
Start.ma
prop_Constrain_
Finish.ma

2 Change to the Animation menu set by pressing F2. Open the Outline and expand the lollipop's rig group. Notice how the group that holds the geometry is actually what is constrained to the lollipop controller.

3 Select Bloke's hand control, and *Shift* select the lollipop's control. Click on Constrain>Parent.

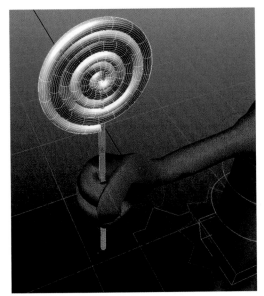

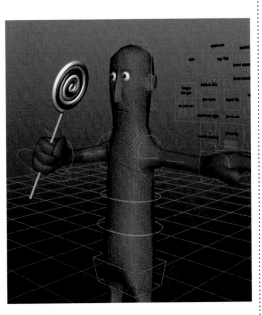

5 It doesn't matter that we can't get it exact. Now select the lollipop geometry and move it to be much more closely in Bloke's hand. This is the freedom we have given ourselves by placing a group in between the controller and the constrained geometry.

6 Test the prop is constrained correctly by moving Bloke's hand around. In the next chapter I will show you how we created this prop.

Constraint Weights

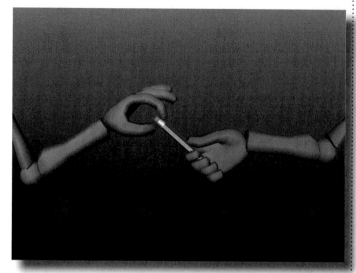

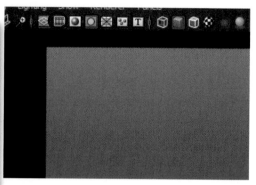

1 Open constraintWeights_start.ma. In a viewport menu, go to Panels > Perspective > shotCam to see the camera for the animation. If you like, press the viewport's Film Gate button to frame the animation more accurately.

WHEN WE'RE USING PROPS and objects in our animations, there will be times when things need to be constrained to multiple characters. If a prop is passed between two or more things, it will have to be constrained to all of them at some point in the animation. To tell Maya which constraint we want active at a specific time, we need to use the constraint's weight attribute.

It may be helpful to think of the weight as an on/off switch. Every time we constrain an object to something else, a weight attribute for that particular object is automatically created in the constraint's node in the channel box. Then we simply need to key it at 1 (on) and 0 (off) at the appropriate times.

In this simple animation of one hand giving another a pencil, we're going to see how to switch the constraint weights over one frame to get a seamless transition.

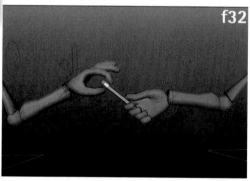

f32

4 Go to f32. We want to constrain the pencil to the hand on this pose, as the blue hand will take control of it from this point on. Select the blue hand IK control, then the pencil control, and go to Constrain > Parent Constraint.

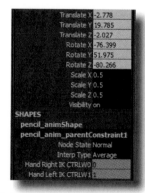

Translate X	-2.778
Translate Y	19.785
Translate Z	-2.027
Rotate X	-76.399
Rotate Y	51.975
Rotate Z	-80.266
Scale X	0.5
Scale Y	0.5
Scale Z	0.5
Visibility	on

SHAPES
pencil_animShape
pencil_anim_parentConstraint1
Node State Normal
Interp Type Average
Hand Right IK CTRLW0 0
Hand Left IK CTRLW1 1

7 Go to f33, then switch the weights values to the opposite, turning off the pink hand constraint and turning on the blue hand's. Select both weights, right click and choose "Key Selected".

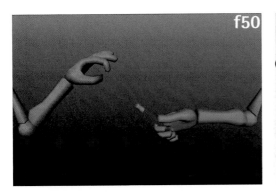

f50

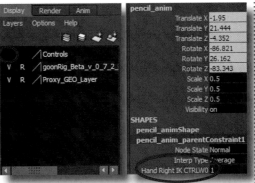

constraintWeights_
start.ma
constraintWeights_
end.ma

2 Scrubbing through the animation, we can see that the hands go through the motion of giving the pencil, but the blue hand doesn't actually take it. Right now there is only a parent constraint on the pencil for the pink hand.

3 In the layer panel, turn on the Controls layer to see the rig controls. Select the control on the pencil and click on "pencil_anim_parentConstraint1" in the channel box. Here we can see the weight attribute for the right hand since it's constrained to it.

HOT TIP

Constraint weights don't have to be switched over one frame. They can blend over however many frames you want by simply setting the weight keys further apart. Then the constraint will gradually drift into the next one. You can even edit the blend's curve in the Graph Editor. For animations like this one, that obviously wouldn't work, but for situations without obvious contact changes it can be handy.

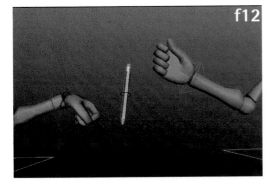

f12

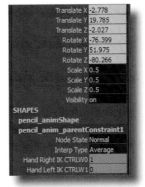

5 You'll see the new weight for the left hand created in the channel box, but now the pencil floats between both hands. This is because both weights are on, therefore pulling the object equally to keep it exactly between them.

6 Select the pencil control. At f32, set the Hand Left weight to 0 (off). Then select both weights, right click and choose "Key Selected" to set a key on both weights. If you scrub through now, the pencil stays with the pink hand the entire animation again.

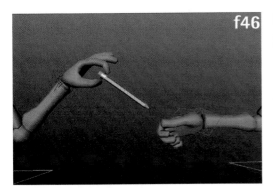

f46

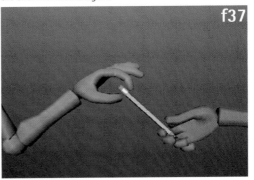

f37

8 The pencil should now get taken by the blue hand after f33. On your own projects, remember to design your animation so you have the right pose to pick up a prop and make the switch look natural.

9 You'll notice that the pencil goes through the pink hand's fingers after it is taken. Once we have the constraint working properly, its much easier to animate the fingers following the pencil as they let go. Open constraintWeightsEND.mb to see the final result.

127

Animating with Constraints

THERE WILL INEVITABLY be situations where the easiest way to animate something is to keyframe it at certain places, and constrain it in others. Maya makes this simple with an attribute called "Blend Parent", which we can key on and off depending on what we need at a given moment. When Blend Parent is set to off (0), Maya will ignore any constraints on an object and follow the keyframe data. When Blend Parent is on (1), it will ignore keyframes and conform to any constraints currently active. The best part about Blend Parent is it's created automatically whenever you set a key on a constrained object, or constrain something that already has keyframes set on it. When either of these situations happens, Maya creates a pairBlend node that allows us to switch between the two modes (or even blend somewhere in between, hence the name...).

Many times, I find animations that need this approach are simplest when done in a rather straight-ahead fashion. That isn't to say the animation isn't planned out, it most certainly is, but I've always found keeping track of things easiest if the constraints are done during the blocking process. We're going to take that approach here, where we'll start by animating an object (a bouncing ball: the cornerstone of animation education), constrain it to a platform, then keyframe it again, constrain it to a claw, and finally keyframe it through the end. Sounds complicated in theory, but this exercise with a living ball as our character will show you how simple it really is.

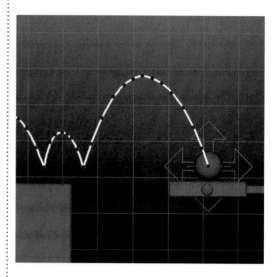

1 Open ballCourse_constraints1.ma and switch to the front view. I've done some preliminary animation of a ball hopping over to a platform, which is also animated. Scrub through and you'll see that the ball doesn't follow the platform after f41.

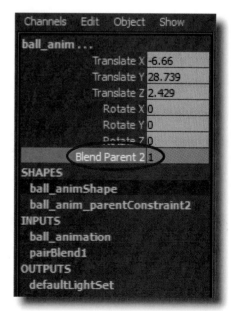

4 At f41, right click on the Blend Parent attribute and do Key Selected to set a key on it. This ensures that we will be at 1 (on) at the frame where we want the ball to start following the platform. The channel will turn orange once you set the key.

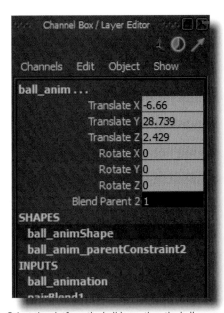

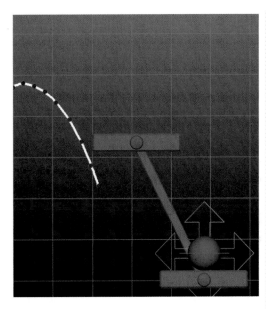

ballCourse_
constraints1.ma

2 Select the platform the ball is on, then the ball move control, and in the animation menu set go to Constrain > Parent. Notice that our channels turn green, indicating both keyframe and constraint data, and the Blend Parent attribute automatically appears.

3 Scrubbing through the animation, we see that the ball now follows the platform, but stays there the entire time. Because Blend Parent is on 1, Maya ignores the keys and follows the constraint. We need to key it on at f41, but have it off up until then to see the animation.

HOT TIP

An "all or nothing" approach is usually best when working with constraints. If it's a more complex character animation, it's often easier to ignore any constraints until the animaton is in its polish phase. Then you can constrain props without worrying about having to shift frames around or make big changes to the movement.

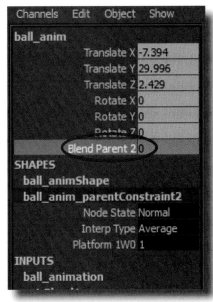

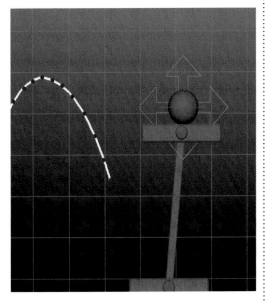

5 Go to the frame before, f40, and set Blend Parent to 0 (off). Right click it and Key Selected again. Since this will be the first key for Blend Parent, all the frames up to it will be off as well.

6 Scrub again and you'll now see that the ball is once again animated until f41, where it follows the platform perfectly.

Animating w/ Constraints (cont'd)

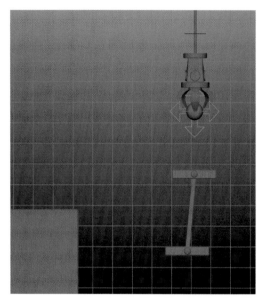

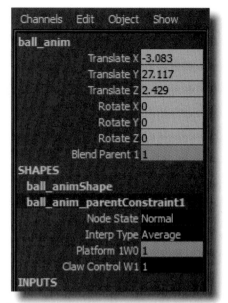

7 Open ballCourse_constraints2.ma. This file has everything we've just done, as well as the blocking animation to get the ball up to where the claw grabs it. Scrub through to f88.

8 Select the claw control, then the ball control and go to Constrain > Parent. Notice in the channel box that we get a Claw Control W1 attribute. Remember that these weight attributes tell Maya which constraint is currently active.

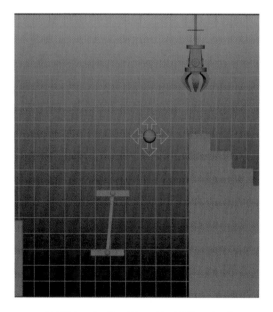

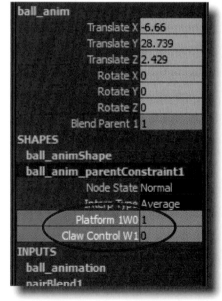

11 At f88, key the Blend Parent to 1. This makes it switch on over one frame, making our transition seamless. The ball still doesn't follow the constraints properly though, as we need to set keys on the weights to tell Maya which constraint we want active.

12 At f41, RMB > Key Selected the Platform weight to 1, and the Claw Control to 0. The ball will snap back to the platform. However, it should follow the claw at frame 88, so the weights need to change there.

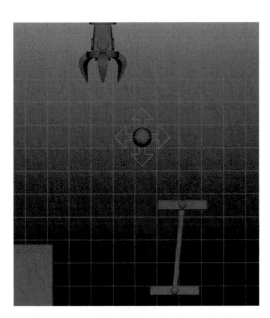

9 If you scrub, you'll notice the ball acting strangely at the constrained parts of the animation. This is because since both constraint weights are on, they both pull at the ball equally.

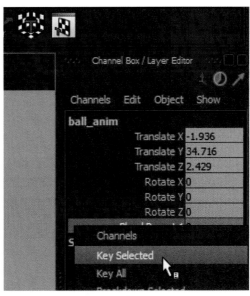

10 Let's key the Blend Parent so the ball starts to follow the claw's constraint at f88. Go to frame 87, enter 0 in the Blend Parent attribute and RMB > Key Selected. At f75, key the Blend Parent at 0 as well. This will make the ball follow its keyed animation from f75-f87.

ballCourse_constraints2.ma

HOT TIP

The reason we use 0 and 1 for turning constraints on or off is that it's like binary: 0 = off, 1 = on. Or you can think of 1 being 100% and 0 being 0%., whatever is clearer to you.

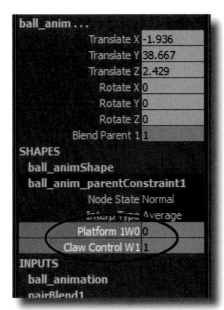

13 Set a key on both weights at f87 so this value holds through there. Then at f88, key the weights at the opposite values, the platform to 0 and the claw control to 1. Also key the Blend Parent back to 1 so it switches to following the constraint.

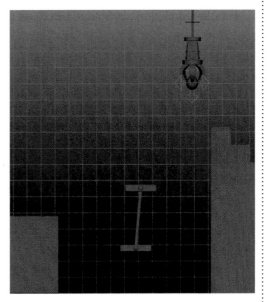

14 Now the ball stays with the platform when it's supposed to, jumps on its own from f75-f87, and follows the claw after f88.

Animating w/ Constraints (cont'd 2)

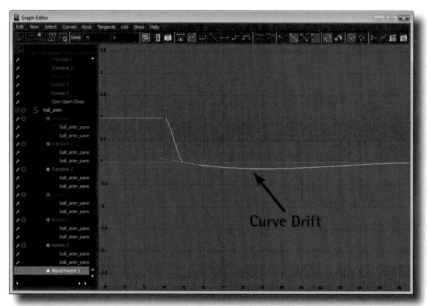

Curve Drift

15 If you notice the ball behaving strangely during the constrained sections, check the Graph Editor. If the curves for the Blend Parent or weight attributes have any drift in them, they will mess up the constraints. Be sure to zoom in and check the curves closely, as they can look flat zoomed out.

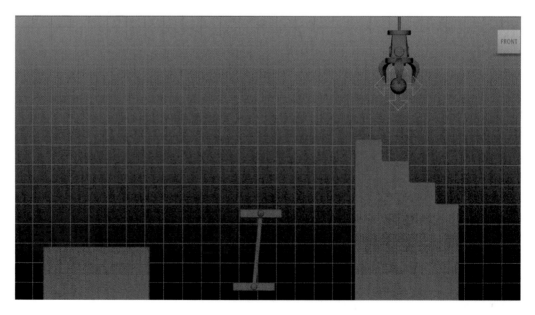

17 Open ballCourse_constraints3.ma and it will have everything we've done, along with the final blocking animation of the ball being released and bouncing down the stairs. We can't see it, however, because we need to key Blend Parent off once more to tell Maya to once again use the keyframe data on the ball.

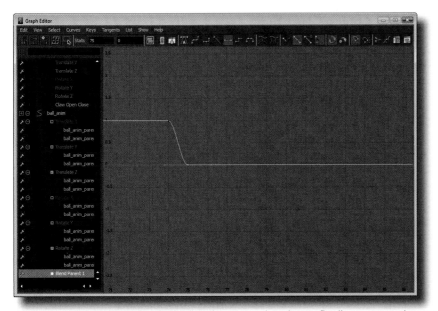

ballCourse_
constraints3.ma

16 If you find this happening, simply select the curves and set them to flat, linear, or stepped tangents using the buttons at the top of the Graph Editor. Any of these tangent types will work for this purpose. See the Spline chapter for more details on how the different tangent types work.

HOT TIP

You can set
the options
for a parent
constraint
in Constrain
> Parent >
options. Here
you can tell
Maya to only
constrain
specific axes, if
you only need
certain ones for
your animation.

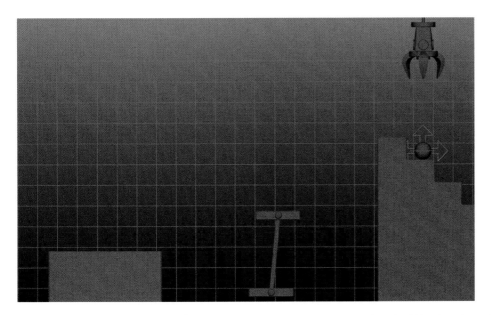

18 At f112, key Blend Parent to 1 to hold it through that frame, then key it to 0 at f113. Scrubbing through you should see the ending blocking animation. We now have blocking of all the animation, including the constraints. If you have more constraints in an animation, remember to always have the active one's weight keyed at 1, and all others at 0. Always set a redundant key at the frame before the weights and Blend Parent change to hold the current state up to that point. Remembering those two steps will get you through any number of constraints, no matter how many there are!

A Well-rounded Approach

by Kenny Roy

I HAD THE CHANCE TO TALK TO SOMEONE RECENTLY who was my boss on a feature film a long time ago. What I learned about the circumstances that led to my hiring made me rethink my entire stance on demo reels, resumes, and overall attitude.

We've talked before about hobbies that contribute to animation; painting, drawing, acting, even sculpting can help you develop your aesthetics. But what we haven't touched on is the fact that being a well-rounded artist is more than just dedicating yourself fully to your craft. It is very beneficial to your animation skill to be constantly absorbing animation, but it can be detrimental to your career in the long run to not find the right balances.

Let's jump back to 2005. I was a bright-eyed and bushy-tailed animator new to Weta Digital, ready to start working on King Kong. By no means was I a super star animator. In fact, the entire show I struggled with my work, and relied heavily on the guidance and help of my supervisors and peers. I made it out the other end of that long, difficult project relatively unscathed, but always had the question in my mind, "How I could have possibly made it onto such a stellar team in a world-class studio?"

Fast forward again to the present day. I had lunch with the Animation Director, Eric Leighton, who let me in on a little secret; he hired me for one reason, and one reason alone: my resume. And not what you might think; it wasn't a slew of amazing credits or a long list of awards and accolades in my wake. No, it was that I had put on my resume my acting and improv interests. To follow that up, the very end of my demo reel had a recording of a section of a comedy show that I was a part of the year before. To be honest, I don't even know why I put it on there, but something told me that a recruiter might find the show interesting and remember me when it came time to hire again. Specifically, Eric told me that rather than fill the last few spots of the animation team with fanboys and copy+paste clones, he was looking for energy, enthusiasm, and a different dynamic. It was my improve experience (which I have been doing since high school) that gave me the edge over better animators.

As an employer myself now, I can relate to the sentiment that Eric was talking about. I too like to see my artists excited about what they are doing after work, on the weekends, etc. Especially when it has nothing to do with animation. An artist that gets a little stoked over an outside interest brings a little bit of the outside world into the studio. In fact, my best artist that I've worked with for more than two years now takes Wednesday afternoons off to be involved with a community group in her area. I don't think I've ever said no to her request each week to leave early to be a part of this. I like the idea that she is completely unplugging from animation to involve herself in something really important to her.

      You need to establish a balance between work and home. But on top of that, your home life cannot just be an extension of animation. I know my story is quite unique, but on the other hand I feel like the trend for aspiring animators is to immerse themselves SO fully into animation that they have little depth to their lives otherwise. It's remarkable to see young animators so engrossed in the craft, but we have to ask ourselves, "Is this how the masters became the best?" The answer is an obvious "no". The best artists in any field are always multi-talented and multi-interested individuals. Just look at any of the people at the top of our industry and you'll be able to find stories of their obsessions outside the field of animation (John Lasseter and his model train fetish, for instance).

      We want to be the best candidates for the job so we can work at major studios and on high profile projects. That doesn't necessarily mean that we should be forsaking all else to be entirely focused solely on animation. Perhaps my story is unique, and perhaps Eric's goals for his animation team are different to the goals of most Animation Directors. But as someone who hires artists myself, I think it's a safe bet that any way you can distinguish yourself from the masses is good. Even better if it's a passion you have after the horn blows at the end of the workday.

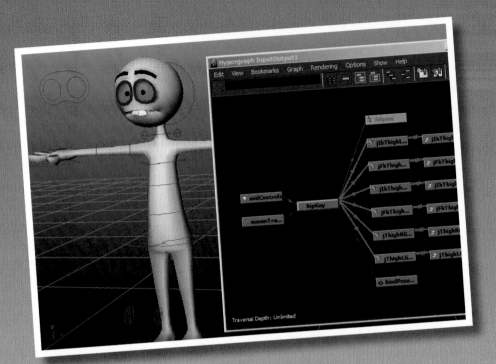

■ The most commonly sought-after skill in an animator besides animation skill is rigging knowledge. This is because animators with a little bit of awareness of the techniques behind the controls can solve production problems on the fly.

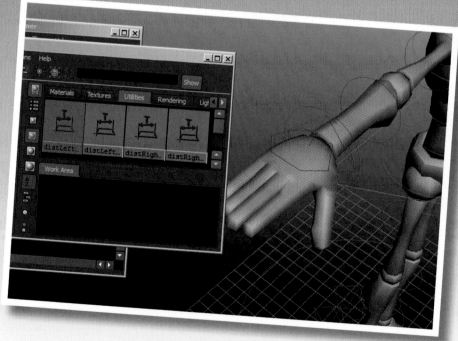

Rigging Cheats

EVERY ANIMATOR HAS RUN INTO PROBLEMS with a rig at some point in their career. Be it a hidden controller or bad weighting, a rig problem can ruin your day quickly. This is why knowing a few cheats about rigs is a good idea. In the latest version of Maya, these rig cheats are ultra stable and time-saving. You'll (hopefully) never again be working on a scene only to be stopped in your tracks by a misbehaving skeleton. We've scoured the web to find a few new rigs to include with this edition of How to Cheat in Maya, so let's go ahead and dive into the best rigs the web has to offer and see what we can find...

Rig Testing

L ET'S FIRST RUN THROUGH a few of the things you should identify in your rigs before you start working with them.

In an ideal production setting, you are given enough time to test your rigs before you have to animate shots. This is in an ideal setting. Not very many productions are ideal! Schedule sometimes demands that you are producing work on day one. When the deadlines are that tight, we need to have a quick list of things to check to make sure our rigs are going to behave how we want them to.

Some of these cheats will reveal characteristics about a rig that aren't necessarily an indication that the rig is broken or low quality. These characteristics might include scaling breaking after a certain point, IK/FK switch channels being on the same control that you are using frequently for posing, or proxy meshes hidden in the rig. It would be quite a shame if you completed a shot using a new rig only to see later on that an attribute or parameter was set incorrectly.

Since all rigs are slightly different, the locations, names, and even geometry type of the controls we point out in the following cheats may not be the same in your production rigs. However, there is a certain amount of standardization inherent in rigging, and we'll expect you can always find the "IK hand controller", or the "FK head controller" no matter what character you're working with. To get used to this, in this chapter we'll use the semi-standardized names to describe the rigs.

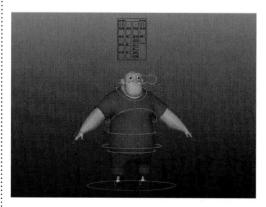

1 Open "Groggy_Test.ma". We're going to test two things right now, controller symmetry, and controller object space.

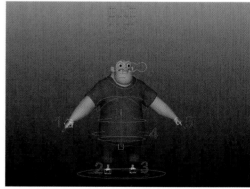

2 Select his IK hand controllers, his IK feet controllers, and his IK pelvis controller. The first thing you want to check is that all of the controllers move in the same world space, and that they are symmetrical.

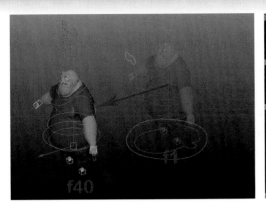

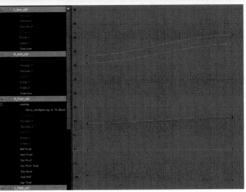

Groggy_Test.ma

3 Set a key on f01 with the controllers in place. On f40, move the controllers forward in world space substantially off of his master controller like so.

4 Now we check if the controllers are in world space. With the controllers still selected, open the Graph Editor. Uh oh. Look at all of the different translations on these controllers!

If you look closely, the arm's object space is not aligned with the feet or the pelvis. What this means is we need to be careful when we are posing the character, especially in cycles, because this rig was not set up with "FORWARD" being represented by only the Translate Z channel. Below you can see that if we move the controllers in the Z channel alone, the results are totally unpredictable. This rig would be very unwieldy if we used IK arms in a walk cycle. If you must use this character with arms IK mode, then it's easiest to pose the character using "WORLD" translation mode by holding down **W** and LMB-dragging to the left on the marking menu that appears. Also, the infinity curve type will be "cycle with offset" for all three translation channels (not just Z like normal) for a character like this. More on that in Chapter 9, Cycles.

HOT TIP

You can also check in the channel box to see if all world controllers are moving in world space by moving them, and then selecting each individually and seeing if the values change.

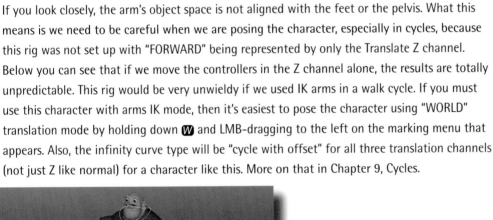

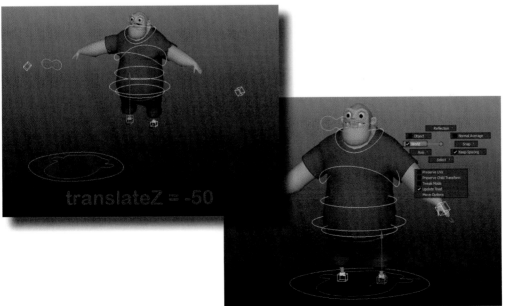

Rig Testing (cont'd)

RIGS CAN HAVE IDIOSYNCRACIES that you come to learn over time. We took a look at the Groggy rig in the last section and found that IK arms will require us to have a few extra steps to make our cycles perfect (again, more on that in the "Stride Length" section in Chapter 9). There are many reasons that rigs have different characteristics though. Different proportions, the rigging pose, and the general use for the rig (some rigs are designed to be able to blend mocap data into a robust control system, e.g.). But there ARE a few things that pretty much all rigs should have under control, pun intended.

The first is that setting all of the controller's attributes to zero, or "zeroing", puts the rig back into the initial pose. This is vitally important for avoiding gimbal lock while animating, dealing with animation curves while you are polishing your scene, and creating cycles with a set stride length.

The second requirement is that animation can be copied and pasted on the rig. With most rigs, this works fine. However, sometimes rigs have very complex hierarchies filled with connections and nested constraints that mean that your animation is not copied perfectly. We'll try both AnimExport and good ol' Copy Keys to get to the bottom of this.

While many of the quirks of a rig are workable , such as the slightly different object space on Groggy's IK hands, some things are show stoppers. Let's see how this rig stacks up on these two essential issues.

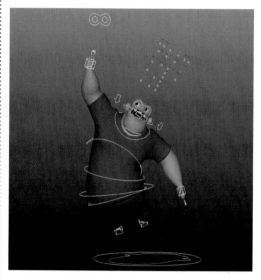

1 Open Groggy_Zero.ma. See how Groggy is in a pose? Let's try "zeroing" him out. Drag a selection around his whole rig to choose all of his controls.

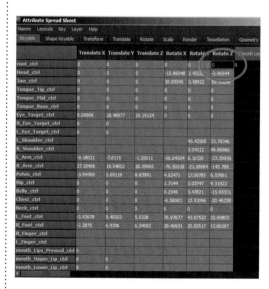

4 Now just type 0. But don't press *Enter* yet. You'll see Maya automatically puts the zero in the upper right cell when you have selected multiple cells, rows, or columns.

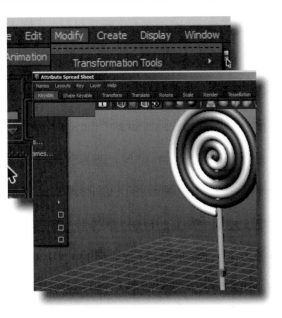

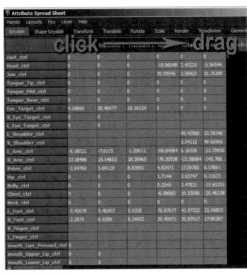

Groggy_Zero.ma

2 Now let's open the Attribute Spreadsheet. This is a very under-utilized panel in Maya. It displays in spreadsheet format ALL of the attributes for the selected objects. Nice!

3 Now to zero all of the controls back to their origins, we're going to select all of the Translate and Rotate Columns. LMB click and drag across the very top of the Attribute Spreadsheet, selecting all 6 columns.

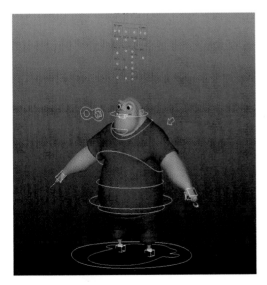

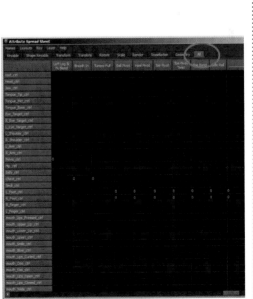

5 Now press *Enter*. Groggy passes the test! He snaps right back to his initial pose. This is great.

6 We only "zeroed" his Translate and Rotate channels. If there were other channels (IK switches, foot roll, etc.) you would have to find them in the All Keyable tab of the Attribute Spreadsheet.

Rig Testing (cont'd 2)

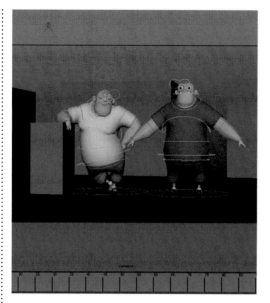

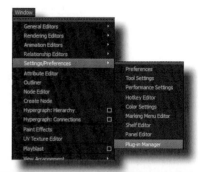

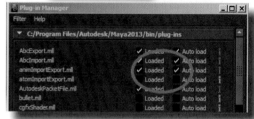

1 Open Groggy_Copy.ma. This is a completed animation scene but what do we do if we need to copy the animation onto another rig? We're going to show you the normal way with AnimExport, and a great cheat using Copy Keys that works even faster.

2 First we need to enable the AnimExport plugin. Go to Window>Settings/Preferences>Plugin Manager. Find animImportExport.mll and check both the "Loaded" and "Auto load" boxes.

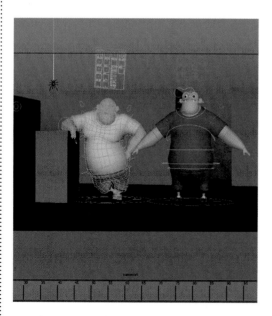

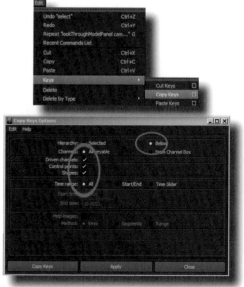

5 Let's try this using just the clipboard. This is much quicker and useful if you don't need to save the animation, just need to copy it fast. (Very common if there's a rig update in production.) Open Groggy_Copy.ma again and select "groggy:root_Group" in the outliner.

6 Go to Edit>Keys>Copy Keys □. This dialog is the same as the AnimExport dialog, because what you are doing is the same, except you are only copying keys to the clipboard and not saving them for later. Copy the settings above.

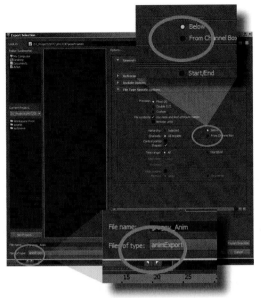

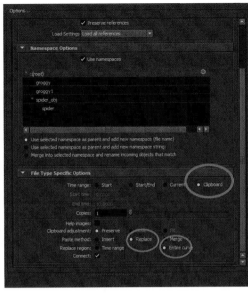

Groggy_Copy.ma

3 Now in the outliner, select the animated Groggy's rig group node, "Groggy:root_group". Go to File>Export Selected. In the Export dialog, change the type to "animExport" and leave everything default except change "Hierarchy" to "Below". Name the file groggy_Anim.

4 Now we'll import that animation onto the static Groggy rig. Select his main rig group "groggy1:root_Group". Go to File>Import. Make sure the file type is set to "animImport", and copy the rest of the settings circled above. The animation copies perfectly.

At its core, Maya handles AnimExport and Copy Keys the same way. One just writes a file and the other stores it in your clipboard. The nice thing about Copy Keys is you don't have to hunt for the saved file, AND, you can copy keys from one scene and open another scene to paste them into – Maya keeps the curves in the clipboard.

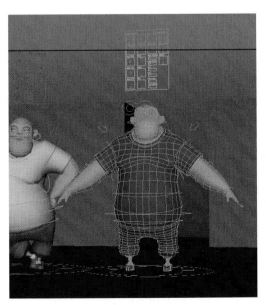

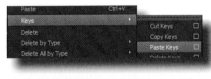

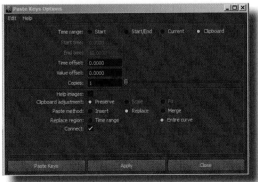

7 When you press the "Copy Keys" button, the script editor returns "// Result: 281" in the Command Line. That means 281 curves were copied to the clipboard. Now select the static groggy's rig group "groggy1:root_Group".

8 Go to Edit>Keys>Paste Keys ☐. Copy my settings above and hit Paste Keys. Beautiful. The curves in the clipboard are pasted onto Groggy and he moves as expected. This is extremely useful if Replace Reference does not work and you need to copy animation onto a new rig!

Sprucing It Up

ONE OF THE BEST WAYS to cheat in animation is to take advantage of the fact that Maya interpolates motion for you. For example, in 2D animation done for TV, it is still typical for the animation to be done on "2's" – every other frame is held for two frames, giving you effectively 12 frames per second instead of the normal 24. Well, this looks choppy to the well trained eye. In 3D, unless we are using stepped mode, there will ALWAYS be motion on every frame. When people say "on 2's" in Maya, what they mean is they have set key poses every two frames – but there is still motion on every frame.

The way we can cheat using this property of 3D is to "spruce up" a rig with some dynamic objects. We can get away with using far fewer poses and less movement, because the dynamic objects will be constantly moving. It will take away the choppy feeling and make it look like the "world" in which the character is living is smooth and continuous, even with staccato movement in the character itself.

We're going to take a scene that has VERY crude animation on Moom, and add a ponytail and earrings using two very different dynamic methods. You will then see when we play back the animation, that the scene has taken on a more dynamic quality. The mere addition of these dynamic objects and the secondary motion they create helps us cheat the animation. When you are on extremely tight deadlines and can only afford the time to set a few key poses in a shot, this cheat will save you.

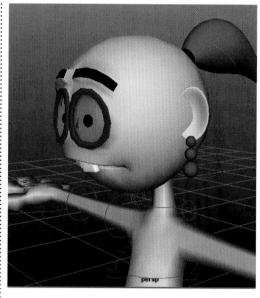

1 Open moom_Dynamics_Start.ma. I've done a lot of the work for you, by setting up the earring and ponytail geometry and starting the process of creating the dynamics objects.

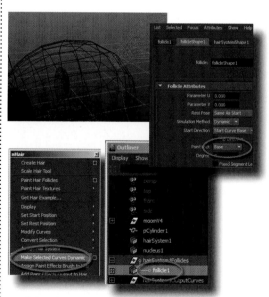

4 Select the curve and go to nHair>Make Selected Curves Dynamic. In the Attribute Editor under the Dynamics tab of HairSystemShape1, change Bend Resistance to 10. Select FollicleShape1 in the Outliner in the hairSystem1Follicles group, and change the Point Lock attribute to "Base".

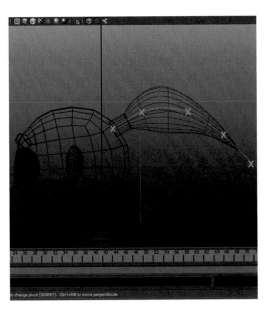

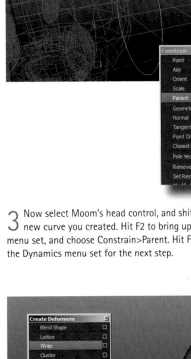

moom_Dynamics_
Start.ma
moom_Dynamics_
Finish.ma

2 Let's first create the ponytail dynamics. We're going to use a simple hair curve and wrap the geo to it. Switch to the side view and draw a Nurbs curve through the ponytail like so using the EP curve tool.

3 Now select Moom's head control, and shift select the new curve you created. Hit F2 to bring up the Animation menu set, and choose Constrain>Parent. Hit F5 to switch to the Dynamics menu set for the next step.

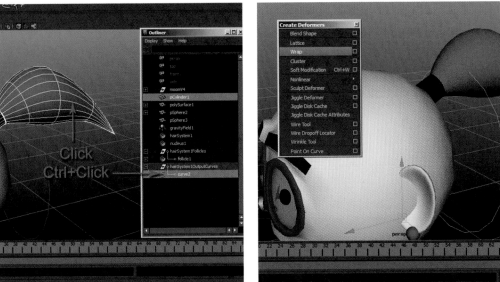

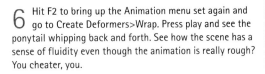

5 On f01, select the ponytail mesh. In the Outliner, find the newly created hairSystem1OutputCurves group. Curve2 inside is the result of the dynamics applied to curve1 that you created. *ctrl*+click curve2.

6 Hit F2 to bring up the Animation menu set again and go to Create Deformers>Wrap. Press play and see the ponytail whipping back and forth. See how the scene has a sense of fluidity even though the animation is really rough? You cheater, you.

145

Sprucing It Up (cont'd)

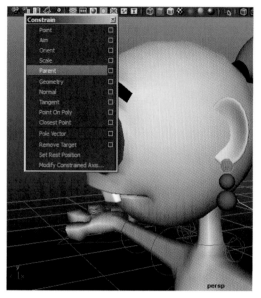

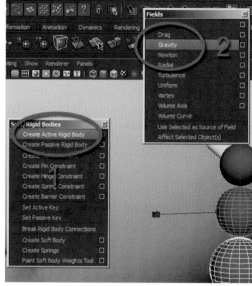

1 Hair curves are a quick solution but are not ideal for meshes that shouldn't deform. We're going to use rigid bodies to make the earrings dynamic . On f01 select the head control, *Shift*+select the top of the earring, and go to Constrain>Parent.

2 Now let's make the two other spheres rigid bodies. Select both of them, and hit F5 to switch to dynamics. Go to Soft/Rigid Bodies>Create Active Rigid Body. With both of them still selected, click on Fields>Gravity.

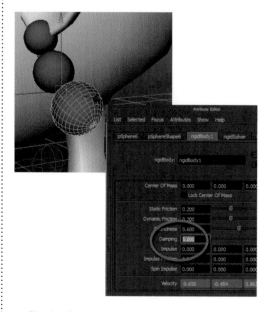

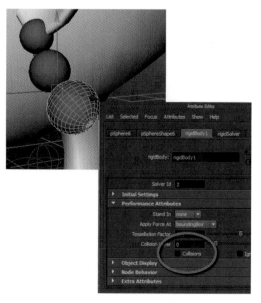

5 There's a few settings we need to change to make the earrings move correctly. First in the rigidBody1 tab with the bottom sphere selected, find the "Rigid Body Attributes" section and change "Damping" to 5.

6 Next, scroll down in the Attribute Editor to find the "Performance Attributes" section. Turn off collisions. Select the middle sphere, navigate to the rigidBody2 tab and repeat the last two steps.

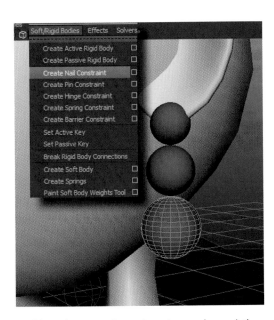

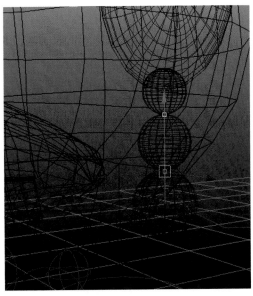

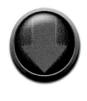

moom_Dynamics_
Start.ma
moom_Dynamics_
Finish.ma

3 We need to set up these spheres to move in correlation with each other. The Nail Constraint is perfect for this. Select the bottom sphere and go to Soft/Rigid Bodies>Create Nail Constraint.

4 Move the new Nail Constraint to the bottom of the middle sphere, **Shift**+select the middle sphere and hit **P** to parent it. Now repeat the last two steps for the middle sphere, creating a Nail Constraint and then parenting it to the top sphere.

HOT TIP

The Nail Constraint is the perfect dynamic constraint for swinging objects like earrings. There are many other types of dynamic constraints and I encourage you to try them all. Hinge Constraints are like Nail Constraints but they only rotate on one axis, and Spring Constraints are like Nail Constraints but they stretch!

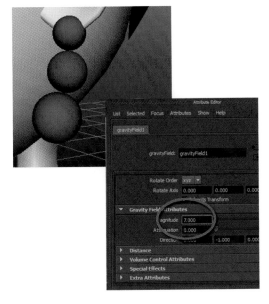

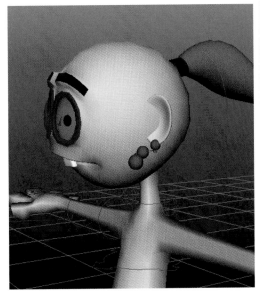

7 Select gravityField1 in the outliner and change the Magnitude attribute to 7.

8 Now hit the play button! Watch how the ponytail flops around with the head movement, and how the earrings swing nicely from Moom's ears. As crude as the motion is in the scene, there's something soothing to the eye to see nice smooth dynamic movement.

Rigging Props

NO MATTER WHAT TYPE OF ANIMATION YOU DO, chances are your character will interact with props quite often. To make sure that you are not animating the wrong object, most props should be rigged. There's a little bit of an art and a science to rigging props, but I've simplified it down to this simple cheat to get you back to animating as soon as possible.

Since we are also using a referencing pipeline, rigging props allows you to turn the prop file into a format that can be standardized across multiple scenes. Instead of bare geometry floating around in your shot, using this cheat you will be able to create an asset that all the animators working with you can utilize.

We start by creating a group that will hold all of the geometry for the prop. This is done so that no matter what is added to the prop, the rig will still function in all of the scenes that it has been referenced into. Next we create a simple controller that will move the prop around. Last, we group all of the controls, geometry, and other nodes into a single group and name it our rig.

In a production, animators should know how to rig their own props so that if there is a need to do so, you are not taking valuable time away from the character riggers. Any time you can troubleshoot your own scenes, take care of problems, and put out fires yourself, you are proving how valuable an asset you are to your company. Cheating is job security!

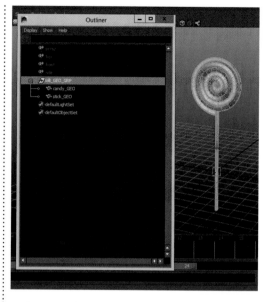

1 Open prop_Start.ma. There is a lollipop sitting lonely in our scene. Start by selecting all of the geometry and hitting Ctrl+g to group it. Name this new group "lolli_GEO_GRP".

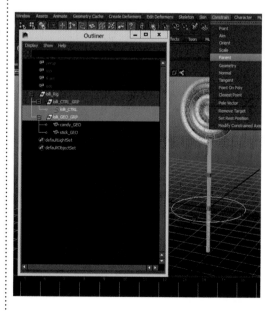

4 We want the circle to control the geometry, but we are going to constrain the group. Press F2 to change to the Animation menu set. Select the circle, **ctrl** **Shift** "lolli_GEO_GRP" in the Outliner, and click on Constrain>Parent.

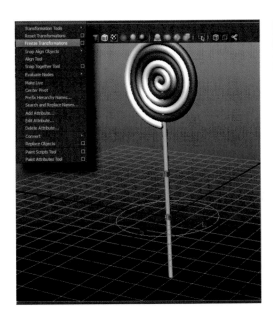

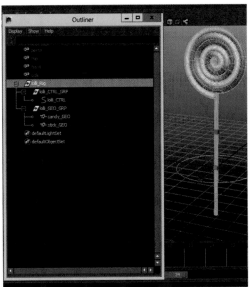

prop_Start.ma
prop_Finish.ma

2 Now create a Nurbs circle at the origin. Rename the circle "lolli_CTRL", and when you are done scaling it to an appropriate size, click on Modify>Freeze Transformations.

3 Group this circle as well and name it "lolli_CTRL_GRP". Select this new group and the lolli_GEO_GRP and group them once again. Call this group "lolli_Rig".

In general, you want to use the scale of the controller only if it is animated. The overall scale of the prop (sizing the prop relative to the scene) should be done using the rig group, not the controller.

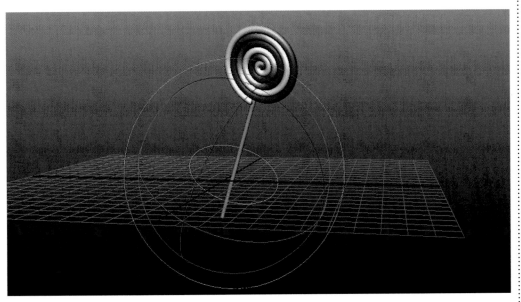

5 You are done! Select the control and move and rotate the lollipop around. You may even want to test the feature of the geometry group by dropping some geo into that group and watching how the controller still moves the objects inside. This is great for when you need to update the geometry of a prop that is referenced into many scenes.

Listen Closely
How to REALLY Break Down Your Dialog
by Kenny Roy

IN ORDER TO GET ALL OF THE NECESSARY INFORMATION from a piece of dialog, you need to listen closely. VERY closely. Now even closer still. You are probably already breaking down your audio files phonetically, and making notes on the inflection and intonation, but you are missing a lot of the magic in the noise...

Have you noticed that some animation just really seems to "nail" the dialog? That's because the animator is picking up on a myriad of other things in the sound file that go unnoticed to the novice animator. While they are nearly impossible to point out, combined these little nuances really bring the audience into the scene. Here's how to find them.

First, listen for the "anchors". Anchors are what I like to call all of the NON-VERBAL sounds that the character is making. These could be breaths, pauses, stutters, mutterings, lip smackings, breathing sounds, puff sounds, teeth clicking, tongue snapping, interrupted words, repetition, grunting, growling, harsh delivery or odd emphasis in the middle of a word, a rasp in the voice, loss of air or voice cutting out, and many, many more. These non-verbal sounds, when animated correctly, really "anchor" the character into the scene, which is why I like to call them that name. It solidifies the character by making them seem like they truly are breathing the air in the scene, and creating noises with their bodies. Without anchors, characters seem to be opening their mouths only to let us hear a radio that is playing sound in their bellies. If you can get the audience to feel like the character is actually creating all of the sounds that we pick up on subconsciously, then your engagement of their attention will be far greater. They will be far more immersed in the scene. Anchors have the power to do that. The trick is to animate these anchors much too large for the sound they create, and then tone it down. Don't try to be subtle with it; create an exaggerated movement to explain an anchor, then go back into the right size.

Next, listen closely next for the ENERGY of a piece of dialog. The energy will clue you in as to where in your shot you need to rely on subtle movements, and where you should have broader gestures. The energy might not necessarily be expressed in volume, but it might be hidden within the anchors. A waviness in the voice might actually be a result of a character starting to get so angry that their body starts shaking. A character's voice cutting out suddenly could actually be a result of them losing the energy they need to go on and stopping short in exasperation. And the voice crack of a boy in his teen years might make us chuckle, but imagine what his energy would do after that happens. The embarrassment he might feel could lead the energy of the scene to do some interesting things. When you have listened very closely for the cues in energy shifts, you can combine that with the anchors and get some very engaging results.

Last, listen for body movement. You don't want to necessarily get caught in the trap of having to "explain" every single little sound of cloth and feet moving, but if you miss a step (pun intended) you will immediately pull your audience out of the scene. Listening very closely to the movement of the character will give you cues as to how the character needs to be posed. That is, some performances just aren't possible sitting down. Other performances would seem forced if delivered by a standing character. All humans are very adept at piecing together the posture of a character from the sound of the voice. It's built into our DNA to pick up on ultra-subtle cues. Things like how much the voice sounds like it is coming from the nasal cavity or deep in the back of the throat can lead us to conclude the character is either standing, or curled into a ball on the ground. A slight muffling of the voice at points in the audio could be explained by a character who is holding their head in their hands, and as the palms cover the mouth briefly, the sound changes. The real point is that animators rarely take all of these clues into consideration and their animation lacks for it.

So first, find literally ALL the sounds the character is making, purposefully or not. If you haven't been adding them before, this first step will add the most to your scenes for the least amount of work. Next, find the energy of the scene in the audio and let the energy dictate some of your animation choices like broadness of movement, and strength of pose. Last, listen even closer to see if you can discern the extremely subtle hints of body position and posture. The audience can detect when you are stretching the character past what the performance can sustain. Implement these three new steps in your audio workflow and see if you are able to get that subtle, hard-to-pinpoint magic that some of the best scenes have.

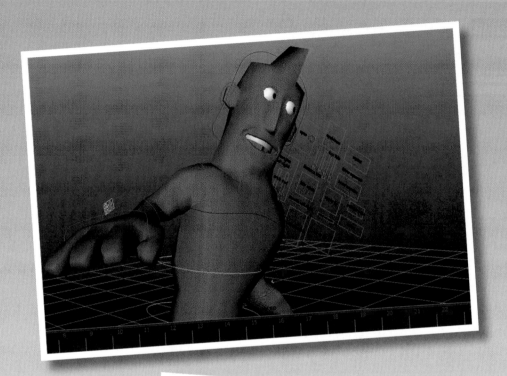

These look like our familiar rigs, but we've customized them in a bid to make our work look unique from the rest.

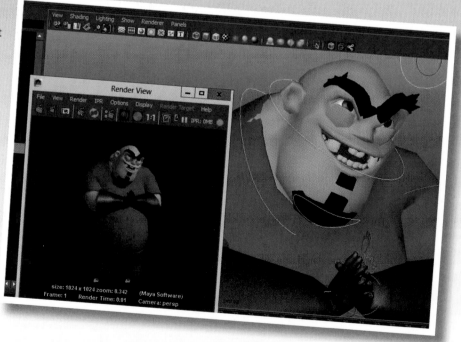

Standing Out

THE ANIMATION FIELD SHOWS NO SIGNS of slowing in the near future. In this growing field, you need to do all you can to distinguish yourself from the crowd. And to set yourself apart from the rest, you have to know a few cheats to spruce up your animation. We'll walk through a few of these cheats in this chapter.

From adding some hair and fur to your characters, to customizing a model with your own embellishments, anything you can do to make your reel look unique may be the leg up you need to get a job as an animator.

Adding BlendShapes

Doubtless you are experimenting with many online rigs to produce work for your demo reel. There is nothing wrong with that, in fact it truly is the best way to expose yourself to different control sets and rigging styles. You will be aptly prepared for production.

On the other hand, using rigs you downloaded means you are opening yourself up to the possibility that recruiters will feel like they've "seen your reel before". Nothing can be more detrimental to your chances of getting a job than a feeling of too much familiarity when a recruiter watches your work.

To combat this, we're going to walk through a cheat of adding a custom BlendShape to an already completed rig. When you have practiced this method enough, hopefully you will customize all of your rigs to give yourself an edge in the job race.

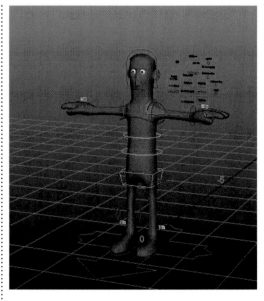

1 Open custom_Start.ma. Good ol' Bloke is standing in T-pose on the grid. He has been around the block a few times, so let's spruce him up.

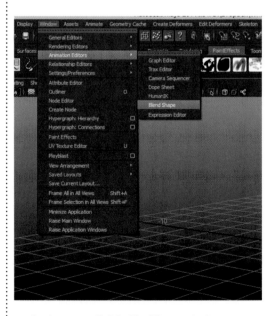

4 Another way to find the BlendShape nodes in a scene is to click on Window>Animation Editors>Blend Shape. Select Bloke's body mesh.

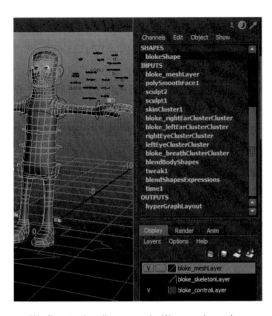

custom_Start.ma
custom_Finish.ma

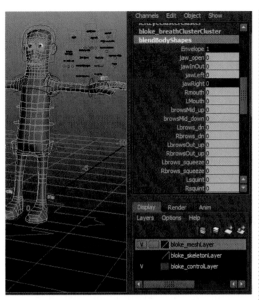

2 We first need to diagnose a rig. We must determine where the BlendShapes are going to be inserted. Select Bloke and look at the channel box.

3 ¾ of the way down the Inputs we see he has an input called blendBodyShapes. Click on that and see all of the facial blends there are.

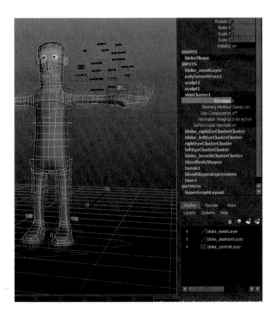

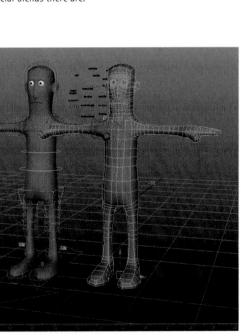

5 We need to be sure we are working from a clean base mesh. One by one, change the "Envelope" channel to 0 in the channel box on all the deforms from the BlendShape node upwards.

6 With Bloke selected, hit *ctrl D*. Select all his transform channels in the channel box and right click and choose "Unlock Selected". Rename this new copy "custom_Blend" and move it to the side.

Adding BlendShapes (cont'd)

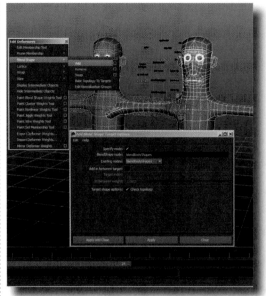

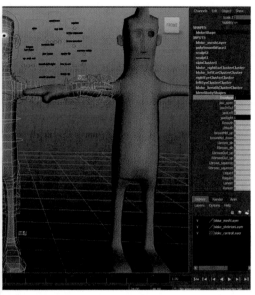

7 Now we add the new BlendShape to the character. Select custom_Blend, **Shift** select Bloke's body mesh, and in the Animation menu set (F2) click on Edit Deformers>Blend Shape>Add and click on the Options box ☐.

8 Check the option "Specify Node" and choose blendBodyShapes. Hit Apply and Close. Now go back through the deformers on Bloke's body mesh in the channel box and turn the Envelope settings back to 1.

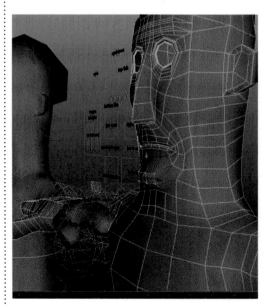

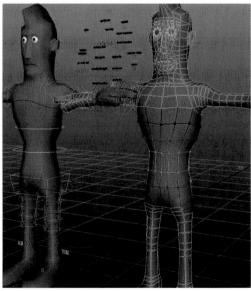

11 We can also give him a prominent chin. Remember that hitting **B** turns on the soft selection allowing you to make smooth adjustments to the mesh.

12 Last, let's slim the waist a little bit so Bloke looks a little more heroic.

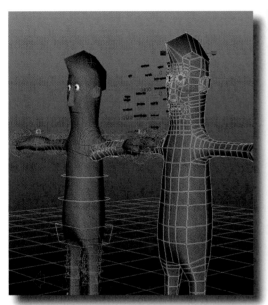

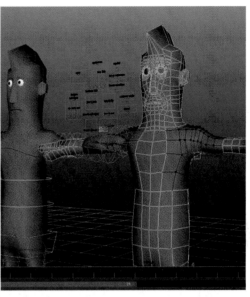

9 Select the blendBodyShapes input in the Channel Box and scroll to the bottom where the custom_Blend channel is and set it to 1. In the panel, switch to component mode by pressing F8, select and move vertices in the custom_Blend's head to make a Mohawk.

10 Let's also give Bloke some muscles, so move the vertices in his chest and arms to give a more muscular physique.

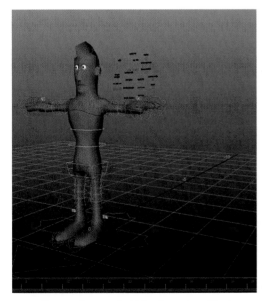

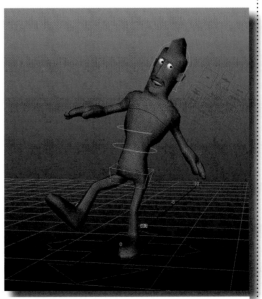

13 Clean up the scene by hiding the custom_Blend (*ctrl* *H*).

14 Test that the BlendShape is working well by posing Bloke and seeing if any vertices are misbehaving. Now enjoy your customized model!

HOT TIP

Don't forget that Bloke has a smooth channel. On characters that have a smooth channel, you should test your custom blends with the smooth turned on, to see the final result.

157

Adding Clusters

W hen it comes to customizing downloaded rigs, BlendShapes are a great first start. But you can't just rely on custom geometry: you need to add control to these customizations or they will be static and boring. Since the rigging is already done, it would be very disruptive to add more bones and controls to the rig. This is where clusters work great.

   Though clusters can add substantial scene overhead, and are finicky with their object space, they do offer some of the easiest control when it comes to customizing a complete rig. To demonstrate the proper workflow for adding clusters, we will add a wobble cluster to the Mohawk that we added to Bloke in the last cheat.

   First, the position of the cluster and the weight of the cluster need to be decided. Next, we have to reorder the deforms on the mesh so that the clusters do not interfere with the BlendShapes or the skincluster nodes. Then we'll set up the controls and link up the clusters into the head rig.

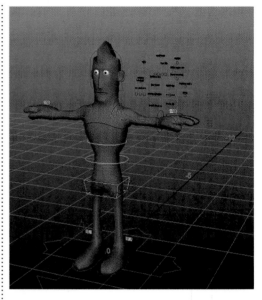

1 Open clusters_Start.ma. Here is the finished customized Bloke with the BlendShape that we added in the last cheat.

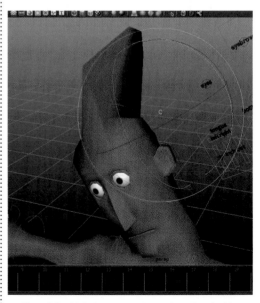

4 You might think that we are almost done, but do this experiment: rotate the head in any direction, then rotate the cluster that is left behind. Yikes, this result is not what we are looking for.

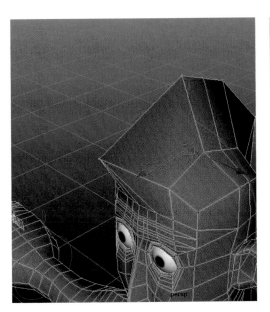

2 We want to create the controls on his new Mohawk. Press F8 to go into component mode, and select the vertices of the Mohawk.

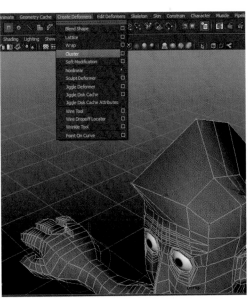

3 Switch to the Animation menu set by pressing F2. Click on Create Deformers>Cluster.

clusters_Start.ma
clusters_Finish.ma

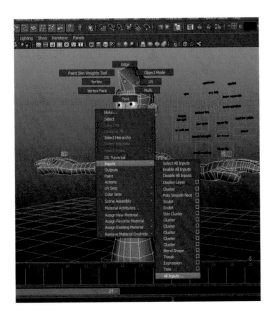

5 We need to reorder the deformers first. Undo the head rotation and then RMB click and hold on Bloke's body mesh. Choose Inputs>All Inputs.

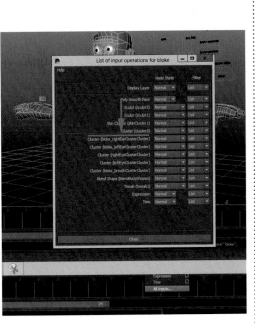

6 See how the cluster is on the very top of the list? This means that it is calculating after everything. We want it to calculate just before the skincluster. MMB-drag the cluster6 node below the skinCluster1 node.

Adding Clusters (cont'd)

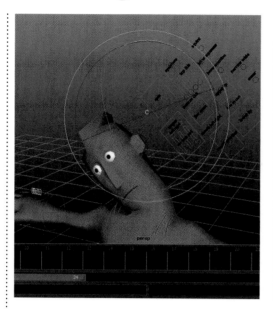

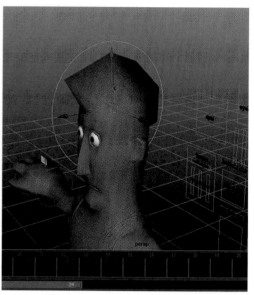

7 Now it's time to hook this cluster up to some controls. Create a Nurbs circle on the origin. Move it up to Bloke's head, rotate it 90 degrees in Z, and scale it to roughly match the size of the Mohawk.

8 Press F8 to go into component mode, and move the CVs in the circle to more closely match the orientation of Bloke's Mohawk. It's a good idea to have controls that resemble the part they move.

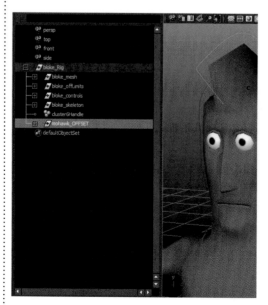

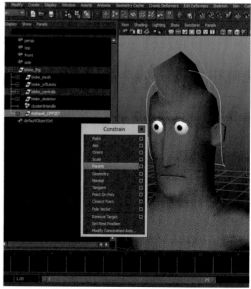

11 Rename this group "Mohawk_OFFSET" and MMB drag it into Bloke's rig group for good housekeeping.

12 Select Bloke's head control, Ctrl+select the Mohawk_OFFSET group in the Outliner, and in the Animation menu set (F2) click on Constrain>Parent.

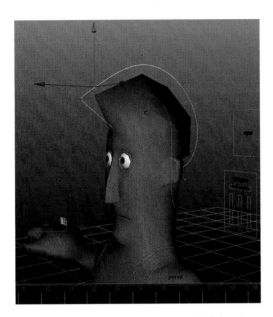

9 Get out of component mode by pressing F8. Select the new curve, rename it "Mohawk_CTRL", delete history by pressing *ctrl* *Shift* *D*, and zero the transforms by clicking Modify>Freeze Transformations.

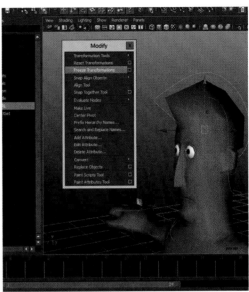

10 We need this control to ride around with the head, but it cannot have values in its channels (you will see why in a minute). So a constraint or a parent won't work yet. Click on the Mohawk_CTRL and press *ctrl* *G* to group it.

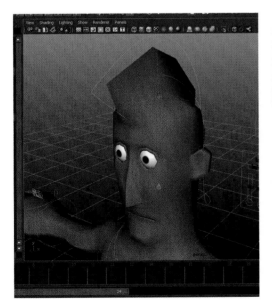

13 Select the Mohawk_CTRL and press *W* to switch to the Move tool. Hold down the *D* key to activate the Move Pivot mode, and hold down *V* to snap to points. Snap the control's pivot to the cluster by MMB clicking on it, still with *D* and *V* pressed.

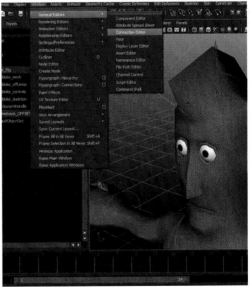

14 We can't use a constraint right now or the cluster will have double transforms again. Instead we will use a simple connection of the transforms of the control and that of the cluster. Select the Mohawk_Control and click on Window>General Editors>Connection Editor.

HOT TIP

Clusters' pivot point is slightly below where the "C" icon shows up for the cluster. Don't let the slightly odd pivot placement trick you into thinking you haven't snapped the Mohawk_Control's pivot correctly.

161

Adding Clusters (cont'd 2)

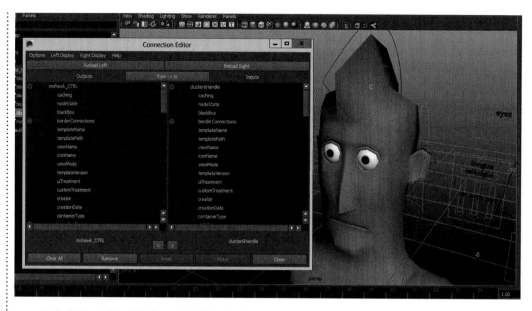

15 In the lefthand side of the Connection Editor, the Mohawk_CTRL's attributes will automatically load up. Select the cluster in the persp panel, then click on "Reload Right" in the top right hand side of the Connection Editor. The cluster's attributes should load in the right column.

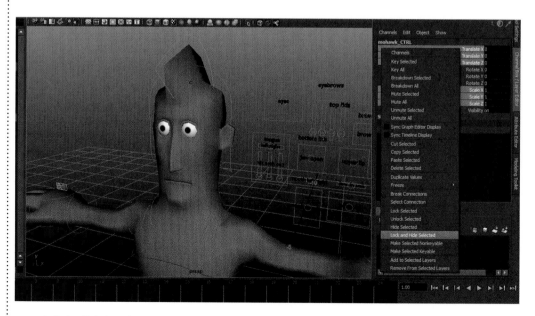

17 Let's do a little housekeeping again. Select the Mohawk_CTRL and in the channel box, select the translate and scale channels, right click on them, and choose "Lock and Hide Selected".

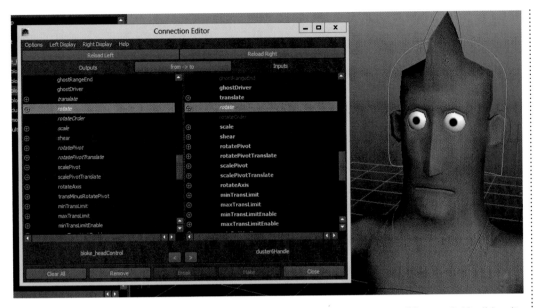

16 On the left-hand column, scroll down until you find the Mohawk_CTRL's rotate attribute. When you find it, click on it. Find the rotate attribute in the right column as well and click on it. When both attributes are selected, Maya creates a connection between them.

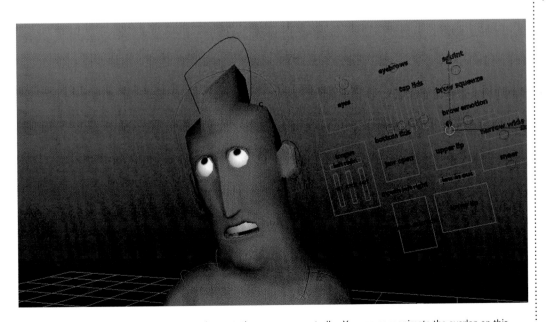

18 Test it out! Move Bloke into a pose, and try rotating your new controller. You can now animate the overlap on this Mohawk and give your scenes some customized animation that no other animator has.

Wrap Deformer

To FURTHER CUSTOMIZE YOUR CHARACTERS, you may
want to add new geometry to the rig. Sometimes
constraining the geometry won't work, especially if you
are trying to attach new geo in an area that is deforming.
Parenting has the same issues, and adding the new geometry
to the skin deformer is normally not an option either. So
what can you use to make further customizations to your
rigs? The Wrap Deformer saves the day.

I will start off by saying that this deformer can be
a little finicky in that certain conditions need to be met.
First, you should only wrap a piece of geometry to one other
piece of geometry. Meaning, if your character has separate
geometry for the head and the neck for instance, then you
would not have much luck wrapping a scarf that covers
the seam between the objects. Next, if your geometry has
parts that are very close together, the wrapped geometry
may not work. For instance, you will probably not be able
to wrap eyelashes on closed eyelids; the upper and lower
lid will 'fight' for the vertices of the lashes. If the eye was
open, however, it may work fine. Next, the Wrap Deformer
works best if the source and the target are close together. So
while it causes problems if geometry is close together on the
source (the one deforming the wrapped geometry), you also
run into trouble if the wrapped geo is too far away from the
mesh. An example would be the Mohawk that we created
in the last cheat. If that Mohawk was a separate piece of
geometry, then it would not be a good wrap candidate
because of how far away the tip of the Mohawk is from the
scalp. The bottom would deform fine, the top would get
funky. In general, Wrap is commonly used for things like
adding geometry to clothing or to the skin of the character.

Last, the Wrap Deformer can cause scene slowdown,
so you should add it later in the lifespan of the shot, and
add it in the referenced rig file instead of the scene file.
Referencing is covered in Chapter 10.

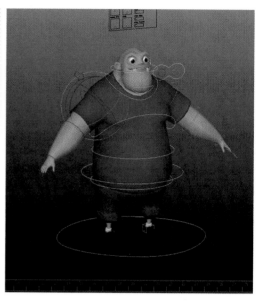

1 Open wrap_Start.ma. Groggy is standing in the scene,
and looking like normal. Let's turn him into EVIL Groggy
for a scene we might be working on.

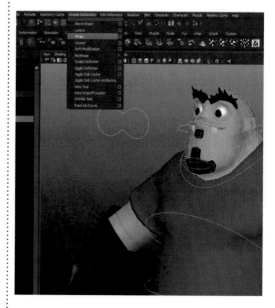

4 Now let's add the evil goatee. Select the goatee
geometry, then Groggy's head, and click on Create
Deformers>Wrap.

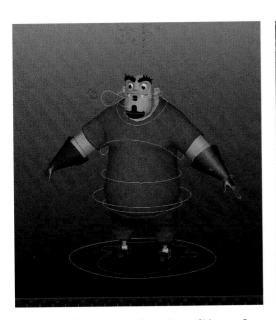

2 Click on File>Import and choose "wrap_Objects.ma". You will notice a few objects import into the scene to make our "evil" version of Groggy.

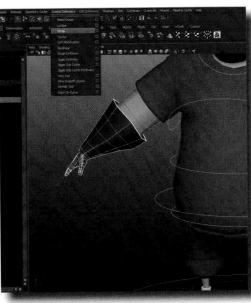

3 Let's do the gloves first. Hit F2 to switch to the Animation menu set. Select the right glove, then the right arm, and click on Create Deformers>Wrap. The default options are fine for us. Repeat this step for the left side.

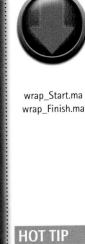

wrap_Start.ma
wrap_Finish.ma

HOT TIP

The gloves were made by duplicating the arms, moving the vertices around the cuffs outwards to create a flare, and then doing a tiny bit of sculpting to get the geometry to be slightly off the skin. Duplicating body parts is a common starting point for using the Wrap Deformer.

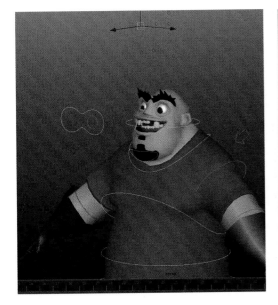

5 We should test that the Wrap is working correctly. Use the facial controls above Groggy's head to dial in some face poses, and make sure the goatee is being wrapped correctly.

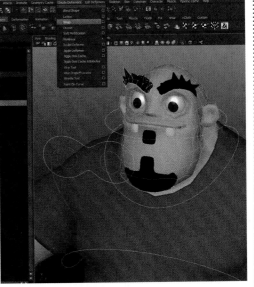

6 Let's do the eyebrows now. Select the right eyebrow and the head, and then click Create Deformers>Wrap. Repeat on the left side.

Wrap Deformer (cont'd)

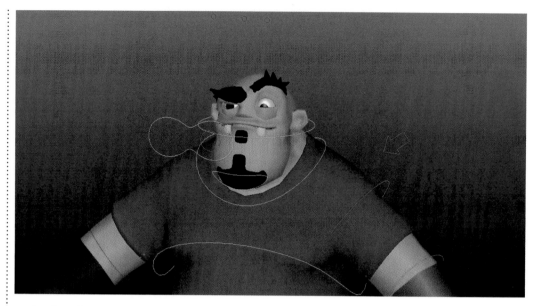

7 Test the eyebrows by using Groggy's facial controls again. They look like they're working great.

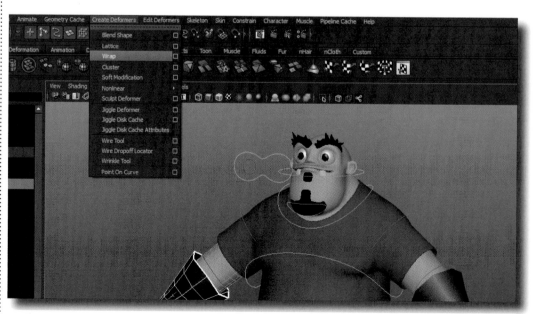

9 As you can see, the Wrap doesn't work. We need to wrap higher smooth levels. Undo the arm movement, and start over wrapping the geometry to the smoothed Groggy again.

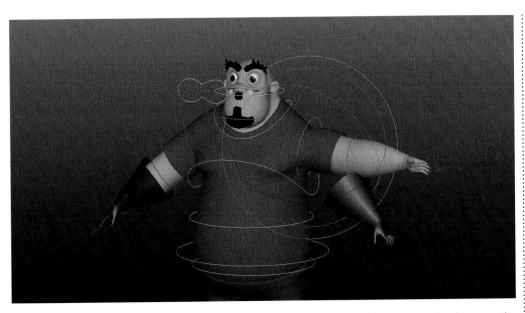

8 The Wrap deform only works on the smooth level that you created it on. Select Groggy's master control and turn smooth to 1, then move his arm.

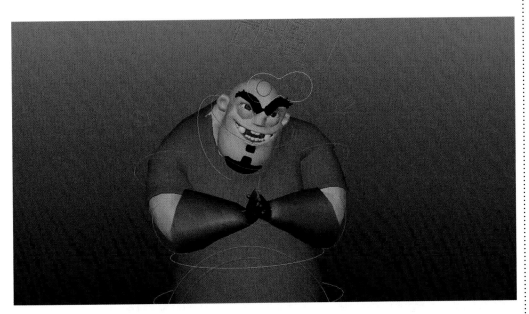

10 If you want to wrap the geometry to an even higher smooth level, just create new Wraps at that level. Text all of the wrapped geometry out by posing Groggy in an evil pose. Et voila, instant villain!

HOT TIP

You can smooth geometry that has been wrapped to another object without it breaking. Just hit **3** to use the Mental Ray Smooth Mesh Preview, as I did on the goatee.

Adding Hair & Cloth

HAIR AND CLOTH WERE SO TECHNICALLY difficult and computationally expensive that it would be crazy to attempt putting them on your reel. Today, however, adding these effects to characters is achieved through a few mouse clicks. And though the animation quality will actually be what makes your reel stand out from the crowd, knowing how to add these effects to your characters can serve you on the job.

If you are using characters that have been downloaded from a free site, normally the artists that created them do not want to confuse animators with things like hair and cloth. That doesn't mean that adding these effects are overly difficult. Actually there are just a few considerations to keep in mind. For example, you normally want to start your animation on f101 when dealing with hair and cloth. The reason for this is that you want to have enough frames in the beginning of the scene to run the simulations and let the effects settle. Also, you will want to learn how to turn off evaluation of dynamics so you can animate at 24fps until it's time to view your effects.

Hair and Cloth also add a layer of animation in your scene, just like how in the Rigging chapter we talked about adding dynamic motion to your scenes as a way to visually "fill in" the gaps in the animation. It may be a cheat, but it works.

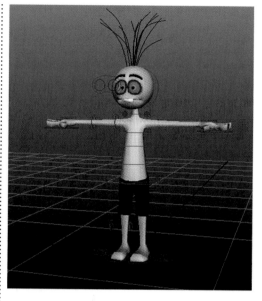

1 Open hair_Cloth_Start.ma. Our pal Moom is standing with some shorts and Nurbs curves sticking out of his head. We will apply hair and cloth to these objects.

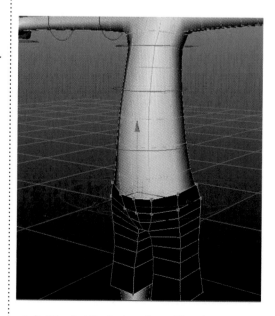

4 On f01, select the shorts, and press F8 to change to component mode. Select the vertices of the belt loop (top two edge loops). Then **Shift** select Moom's body geo.

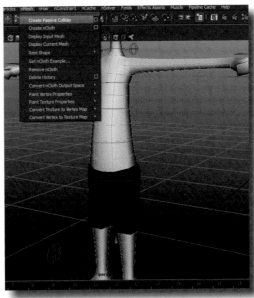

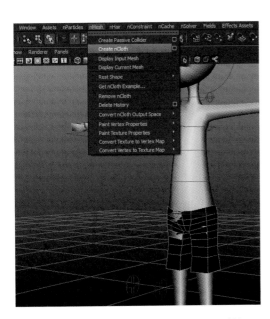

2 Let's start with the cloth. Select the geometry of his shorts. In the top left corner of the Maya UI, choose "nDynamics" from the Menu Set drop-down box. Click on nMesh>Create nCloth.

3 Select Moom's body geo, and click on nMesh>Create Passive Collider. Now if you press play, you will see the shorts stick to Moom. They can still fall down though, so we'll also add an nConstraint.

hair_Cloth_Start.
ma
hair_Cloth_Finish.
ma

HOT TIP

You may have to adjust the "thickness" setting in the nCloth collision settings to make sure the pants do not intersect the leg when it animates. Also, explore the presets in the nCloth shape to get different effects on this cloth.

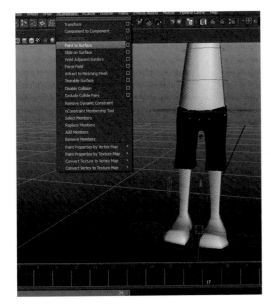

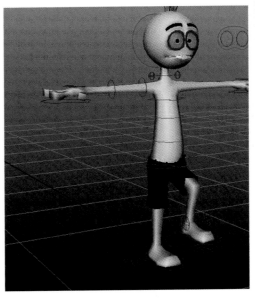

5 Click on nConstraint>Point to Surface. This creates a constraint, almost like a Wrap deform, where the selected vertices are linked to a nearby surface. Now Moom's pants won't fall off.

6 Test that the clothes are working by setting a keyframe on f01 with the foot on the floor, and then raised on f48. Looks pretty good!

Adding Hair & Cloth (cont'd)

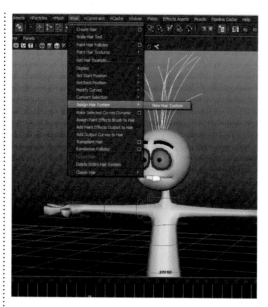

7 Select all of the curves sticking out of Moom's head. Click on nHair>Assign Hair System>New Hair System.

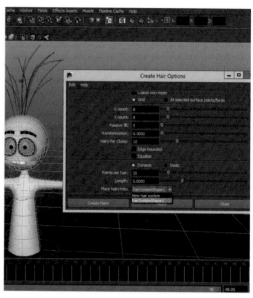

8 Select Moom's head and click on nHair>Create Hair> . In the dialog box that opens, select HairSystemShape1 at the bottom where it says "Place Hairs Into". Click "Create Hairs".

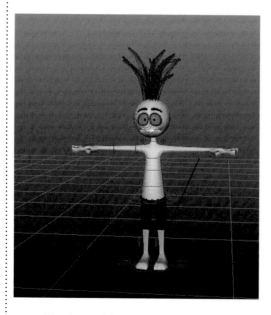

11 After they are deleted, the hair is looking how we designed it to with the crazy curves coming out of the top of his head.

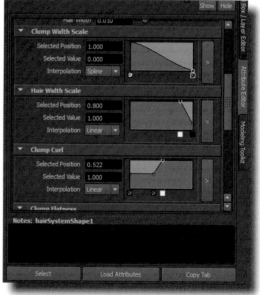

12 Let's customize the hair just a little bit. Select the hair, go into the Attribute Editor (*ctrl* *A*) and go to the hairSystemShape tab. Change the Clump Width Scale and the Clump Curl attributes to match mine.

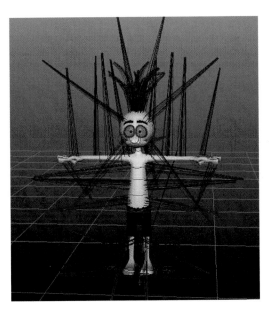

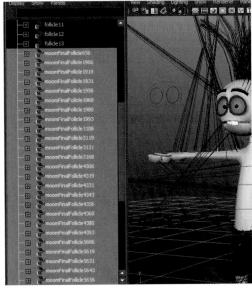

9 The result is a little whacky, but that's ok, we'll fix this.

10 In the Outliner, open the hairSystemFollicles group. Select all of the follicles in the group with the prefix "moomFinal". Delete them.

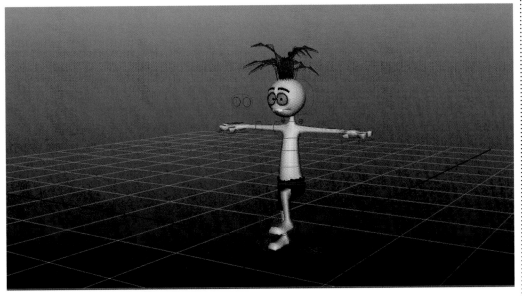

13 Check out your custom Moom! He has snazzy shorts and a rockin' hairdo. Not only is this character customized for you, these dynamic objects really add some visual continuity to your scene, letting you get away with snappy movements.

Shoot Right
Make the Most of Your Reference Video
by Kenny Roy

REFERENCE VIDEO IS THE MAINSTAY OF MANY animator's planning process. It can also provide some of the most unexpected "happy accidents" in the lifespan of a scene. Regardless of how much you use reference video in your workflow, you should be aware that workflow itself extends to the process of shooting your own reference video. Yep, workflow pervades all!

Let me start by describing what most beginner animators do when they shoot their own reference video. We'll take a dialog shot as an example for this scene. Most animators turn on the camera, play the dialog in the background, and try to lipsync and act out the scene at the exact same time. There are many problems with this approach.

The first problem is that the memorization of the lines was not done prior to turning on the camera. In the Meisner Technique (a-well known method approach to acting), memorization is done by stripping away all of the emotion in the words, and running through the dialog repeatedly. Then doing it again, and again, and again. Pretty soon you can run through the dialog without thinking; and this is the trick. Practicing the dialog so much that it becomes automatic is how you get PAST the words that are being said, and start focusing on the characters themselves. Practice running through the dialog with no intonation, inflection, or a hint of emotion and watch how as you gain speed and accuracy, your brain is now freer to do things like control your posing and movement. When done correctly, it's almost like a magic trick.

Once you have memorized the dialog ad nauseum , it's only now time to get in front of the camera. But wait! Keep the audio turned off on your computer for now. That's right; we do not want the audio from the scene distracting us. It is highly disruptive to hear the words and try to match the timing perfectly, and there is no better way to lose all of the freedom you have gained by memorizing the lines so thoroughly. So while the lines are fresh in your head, do some takes on camera of YOU doing the performance. No audio to fall back on, no cues, just you doing your absolute best performance of the line. What you will later go back and look for in these takes are subtle actions and movements that you would otherwise have not performed if you were caught up in matching the audio with your voice. Do some takes that are absolutely over the top! Who knows, you may see a pose, an arc, a facial expression, or something else that clues you in to where you can exaggerate in this shot. Do some takes that are totally out of character too. Even the bad takes will have something that is valuable in them.

The third step in the workflow is to do some takes with the audio playing again. However, rather than let yourself get caught up trying to match the voice perfectly, do your performances without speaking this time. Instead, gesture with your arms and legs and move around the scene, just without speaking. Again, we are trying to free our minds to come up with beautiful accidents that will improve our finished animation immensely. Do multiple takes where you are trying to simply let your weight rise and fall with the energy of the dialog. Zero in on the body language of the character as you hear it in the delivery, and exaggerate it fully. The great advantage of this second type of performance is that it will give you some very solid clues as to the timing of your scene. Whereas the first type (spoken by you, no audio cues) allows you to be free with pose and unrestricted by timing, this type of video will be priceless for extracting valuable timing tricks for use in your shot. Look closely at weight shifts and how you are leading up to the big actions. Watch the eyelines, head directions, and even the timing of the micro gestures that you do with your fingers. All of these little things can be a nightmare to try to guess the timing of so you can save yourself hours by spending just a few minutes of extra takes of the second type of video performance.

So let's recap. No more turning on the camera and jumping in front of it, unprepared! Take on this three-step workflow to get the most out of your reference video:

1.   Memorize the lines without emotion, getting just the words CEMENTED into your brain.
2.   Turn on the camera, but keep the audio on your computer off! Do many takes where you are performing the line as if you are the original actor in the film.
3.   Next turn the audio back on, but don't bother lipsyncing. Just focus on getting great poses, and look back on this footage with a keen eye for timing – your choices will be inspired.

Remember reference video is not cheating, it's just plain smart!

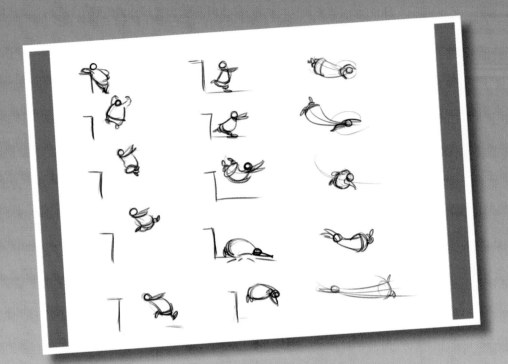

When you have a process that you repeat over and over, the inefficiencies are eliminated very quickly. Shots like the one pictured here just "come together".

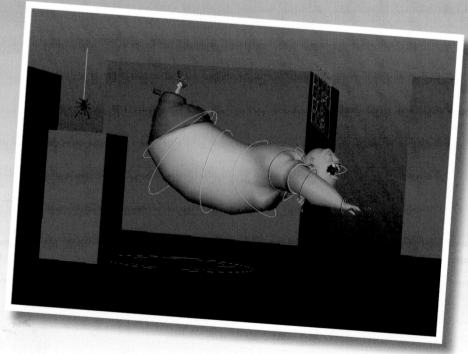

8

Workflow

YOU'VE READ THE INTERLUDE, so you know: simply put, workflow is the step-by-step process that you follow every time you create animation. It is your go-to guide. It is your savior when things go wrong. It is the ever-evolving and improving rubric for success that you depend on.

No? Still not sold on workflow? Fine, maybe this chapter will change your mind. We're going to walk through a shot and demonstrate all of the great cheats that repeatedly make an appearance in a professional's workflow. If by the end you are still not convinced, then consider this: before I started committing myself to improving my workflow, this shot would have taken me over a week to complete. With workflow? This shot took three afternoons without a single headache!

Planning/Reference

T HE BEST WORKFLOWS START with a strong foundation. This means thoroughly planning out your scene. There are a lot of planning methods but the most common and beneficial planning tools are definitely thumbnails and reference video.

With thumbnails, it's important to your workflow that the drawings are very strong. Focus primarily on the body positioning and pose, and less on the staging and camera. You want these drawings to be your guide through the entire shot, so getting too caught up in the staging and direction of the shot at the thumbnail stage will get in the way. With the focus solely on the character's body and pose, you can be sure these thumbnails will be helpful through the whole life of your shot.

Reference video is easy to gather on YouTube. Spend some good time finding as many related clips as you can. The more the merrier. You should also be creating your own reference footage. For this shot, the animation needed to be very cartoony. I've found the best way to make a reference video for really cartoony actions is to 'puppet' your hands around and create a 'sound effects track' by making noises with your voice. It may seem a little silly to be yelling and screeching at your desk, walking your fingers around like legs, but when you see how closely the animation was timed to my reference video, I think you'll see the benefits outweigh the embarrassment.

We're going to go through a few cheats that are great for making sure your drawings and reference video are at your fingertips. We're then going to import your reference video as well and keep it handy.

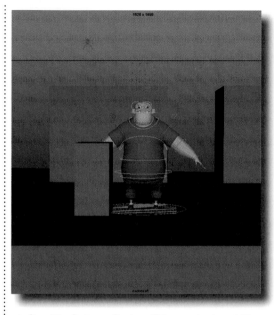

1 Open 01 - Cartoony_Start.ma. This scene has been laid out with the character and set, and is ready for our awesome planning to be imported in a way that will keep it at our fingertips.

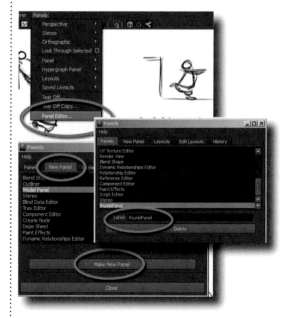

4 Let's save this view for later. Go to Panels>Panel Editor. Go to the New Panel tab, select "Model Panel" in the list and hit "Make New Panel". In the Panel Editor go back to the Panels Tab, select the new panel you just made (at the bottom of the list) and name it thumbPanel, and press *Enter*.

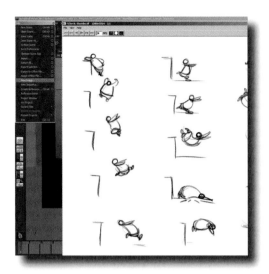

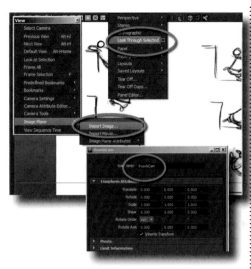

01 – Cartoony_
Start.ma

2 You can simply view a file. Go to File>View Image. Select "Thumbs.tif". Maya opens the image with FCHECK by default. The only advantage of using this method is Maya remembers the file path in case you close it accidentally. Instead let's make sure that isn't an issue.

3 Go to Create>Cameras>Camera. Name your new camera "ThumbCam". In any panel go to Panels>Look Through Selected. In the panel go to View>Image Plane>Import Image. Select Thumbs.tif. Very nice. The image is now loaded into this Maya camera.

HOT TIP

If you ever accidentally close this panel, get it back by going into any panel, switching to the thumbPanel you created, and tearing off the panel for easy use. Your thumbs are never far away...

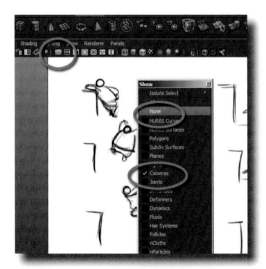

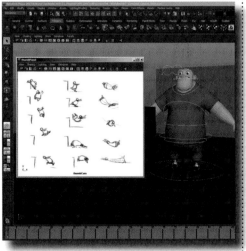

5 Maya may change your panel back to Camera1. Go to Panels>Panel>thumbPanel. In the Panel menu go to Show>None. Then again to Show>Cameras. Lastly turn off the grid by hitting the Grid button at the top of the panel.

6 Now go to Panels>Tear off. The panel now floats and you can move, minimize, and maximize it. This is a great way to work with your thumbnails right at your fingertips.

Planning/Reference (cont'd)

ONE OF THE BIGGEST CHEATS of all involves timing your scene. In the old days, animators would use stopwatches to time their animation. By repeating an action over and over in their head and timing it with the stopwatch, they could write down the specific frame numbers and always have this timing reference close by. I find it alarming that now that we've moved into the digital age, this cheat hasn't been updated as well! We are going to use a piece of video reference created specifically to give us really high-energy timing to our scene.

Maya 2014 imports all kinds of movie files, making video reference accessible and valuable deep into the production of your shot. With multiple codecs and formats supported, you will always have your video reference at your fingertips.

The movie file we're going to load was created to give a very specific sense of timing that could not be acted out. Hence the reason why I use my hands and sound effects (whistles and screams) to get a feel for the energy. "Acting out" your scenes like this, especially when they are cartoony-styled shots, is an invaluable piece of reference. Don't be shy, the more energy you put into this "timing reference", the better the shot will turn out!

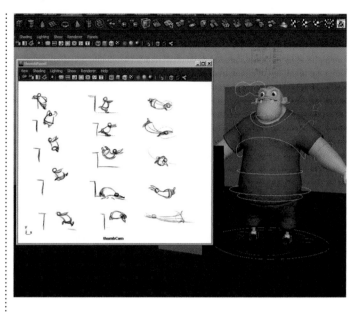

1 Open 02 - Cartoony_Timing_Start.ma. Here is our scene with the thumbnails loaded that we created in the last cheat. In order to nail the timing and energy, let's load the reference video.

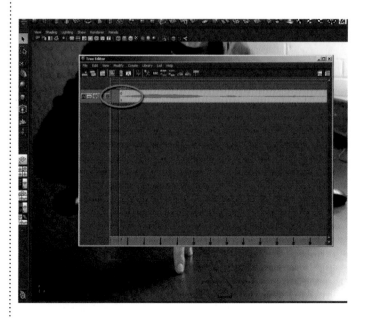

4 Slide the audio to the right in the Trax Editor so that it starts on f01. Retrace the steps in the previous cheat to create a new model panel so that you can always get back to the "refVideoCam" in case you close it.

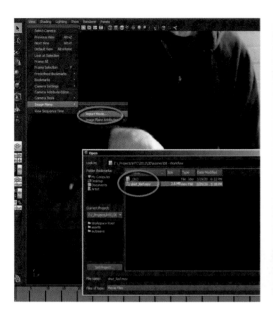

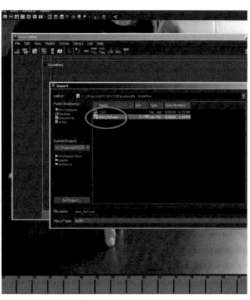

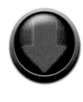

02 – Cartoony_
Timing_Start.ma

2 Create a new camera, name it "refVideoCam", and look
through this new camera. In the panel select View>
Image Plane> Import Movie. Select "shot_ref.mov" in this
chapter's "scenes" directory.

3 Open the Trax Editor by going to Windows>Animation
Editors>Trax Editor. We want to see the footage in a
camera, but also the audio in the Trax Editor for timing.
In the Trax Editor go to File>Import Audio, and choose
"shot_ref.wav".

HOT TIP

If you go into
Panels > Saved
Layouts > Edit
Layouts you
can save this
panel layout
as well, and
get even more
time-saving
customization in
Maya.

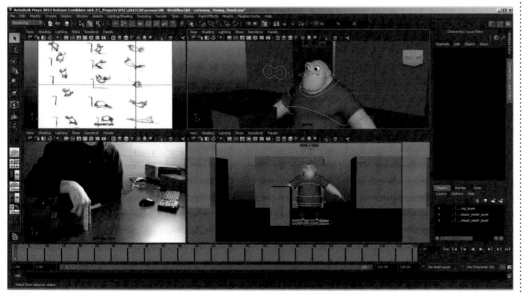

5 Look how awesome we are set up if we open the thumbCam and the refVideoCam alongside our Perspective and
Camera panels! Ready to Block and Roll!

Converting Cycles

WHEN YOU HAVE A WALK CYCLE, you have to decide if the character is going to be walking in world space, or if the character is going to be cycling in place. In general, world space cycles are used in film and television, and most game engines use cycles that are in place.

The reasons are fairly simple. In film work, complex interactions between the characters and the environments mean that the footfalls and contacts need to be happening in a precise way. It makes sense that the character is actually going to progress through the scene. In order to preview the walk cycle and assess the fluidity of the movement, we counter-animate the master controller against the Z-axis movements of the IK controllers (hands, feet and root).

In games, frequently the movement of the character is controlled by the player. Which means that you have to sacrifice the extremely detailed contact and floor interaction in lieu of fast reaction from your character. So walk cycles are 'in place' and the character's feet slide within the object space of the master controller (which the player is actually moving around when they play).

Here is a step-by-step cheat to change your walk cycles from world space to be within the object space of the master control.

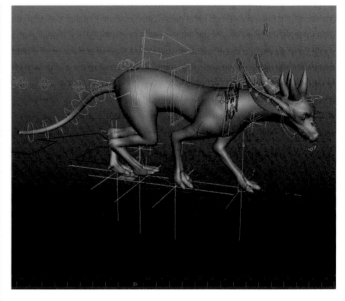

1 Open convert_Cycle_Start.ma. This is a film-style cycle that we are going to convert to a game-style cycle. I've taken the liberty of doing the first step: parent constrain locators to all the IK controls with "maintain offset" OFF.

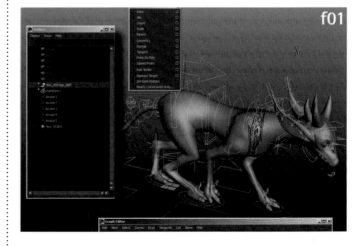

4 Go to f01. Select all of the IK controls AND the master control on the floor (the world "con", the "cog", both feet and both paws). In the Graph Editor, select all of their curves and delete them.

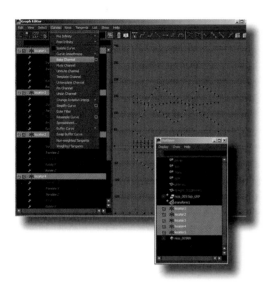

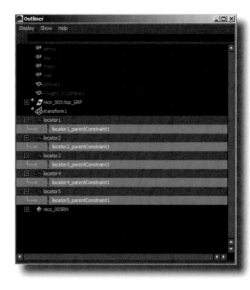

convert_Cycle_
Start.ma
convert_Cycle_
Finish.ma

2 Select the locator1 through locator5 and open the Graph Editor. Click on Curves>Bake Channel. The default settings will suffice. Now there is animation information on these locators based on their WORLD position.

3 In the Outliner, delete all of the parent constraints on the locators by expanding their hierarchies and deleting the parent constraint node.

You have to finish all the steps without changing the frame number after you delete the animation on the IK controls. If you change the frame, the animation will not bake correctly.

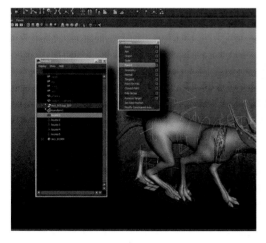

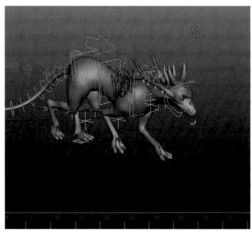

5 Now one by one, constrain the IK controls back to the locators. Select the IK controls and open the Graph Editor. Click on Curves>Bake Channel.

6 Delete the locators. Now your animation has been converted to the object space of the master controller, and Nico is cycling in place. Beautiful.

Stepped Keys

W E KNOW FROM THE GRAPH EDITOR **CHAPTER** that stepped keys give us instantaneous transitions between values. When you key all of the body's controls in stepped mode, you could say that the resulting keyframes are almost like "images" that you can retime at will to give yourself the best result.

Workflow-wise, blocking is the most efficient stage to be doing this retiming. Maya 2014 has awesome tools for retiming keys. We'll practice this by using both the Retime tool in the Graph Editor, as well as the Dope Sheet.

With the Retime tool, our goal is to retime whole sections so that they line up with the energy of the beats much better. This is achieved easily because the Retime tool is intuitive and rock solid.

With the Dope Sheet, a very underutilized tool in Maya, we get a top-level view of the distribution of the keys in our scene. It's very important at the blocking stage to make sure you are hitting your beats exactly. We'll use the Dope Sheet to make sure the impacts of the feet are right on the same frames as the sound, and the impact of the body on the ground also matches the audio we've recorded.

Many novices think that the best animators create perfect timing on their first try. It is quite the contrary! The best animators are normally really good at quickly RETIMING and adjusting their animation. If you can go through a dozen iterations in the time it takes another animator to do just one version, you will be far ahead of the pack. Some might say it looks like you're cheating...

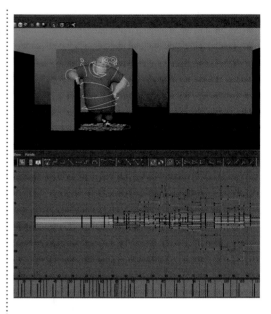

1 Open up 03 – Cartoony_blocking_start.ma. This is our Stepped-Key Blocking. Hit play and see how, although the key poses are all there, the timing is off. Now select all of Groggy's controls and see how tidy stepped keys look in the Graph Editor.

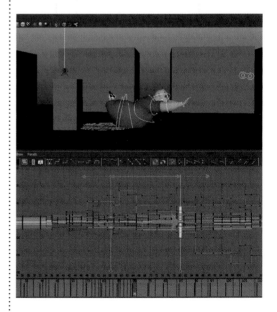

4 Now let's find the moment of impact in the audio. It seems to be somewhere around f80. Drag the middle of the right Retime handle to the right until it's sitting above f80.

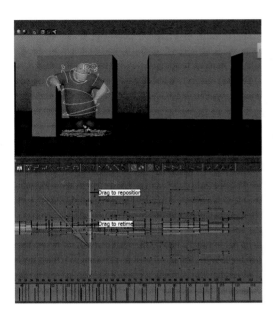

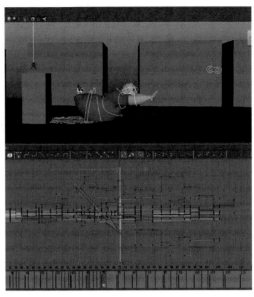

03 - cartoony_
Blocking_Start.ma
03 - cartoony_
Blocking_Finish.ma

2 The section of Groggy running and falling is timed too quickly. The Retime tool is perfect for retiming sections of keys and preserving the rest. Select the Retime tool and Double click on f56 in the Graph Editor.

3 We need to choose a moment that is easy to pick out from the audio file. The moment of impact when he falls is a good choice. It is currently happening on f70. Let's create another retime handle there by double clicking on f70.

HOT TIP

If you right click on a Retime handle, you can insert a key on all channels of the selected objects. This is a great, quick way to create a hold.

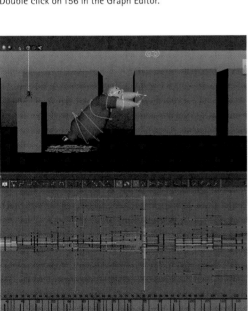

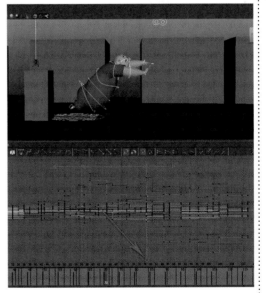

5 It's a good idea to snap your keys to frames, so let's do that. Go to Edit>Snap. Play the animation and see how much better the timing is working now.

6 The Retime handles are preserved. To delete them, click on the little X at the bottom of the handle. You will want to put your handles on integer frame values if you do more retiming from here on out.

Stepped Keys (cont'd)

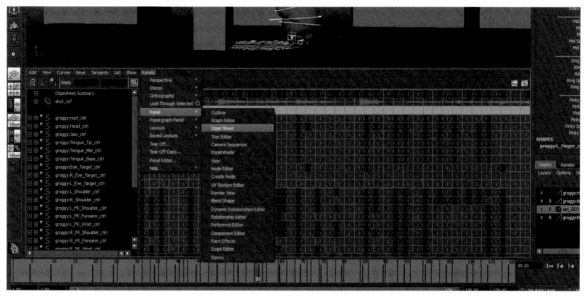

1 First let's switch to the Dope Sheet. The Dope Sheet is the most top-level view of the keys in your scene that we have in Maya. While it can be cumbersome once you get too far into the progress of your shot, the Dope Sheet offers some very quick keyframe editing capabilities. Specifically, the ability to slide around all of the keys on a frame by selecting only a single block in the "Dopesheet Summary" row is a great way to cheat having to select multiple keys in the Graph Editor, or even more time consuming, shift click a range of keys in the timeline. Another little cheat is that moving the keys around in the Dope Sheet snaps the keys to integer frames.

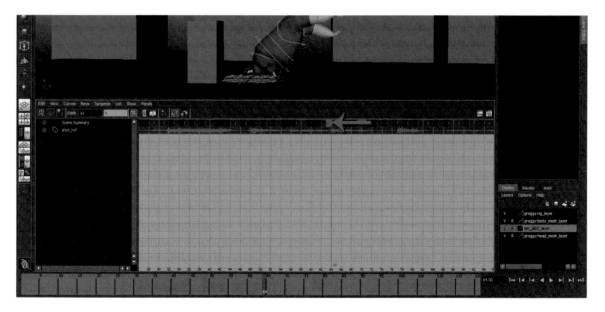

4 The third hit in the audio is happening on frame 64, but our keyframe is only on f65. Select it and move it one frame to the left.

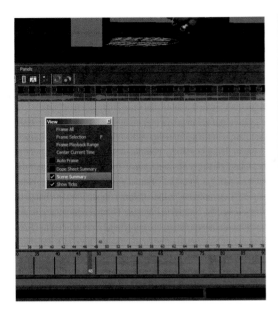

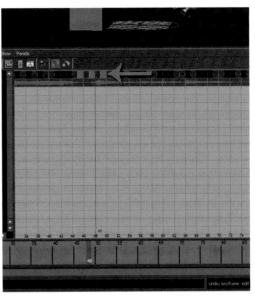

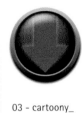

03 - cartoony_
Blocking_Start.ma
03 - cartoony_
Blocking_Finish.ma

2 Let's unclutter our workspace. Deselect everything and in the Dope Sheet uncheck View>Dope Sheet Summary, and check View>Scene Summary. Now we see all of the keys in the scene.

3 Let's use this top-level view to improve our timing. Select the keys on f46, F48, and f50, and hit **W** to switch the move tool. These keys are a touch late, move them a frame to the left by dragging with the MMB.

HOT TIP

If you notice in the top right corner of the Dope Sheet, there are buttons for the Graph Editor and the Track Editor. Maya makes it easy to switch between these common editors. Using these quick buttons frequently will save lots of time!

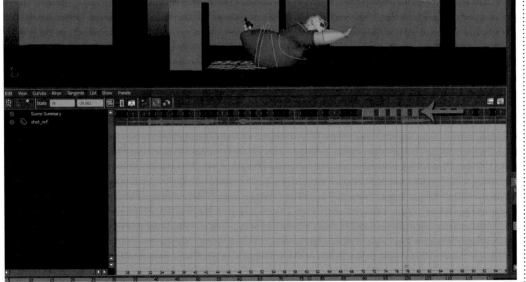

5 The last moment is the big splat on the ground. Let's fix the timing there too. Select all the keys from f71 to f81 and move them a frame to the left. Play it back and see how these small changes make all the difference.

Stepped Preview

Stepped keys offer animators the convenience of pose-to-pose workflow in a digital medium. Like we learned in the last cheat, they are super useful for blocking your work, retiming poses, and keeping good keyframe economy.

We will now use the feature in Maya 2014 called "Stepped Preview". It is an awesome tool that allows us to work in a hybrid mode between stepped and spline. Best of all, it makes it so that you do not risk ruining all of your keyframes if you want to go back and forth between stepped and spline.

Normally, if you wanted to see a splined version of your stepped animation, or wanted to go back to splines to add more breakdowns, you would have to convert the curves themselves to do so. Not so anymore. This is a HUGE workflow improvement for character animators. Why? Now you can keep your tangent in and out types set to Auto, but work in stepped mode by enabling Stepped Preview. When you are confident that you are ready to move onto splined curves, then you can turn off the Stepped Preview Mode, and see if you have enough breakdowns and in-betweens. If not, simply turn it back on and refine a little bit more. It's that simple.

Gone are the days of doing your animation in stepped, then holding your breath as you click the spline button, wondering what your animation is going to look like after it has been completely changed by Maya.

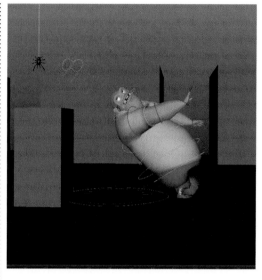

1 Open stepped_Preview_Start.ma. Groggy is pretty much through blocking on his crazy exit, but let's use Stepped Preview to practice this new workflow.

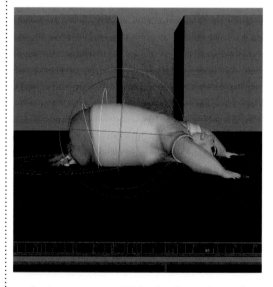

4 Create a new pose on f83 that has Groggy flattened out on the ground.

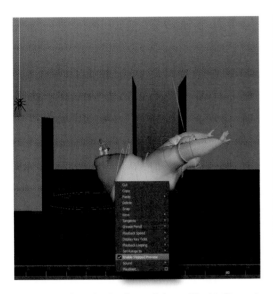

2 Right click on the timeline and choose "Enable Stepped Preview". Playback the animation and you will see that all of your keys are being displayed as if they are stepped.

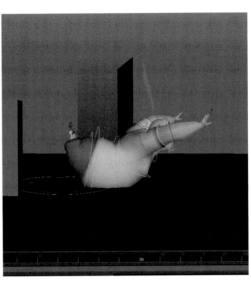

3 Where are there problems? He looks like he's on the ground too long between f80 and f85.

stepped_Preview_
Start.ma
stepped_Preview_
Finish.ma

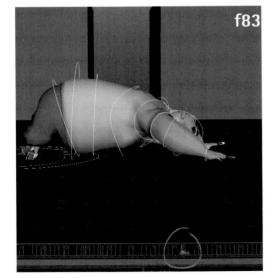

f83

5 Since we are in Stepped Preview mode, it is very easy to see that the pose is a teeny bit too early. Select all of Groggy's controls and move the keyframe on f83-f82. That looks a little better.

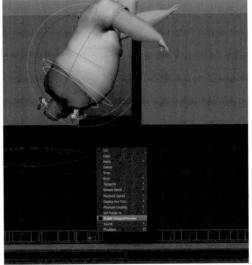

6 Now for the magic of Stepped Preview. Right click on the timeline again and disable Stepped Preview. Playback the animation. Whereas before your splines would be all wiped out if you converted back and forth to stepped, the animation is preserved!

187

Moving Holds When Splining

THE SPLINING STAGE IS SO TERRIFYING; it's very hard to
know what you are going to get! When you are done adding
essential breakdowns in stepped mode, most animators hold their
breath, close their eyes, and click "Spline" in the Graph Editor
only to fret when the resulting mush doesn't carry any of the old
appeal of the stepped version. Transitions seem slow and floaty,
the character cruises "through" poses without any of the snap
that you imagined in stepped, and overall it seems that all of
your amazing timing choices have changed.

This is fine and normal, but it won't do for production.
Pros know that when you are going through your workflow, you
can't have a step that basically leaves the success of your shot
up to chance! And one of the most striking difference between
stepped animation and keys that have been freshly splined is the
absence of any moving holds.

In the last edition of How To Cheat in Maya we showed
you how to do copied pairs. This cheat is an expansion on that
thought; we'll start with a copied pair but this time in stepped
mode. Then we'll use a fancy cheat I've devised to give just the
right amount of movement on a character in a moving hold. It's
the best kind of cheat – one that you can and should use over
and over in your workflow, but more importantly one that takes
all the guess work out of a scary stage in your shot!

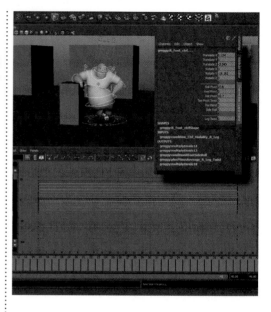

1 Open 05 - cartoony_Moving_Holds_start.ma. This scene
has only the two poses that represent the beginning of
the animation. Select all of Groggy's controls and in the
Graph Editor you'll see the keys are in stepped mode.

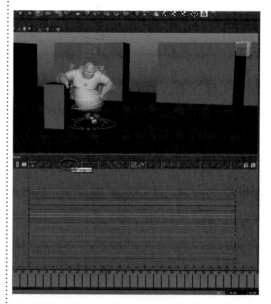

3 Click "Stepped" again to get us back to stepped keys.
We'll build the pose now that gives us a good moving
hold.

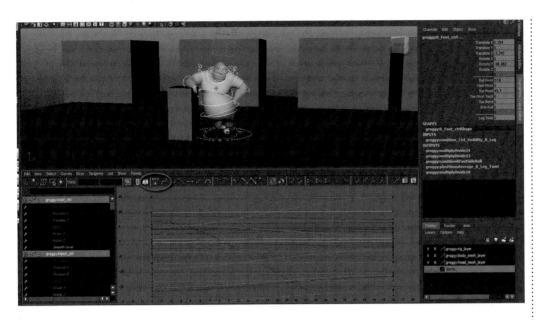

05 - cartoony_
Moving_Holds_
start.ma
05 - cartoony_
Moving_Holds_
finish.ma

2 Now let's take a close look in the Graph Editor at what happens when we spline the animation. Press **alt**+**Shift**+RMB
and drag upwards to zoom in vertically a bit. With all the controls still selected, hit the AutoTangent button and see
what happens to your curves. This is expected. Maya thinks you want to ease in on each of these keys, so it chose flat
tangents for you.

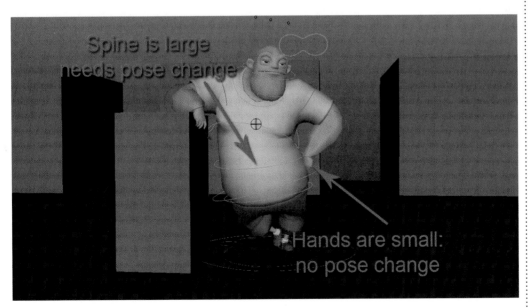

Spine is large
needs pose change

Hands are small:
no pose change

4 Let's build a relaxed pose. With this cheat, we try to imagine the character after he's been holding the pose for 10
minutes. To do this, imagine the big muscles like his legs and shoulders relaxing the most, and the smaller muscles like
the neck and fingers, relaxing least. You'll see why in a second.

Moving Holds (cont'd)

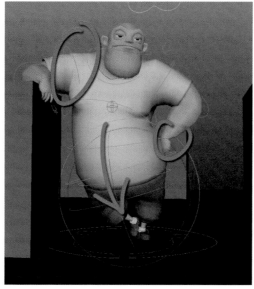

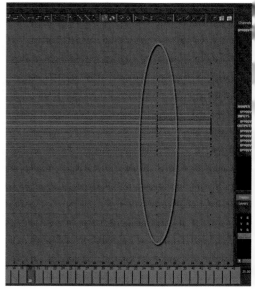

5 On f20, rotate his pelvis a little bit forward, but straighten his legs a tad by moving his pelvis upwards slightly in Y. Rotate the rest of his spine to straighten him up a bit too. Adjust the arms to be back in their resting positions.

6 Switch to the Graph Editor and with all of the controls selected, hit **S**. Make sure a key is placed on all of the curves.

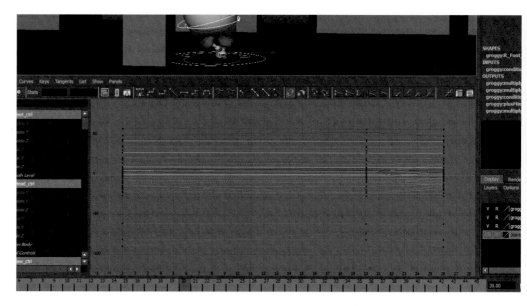

9 Now we're going to use a little cheat to adjust the amount of movement that is happening in our moving hold. Switch to the panel configuration of Persp/Graph as above and play the animation. He's moving too much!

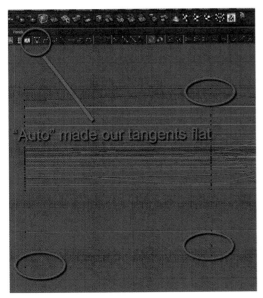

"Auto" made our tangents flat

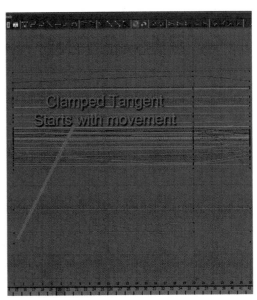

Clamped Tangent
Starts with movement

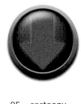

05 - cartoony_
Moving_Holds_
start.ma
05 - cartoony_
Moving_Holds_
finish.ma

HOT TIP

If you go halfway between two keys, you get roughly 50% change, but for more fine-tuned adjustment, you can copy a key only a frame or two before your last frame and get a 5% adjustment. It's common to do a 50% copy and then a couple of smaller copies to get a finely-tuned result.

7 Now hit the AutoTangent button and look at the result. All of the tangents are flat. Maya thinks we need an ease in and out of all of the keys right now. But we don't want Groggy to start from a dead halt on f01.

8 Let's try clamped instead. Clamped will give us much more predictable results when creating moving holds WITHIN stepped mode. I recommend you convert from stepped to clamped as part of your workflow.

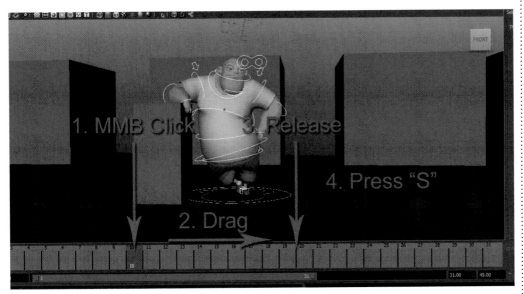

1. MMB Click   3. Release

4. Press "S"

2. Drag

10 To reduce the amount of movement, we're going to use a tried and true cheat, of MMB copying the keys on the timeline. MMB click on the timeline on f10, and drag your mouse to f20. Release your mouse and press Ⓢ.

Moving Holds (cont'd 2)

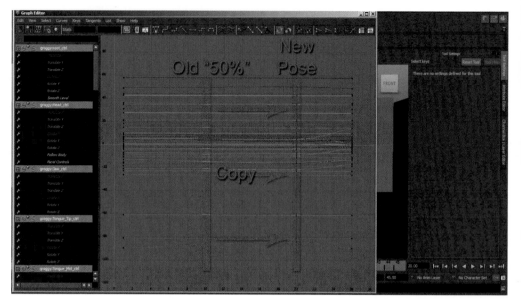

11 What just happened? Since we went about halfway between our two splined keys, we get roughly 50% of the movement we had before when we paste the keys on f20.

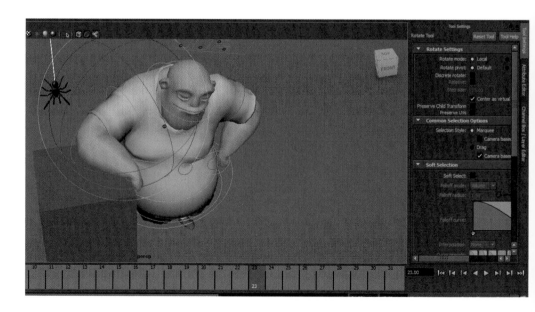

13 Don't forget the arms. On f23 check that his right arm is staying generally still by rotating the shoulder and elbow. Flip back and forth between the three keys (20, 23, and 26) using the comma (,), and period ⬛ keys.

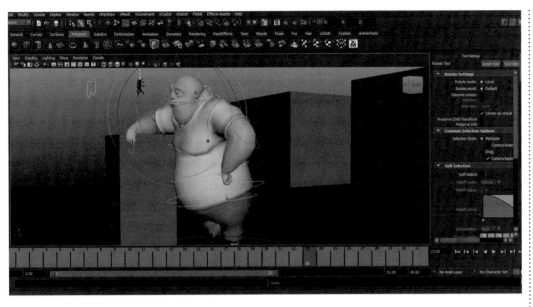

12 If it seems like there's still too much movement, then repeat the last step. Let's add a breakdown in between the end of the moving hold and the final pose. On f23, rotate his spine forward a bit as well as his head.

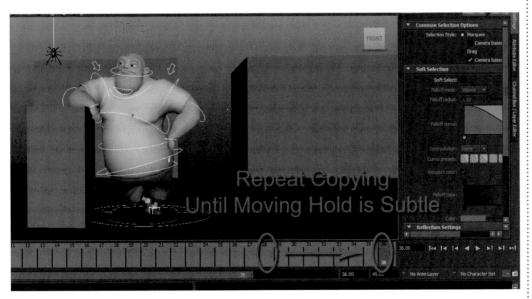

Repeat Copying
Until Moving Hold is Subtle

14 At f110, the body, spine, head and arms are dragging, creating an arced path into the next pose. The R leg is easing out to the extended position. Dragging the R foot in an exaggerated way helps the expanding feel as well.

HOT TIP

Converting your stepped keys to clamped when splining gives the most predictable results if you create your holds using this method. But, change your default tangent to AutoTangent after converting everything to clamped to get the most help from Maya as you move on.

193

Moving Holds w/ Retime Tool

THE RETIME TOOL OFFERS a brand new paradigm for manipulating and creating keys in the Graph Editor. We can make broad adjustments to timing, or in this case, repeat the copy+paste method of moving hold creation in a snap.

Most professionals know that the best way to cheat in Maya is to find quick, effective methods of doing tasks that you must do repeatedly throughout the workday. And while Maya offers very powerful scripting capabilities, rarely will a script come in handy when it comes to something like a moving hold.

Instead we must use all of the tools Maya has to offer to refine and perfect our workflow. In the end, your workflow should take full advantage of the aggregate improvements added to Maya in every new version. To ignore these awesome tools is to ignore cheats that could save your shot!

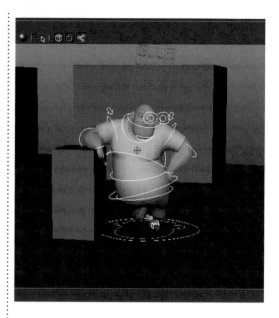

1 Open 06 - cartoony_retime_Holds_start.ma. This is the same scene as before, only this time we're going to use the Retime tool to create the moving holds. Open the Graph Editor and familiarize yourself with the keys again.

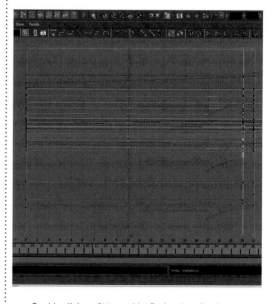

3 Double click on f20 to add a Retime handle there too. Now drag the Retime handle from f10 to f20. The Retime handle we just created will shift over to near f21.

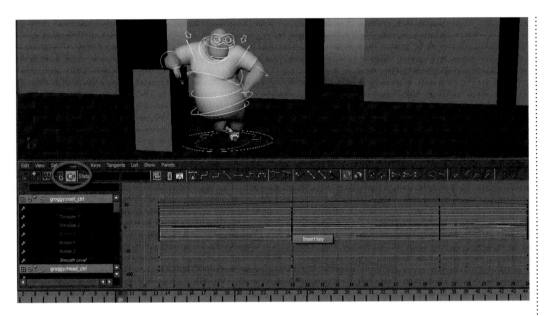

06 - cartoony_
retime_Holds_
start.ma
06 - cartoony_
retime_Holds_
finish.ma

2 In the Graph Editor, click on the Retime tool on the upper left, and double click on f1 and f10. This creates retime handles on those keys. Now right click on the Retime handle on f10 and choose "Insert Key". Now we have a key that represents our 50% point in the animation again.

HOT TIP

Remember
Retime
handles are
not saved into
a scene. You
need to make
your timing
adjustments
before you close
your file or you
will lose the
handles you've
created.

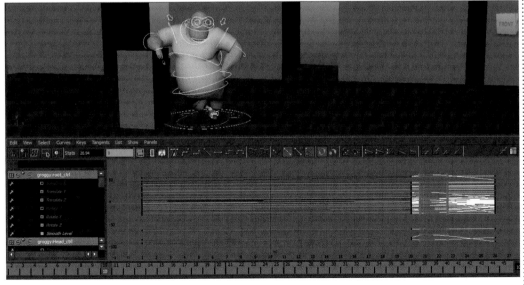

4 Hit **Q** to switch to the select tool. Select the keys on f21 and hit Del. Go to Edit>Snap to make sure your newly retimed moving hold is firmly on an integer frame. Moving hold, done!

195

Refining Arcs in Polish

B Y THE TIME YOU HAVE WORKED THROUGH your entire workflow and have made it to the polish phase, you are most likely dealing with an amount of keyframes that is unwieldy, to put it lightly. To make even the slightest adjustments can take hours of deleting, redoing, tweaking, and frustration.

Arcs are such an important fundamental that we need to make sure at this point in our workflow that we double-check that our arcs look great. However, like I mentioned before, finalizing your arcs in the polish phase means navigating a rat's nest of curves in the Graph Editor.

Fortunately for us, the Editable Motion Trail tool is good for not just creating and defining motion, but for keeping arcs manageable in this time of super dense keys. We took a look at how to use Editable Motion Trails in the Animation Principles chapter and the Techniques chapter so you should be pretty familiar with creating them by now. But unlike in those chapters when we created smooth motion, we will now be using them to finalize arcs among very dense keys. Maya 2014's Editable Motion Trails are rock solid and very stable now.

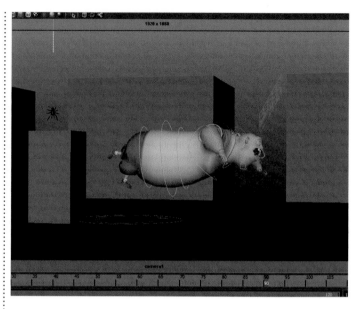

1 Open 07 - cartoony_Arcs_start.ma. This scene is at the end of Blocking Plus and is ready for polish in the arcs. Play a few times through and see if you can pick out the problems.

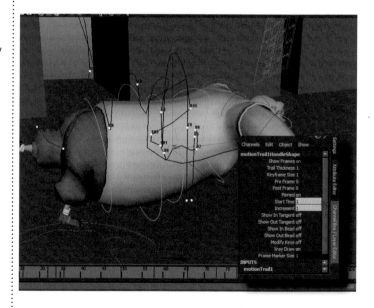

3 By default our trail shows no tangents nor influences on the keys. We'll show those later when it's time to refine. Select one of the keys in the panel and move it to test it.

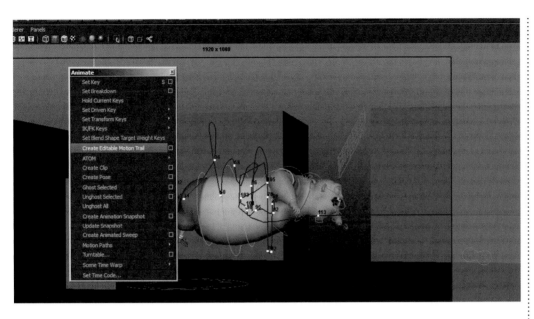

07 - cartoony_
Arcs_start.ma
07 - cartoony_
Arcs_finish.ma

2 We're going to focus on the chest in the frame range 90-102. In these 12 frames, there is a lot of popping and movement. Select his chest control and in the Animation menu set (F2) go to Animate>Create Editable Motion Trail.

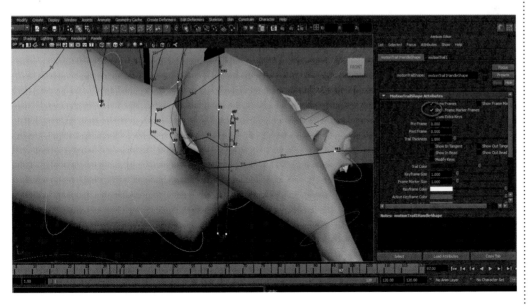

4 Things are easier to follow if you can see all of the frame markers and not just frames with keys on them. Turn them on by checking "Show Frame Marker Frames" in the Attribute panel with the motion trail selected.

Refining Arcs (cont'd)

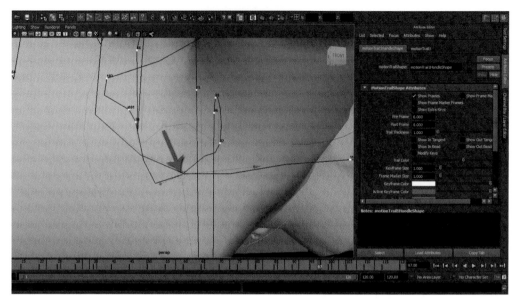

5 Move the key that is labeled "95" down to bring it into more of an arc shape. You'll notice the Editable Motion Trail stays kind of ragged no matter how you move this key. Time to play with the tangents.

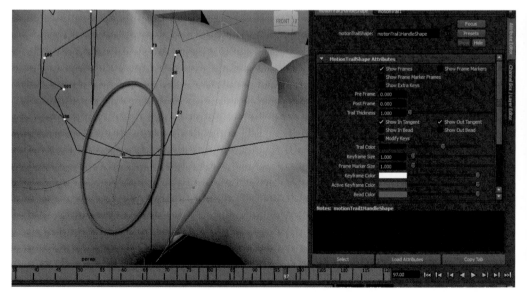

7 Click again on the key labeled "95". The tangents will be selected and you can MMB-drag them around in the panel and see their influence. Adjust the keyframe's position and the tangent's influence until the arc looks smoother.

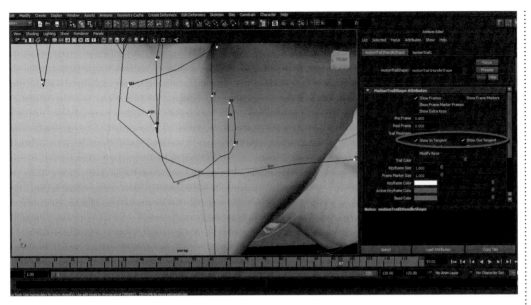

6 In the Attribute Editor check "Show In Tangent" and "Show Out Tangent". This enables influence editing in panel on the entire Motion Trail, not just the select key..

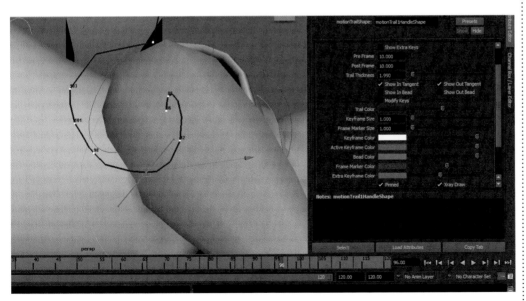

8 Now do the same adjustment to the position and the tangents on the other frames between f90 and f102. Don't stop until you have a nice clean arc in this chest movement.

HOT TIP

Our final check of any arc is looking through the main camera. An arc may look great in perspective but until you see what it looks like to camera, you are not finished finessing.

199

Final Texture

T HE VERY LAST THING YOU SHOULD HAVE in your workflow
is adding final details like little bits of texture to your scene.
This is called non-performance texture; these little details aren't
contributing to the performance choices you've made. Instead
they are making the scene feel full of details and real.

With Maya 2014's animation layers, adding texture
to your polished scene means that you can non-destructively
experiment with ideas. It is crucial that you understand the
importance of workflow at this point; animation layers need to
be planned for very carefully. If, halfway through working on
your shot, you suddenly decide to do some of the animation on
a layer, chances are you will get horribly off track. Instead, you
must either plan on your animation being done in layers (a walk
cycle on the legs for example, and adding torso movement on a
new layer), or you must wait to only add very fine details at the
end.

By adhering to our strict workflow, we are safeguarding
our scene against unforeseen problems later on. Animation
layers give us an immense amount of control over the polished
scene, without any destructive effects on the keys we already
have.

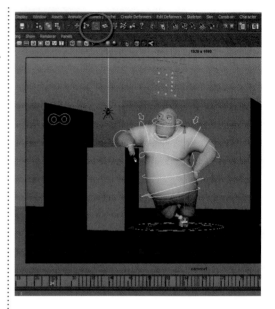

1 Open 08 - cartoony_Texture_start.ma. We are going to
add a little breath at the beginning of the scene. Turn
off all the selection masks except "curves" and then drag
a selection box around Groggy. You will select all of his
controls.

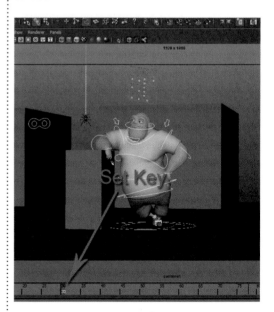

4 Set another key on f30.

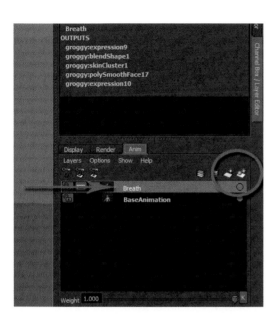

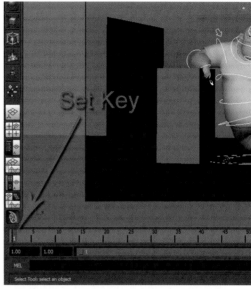

08 – cartoony_
Texture_start.ma
08 – cartoony_
Texture_finish.ma

2 In the channel box/Layer Editor, click on the "Create Layer From Selected" button, and rename the new layer "Breath".

3 Click on the Breath animation layer to make it the active layer. Nothing you do now will affect keys on the BaseAnimation layer. Select all of Groggy's controls. On f01 hit **S** to set a key for the beginning of the breath.

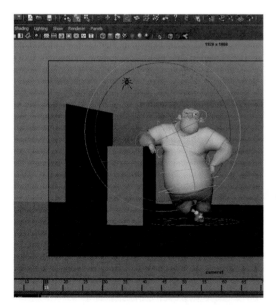

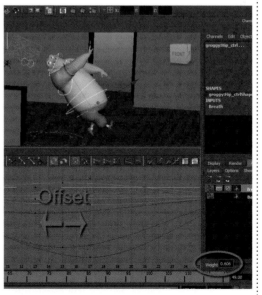

5 On f15, create a pose with Groggy's spine bent backwards slightly like he's taking a breath. Don't forget to adjust his arms back into position. Include the pelvis, belly, chest, and head controls when you are making this pose.

6 Now you have a breath in the animation. You can adjust the amount that this animation is added to the BaseAnimation layer by adjust the weight value in the Layer Editor. You may even want to offset the keys of the spine to have the pelvis move first and the head last.

Spotlight: Michael Cawood

MICHAEL CAWOOD HAS WORKED IN FILM, COMMERCIALS, GAMES and short films. He's won the 'Orson Welles Award' for his short film *Devils, Angels & Dating*, along with 'Best Animated Short Film' at the Burbank Film Festival and 'Best Animation' at IndieFest. Find out more at MichaelCawood.com.

TELL US A LITTLE BIT ABOUT HOW YOU USE MAYA IN YOUR EVERYDAY JOB.

Well, I've been using Maya for about 14 years now for pretty much the entire 3D pipeline on numerous productions. I've used other packages before and since, but I always return to Maya.... it's more ingrained in my work methods... much like a pencil. The only part of the pipeline I've not gotten to go into any depth with is modelling as there's usually more talented modelers on the crew on each project I'm on.

Everyone has their workflow but I've varied the way I use it over the years. Once upon a time I was animating dinosaurs running over great distances, on SGI computers with one monitor. I had to be able to see as much of the 3D view-port as possible so that I could still see the details of smaller characters in the same scene. So I would hide away all the menus leaving only the timeline, hyper-graph and Graph Editor. I used the space bar to bring up all the menus I needed and customized my keyboard keys to cover the most common tools. Even going so far as to assign R to rotate, T to Translate, etc... as they seemed to make more sense at the time. But as I moved around teams and tried different production pipelines I discovered that my custom interface would confuse other artists too much when they came over to my machine to show me something. So, I gradually reduced my customization almost all the way back to the default setup. This was particularly handy as the industry trend switched to shorter contracts and I had to be able to get up to speed quicker and quicker on new machines in new companies. These days I only customize four keys on day one and get right to work.

WHAT ARE SOME OF YOUR FAVORITE TOOLS IN MAYA?

It might seem basic, but I really like the Graph Editor. I've used a few other packages Graph Editors and I prefer Maya's. The last few versions have added a few key features that bring it up to speed on any features the other packages held over Maya, and there's even a nice time-scaling feature that preserves the keys after the time scaling in 2013. It's very slick.

I've noticed many animators using only the red ticks on the timeline to time out their poses, and they're often not looking at the Graph Editor at all, relying instead on a lot of extra keys when they see something looking odd in motion. I like to keep the Graph Editor open all the time and I'll massage the shape of curves using simple, weighted and split tangents. It doesn't take long before you learn the shape of curves in common actions. It can actually be faster to pose the character then simply modify the curves to create those shapes in one complete pass without even reviewing the animation, then watch the whole thing afterwards to correct anything that doesn't conform to that pattern. Generally, the number of corrections you'll have to do are less than the number you would do from simply reviewing the default animation curves in the first place. Lip-sync is a fantastic example of this, and if you're working on a production that requires speed over quality, this technique is a life saver as you'll have something pretty decent looking even before you've had much of a chance to do revisions. It's a bit like using the "force".

WHAT IS A WORKFLOW CHANGE YOU'VE MADE THAT HAS HELPED YOU TO CREATE GREAT ANIMATION?

On the first few projects I used Maya for I was creating a style of animation between realistic and cartoony and I tended to focus on a more physically correct way of animating each body part so I never got into the full body pose to pose workflow initially. This is actually a bit odd, as I studied as a traditional hand drawn 2D animator at university so you would have thought it would have been a more natural transition for me to do pose to pose. But the funny thing was that even in 2D I often animated each body mass in different passes to create physical actions. For 2D it meant I was creating very flowing and natural actions that looked nothing like other animators work and it really helped me stand out. In 3D it was natural to me to continue in this work flow and I almost left pose to pose behind. But one day I started working on a project that was much more cartoony and I'd been watching these fantastically snappy, funny animations from other animators so I forced myself to try the full body pose to pose method again, setting a key on every attribute so that I could focus on the timing and the strength of the poses. It brought back some of the wonder of my 2D animation training and opened up a whole new appreciation for 3D animation. From there I adapted to blend both techniques into my work, choosing when to apply each technique to each given style of movement. It has given me the best of both worlds, combining an understanding of mass, weight, momentum, arcs and anticipation with strong poses, silhouettes and snappier timing.

WHAT ARE SOME OF YOUR INTERESTS OR HOBBIES BESIDES ANIMATION?

Screenwriting, character design, layout (also for print and websites), video editing and pretty much anything that lends something important to the animated film-making process. I've also dabbled in coding for websites. In the past I've taught myself various forms of dance, and these days I'm finding a lot of interest in learning about business. I've hosted my own podcast before and now I'm reciting stories about my short film on my blog for the benefit of future short film animators. Check out AnimatedFilmmaker. com for that.

WHAT ARE SOME TIPS FOR GETTING INSIDE A CHARACTER'S HEAD, UNDERSTANDING THE MOTIVATION AND THE SUBTLETY OF A SCENE?

Taken from my screenwriting studies, if I have long enough to really absorb myself in a story I'll write up a one-page character outline. This will list basic facts about a character's personality, their background, their aspirations, needs, flaws, physicality, relationships, all sorts of things. There are several very good screenwriting books out there that each have different variations on the theme explaining what needs to be included, but just going through those steps really forces you to make a more fully fledged character in your mind. The idea is to get to a point where you know exactly how your character would react to any given situation.

In truth, on most projects you have to hit the ground running and you don't have time to do this, normally you aren't expected to do that much preparation work. So I've usually only had the luxury of going in-depth like this when there's been some down-time and you're waiting for some other decisions to be made before you can really get stuck into the work again. But when it has happened, it's given me the opportunity to really define the character, taking a cardboard cutout of a character in a much deeper and more satisfying direction. My performances have even triggered changes in the script, evolving the style of the written dialog and the performances of the voice actors.

DO YOU HAVE ANY PERSONAL PROJECTS THAT YOU'D LIKE TO TELL US ABOUT?

Well, the obvious one to talk about is my short film *Devils, Angels & Dating* which I started in 2006. I took the project online to attract talent in 2009, running everything online for the public to see. Through the years, over 400 artists from around the world signed up on our development site volunteering their time, over 100 of which were selected to actually contribute their time at one point or another. We finished the film and put it online in January 2012. It's been winning awards at festivals since then and to date it's been viewed well over a million times. We didn't have any funding, but we did get some support from fans, mostly through a crowd-funding site, that gave us enough money to pay for most of the festival run. This also made it easier to pay to keep the development site online for future generations to learn from. It features various behind-the-scenes videos, thousands of work in progress videos, tutorials and images and all the forum threads showing the interaction between the team members discussing the progress of each asset and shot. Check it out at DevilsAngelsAndDating.com.

Since then I've also lent my time to *The Oceanmaker,* another animated short film, for which I acted as Head of Story. In a completely opposite approach from my previous short film, we had a small team of eight that went to an island with laptops for six weeks and we got most of the work done in this idyllic setting. I was mostly focused on translating the script into shots through storyboards, 3D previs, layout, animation and editing. Working very closely with the Director, we were able to really hammer out story points and try lots of approaches to "plus" the story. Since the trip, I've been screening a work-in-progress edit in the various cities to get impartial story notes, which we've then discussed and addressed to refine the film as it progresses. Learn more about that at TheOceanmaker.com.

HOW DO YOU KNOW WHEN YOU'VE FOUND THE "RIGHT" IDEA FOR A SHOT?

You can't, it's never perfect. You have to make something you can be passionate about as you're going to be doing it for years. But ultimately you can work on concepts and scripts for ever and eventually you have to just draw a line in the sand and get into production, otherwise you're never going to get anything made. Once you've learned from a few shorts, you're going to have a much better idea of what works, and asking other short filmmakers can give you some of that perspective but be sure to be making what you're passionate about. Since cultures evolve and audiences change, you can never know what's going to strike a cord with the audience that's a few years ahead of starting production, though, so it's still a huge gamble.

IN TODAY'S INDUSTRY, ARE ANIMATORS A DYING BREED?

The industry seems to need more and more animators as time goes on. But despite that, at the moment, there's more animators than there are jobs. So the smart thing is for anyone wanting to work in animation, to study at least one other area. Being a generalist can be useful and makes you much more hire-able on small teams, but larger studios are still focused on hiring specialists and generally the recruiters don't have the time to think outside the box during the hiring period. However once you've gotten your foot in the door, you're far more likely to keep a job if you know more than just what you were hired for. So you always have to present yourself in very different ways to different companies during the hiring period. It feels a lot like you're not presenting yourself completely honestly but really you're just making their job easier. Later on you can shine in all the other ways that make you stand out.

An interesting side observation to this is that companies in each branch of the animation industry (film, commercials, TV, games, etc.) tend to focus on the areas of your career that fall into their "world". So when I'm working in games, conversations tend to focus around my work in games, completely overlooking my film and commercials work. Similarly, the same happens in film and commercials. It's a very irritating early in your career when you don't have as much experience in the area you've been hired for and you can be treated like a junior, even if you have loads of equivalent experience in one of the other areas. Now that I've done quite a bit in various areas, it means I have enough to bring to the table in any conversation, and it's as though I've lived three separate careers!

IF YOU HAD TO GIVE ONE PIECE OF ADVICE FOR A DEMO REEL, WHAT WOULD IT BE?

Doing character performance pieces like the work that the 11 Second Club encourages is a great staple of the common demo reel. But I'd also recommend that everyone makes the effort to create something really unique for every other shot in their reel. So, animating creatures, robots, unique physical situations and interactions, just put some thought into what studios need to see, and balance that with things they've never seen before that could be useful to them. That's what's going to make your reel stand out. For a while I had a very good routine of promising myself that I'd make something new and creative for my portfolio every month. It could be something as small as a sketch for my gallery or as ambitious as a new shot for my reel. Each month I was creating something completely different though and I quickly started to get more attention from high-profile companies. The other key thing about this approach is that you're bringing something unique to each team. You shouldn't always be trying to be the best animator on a team, but instead you want to be bringing a specialist skill that compliments the your future co-workers and makes the team as a whole capable of something great. Somewhere out there there's an animator who's really good at Spiderman swinging between buildings and he's in a lot of demand, but now that he already exists, you need to find a different type of shot to make yourself equally as in demand.

ARE WE IN THE GOLDEN AGE OF ANIMATION? IF YES, WHY DO YOU THINK SO? IF NO, WHAT WAS/WILL BE THE GOLDEN AGE OF ANIMATION?

It's an interesting question since the industry is producing so much more animated material than it was when I started back in the late 90s. Only time will tell whether what's produced now will stand the test of time. What's clear is that the talent pool is very different from that of a decade ago and the quality bar is set considerably higher in terms of character performances. The question is whether things have really changed in terms of design, story and subject matter. In those terms some things have evolved a little but I'd like to see some real changes shake things up over the next decade. Right now the tools have created a Golden Age of sorts because the films look so different from those of a decade ago, but when the subject matter becomes more sophisticated that's when the real Golden Age of animation can begin.

DO YOU HAVE ANY ADVICE FOR ANIMATORS?

Talk to animators that have really lived the life and done things. But don't just ask them about techniques in creating animation. Make sure to talk about what it's actually like to live and survive as an animator. Learning all the buttons in Maya can only get you so far. It's important to balance life and work. Find your creative sweet spot and mine it without burning out at a rate that compromises your life.

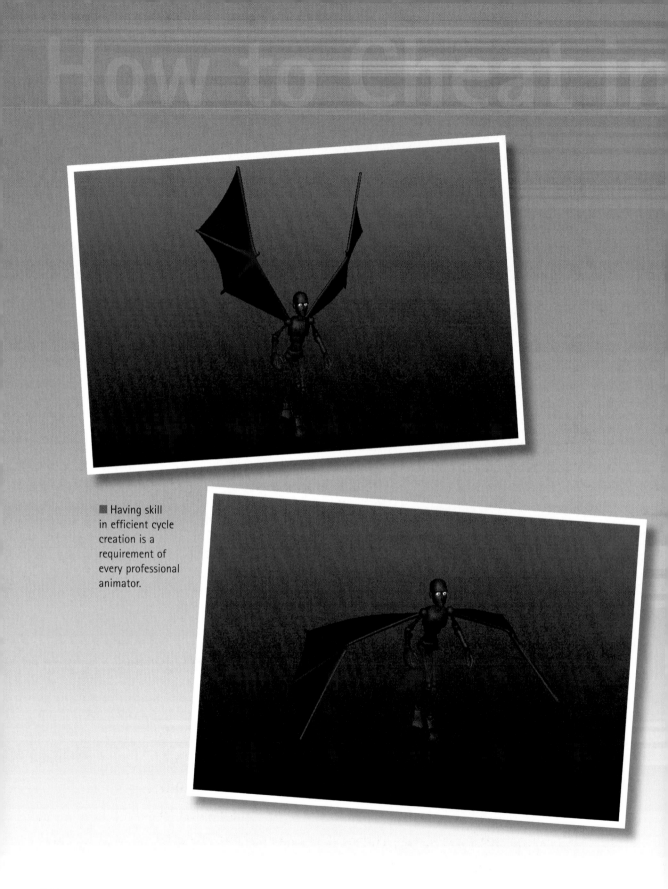

■ Having skill in efficient cycle creation is a requirement of every professional animator.

9
Cycles

CYCLES, or animation meant to loop or repeat, are a
mainstay of the animation industry. From games to film,
to TV, cycles will most certainly be a part of your career
in animation to a varied extent. The ability to quickly
create realistic and appealing cycles is the hallmark of
the experienced animator. To do this you must be familiar
with all of the tools that Maya 2014 has to offer. In
production it is common for an entire animation team to
share cycles, and so having cheats to avoid little technical
problems can have a large impact on a project.

We're going to look at the technical aspects of creating
a cycle with Pre- and Post-Infinity curves. Then we'll
manipulate a walk cycle and create a flying cycle from
scratch. With both of these cycles the plan is to use the
simplest method to get the best results; with cycles, that
cheat is called "offsets".

Cycle Basics

WHEN WE TALK ABOUT cycling in animation, there are a few terms and technical rules you should be aware of. We'll run through them here in this chapter.

First of all, when dealing with cycles where a character moves "forward", the Z axis is the axis that is used to show forward movement.

Next, you will be dealing extensively with Maya's Pre- and Post-Infinity curve types. Maya uses these settings to determine how to cycle animation before your first, and after your last keyframe. We'll test out all of the different types here.

Another rule is that all of the controls of your animation need to have the same duration of frames between the first and last frame of the cycle. They don't have to necessarily be the same frames, however. For instance, as long as you have set your animation to cycle correctly, your head could be animated between f01 and f24, and your arms could be animated from f18 to f41. Also, it is typical to counter-animate a master control against the Translate Z to make it so that the cycling animation stays centered over the world origin, as if it's on a treadmill. This is extremely handy when you are working with a cycle that covers a lot of distance, like a run cycle. It is easy to create this treadmill: simply cycle the master controller backwards the same stride length and frame range as the character cycle (we'll talk all about stride length soon).

Finally, cycling is a lot more manageable when you are familiar with the idea of "offsetting" your keyframes in the Graph Editor. The basic idea is to create animation on controllers within your set frame range (1-24 for example), and then move the keyframes backwards or forwards in time. These new offset keys are the same total duration of the cycle, but you don't have to worry about getting some hard-to-create curves cycling on the same frames as your base animation. An example of this is if there is an extremely wobbly antenna on your character; it's hard to imagine exactly at what point in the overall motion that antenna should be started at on f01, whereas it's easy to key the entire flopping motion and then offset it.

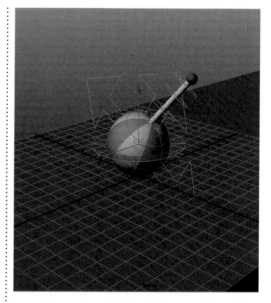

1 Open cycle_basics_start.ma. In this scene we're going to have this ball move up and down, and tilt left and right. You'll see two keys are already created for you. Our cycle length is 24 frames, and there is a key on f1 and f12.

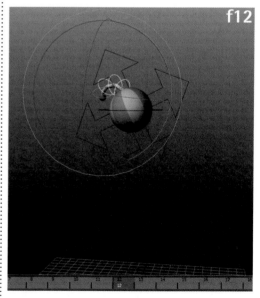

f12

4 Expand the timeline to 48 frames and watch how nicely the animation loops. Now let's key the antenna flopping over from the left to the right. On f01, key the antenna over to the right, and on f12 key the antenna bent over to the left.

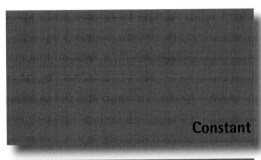

Constant

Cycle

cycle_basics_start.
ma
cycle_basics_finish.
ma

HOT TIP

When working
with cycles,
it's easy to
inadvertently
change some
of the curves'
lengths when
editing them.
If you select
a curve, the
frame field in
the Graph Editor
will display the
curve's frame
length. This is
really handy for
hunting down
cycle hitches
caused by an
extra or missing
frame, especially
when many of
the curves are
offset.

2 Let's look at the different cycle types. Select the ball_ anim control, and open the Graph Editor. Click on View > Infinity. As you can see, the value is constant before the first and after the last keyframe by default. Select the Ty and Rz curves and go to Curves > Post Infinity > Cycle.

3 "Cycle" means that when it gets to the last keyframe, Maya will loop the animation by going back to the first keyframe. In order for the cycle to work, the first and last keyframes need to be identical! In the timeline, MMB drag f01-f24 and hit **S** to paste the key at the end of the animation. Flat all tangents.

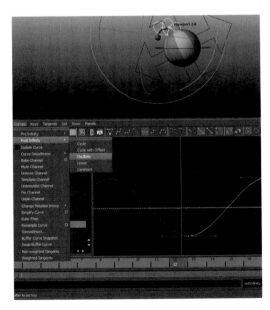

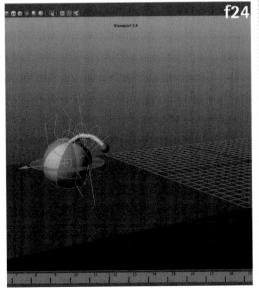

5 In the Graph Editor, select the antenna control's rotation channels. Go to Curves > Post Infinity > Oscillate. Also go to Curves > Pre Infinity > Oscillate. This infinity curve type tells Maya to "bounce" backwards and forwards through the animation when it gets to the first and last key.

6 Now let's make the character move forward. Set a key in Translate Z on the ball_anim control at f01. On f24, move him forward in Z about 10 units.

211

Cycle Basics (cont'd)

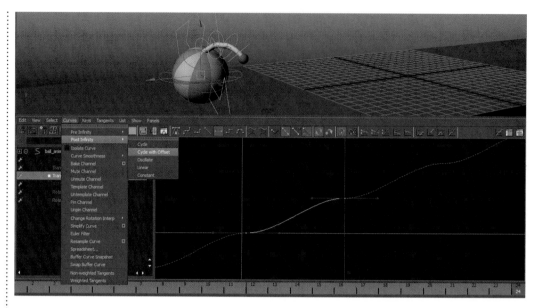

7 The rule of thumb is that Translate Z channels on your MAIN character controls (body, feet, etc.) should be "Cycle With Offset". Set the Translate Z curve to this type in the Graph Editor. Flat the tangents on the Z channel and notice that Maya takes the last frame as the "new" start frame and "goes from there".

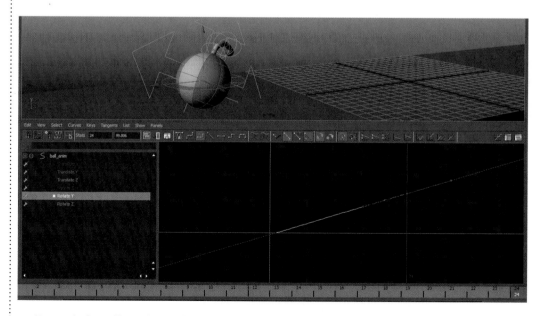

9 Now set the Rotate Y curve Pre- and Post-Infinity type to linear and see the resulting curve. The rotation continues linearly forwards and backwards for infinity. Let's do our first offset. Remember, offsetting animation is a great way to build layers in a cycle.

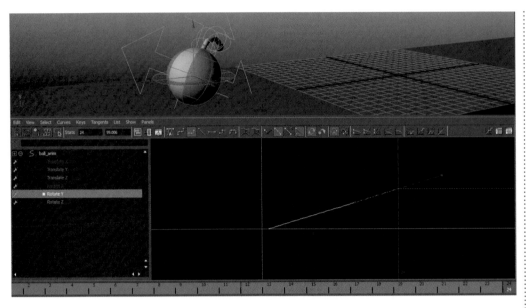

8 The linear infinity type extends the animation as if a linear tangent were applied to the keys. Select the ball_anim control and hit **S** on f24 to make sure there is a key on the Rotate Y there. In the Graph Editor, select the key on f24 on the Rotate Y channel, and move it up to a value of 100.

HOT TIP

Now that you know all the cycle types, be aware of the simplest way to get the motion you need. Pros are always using offset animation curves to build complex motion that would be immensely difficult to create working only within a set frame range.

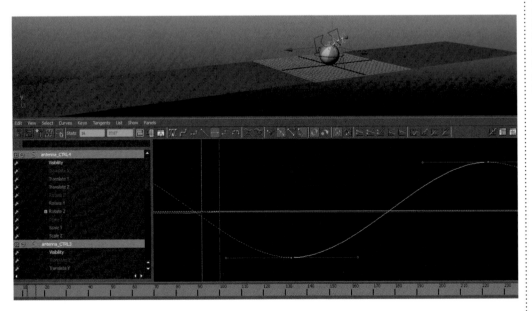

10 Select the controls of the antenna. In the Graph Editor, select the rotation curves and move them forward four frames to make the motion more overlapped. Notice how the curve retains its shape, but also how hard it would be to create the curve shape that exists between f01-f24 from scratch.

9 Cycles
Stride Length

W HEN CREATING ANIMATED CYCLES, we'll first want to quickly sort out a few decisions, namely cycle length (frame count) and stride length (how far one complete cycle "travels" in space). These two decisions are essentially the principles of timing and spacing applied to walk cycles. However, unlike a performance shot in which these decisions can be eyeballed and changed, you'll want to be sure you are working within your set standards so that the result is predictable, manageable, and most importantly, usable.

What is stride length? Simply put, stride length is the distance that a character travels in one complete cycle. If you are animating a biped, one stride would be two steps. If you are animating a quadruped like a dog or a cat, the stride length is the distance the character covers after all four paws have stepped. Another way to think about stride length is that it is the distance the character travels in the time it takes for any one of its feet to complete one cycle (go from being on the ground, to lifting, to moving forward, up to the instant it touches the ground again). This way of thinking about it works no matter how many feet a character has, assuming that all of its feet move only once in a complete cycle.

Why is calculating stride length so important? If you are working on a project with many animators who are all going to share cycles on the project, then it is extremely important that you create a cycle that will loop perfectly for infinity. Without knowing your EXACT stride length, it is impossible to truly create a perfect cycle. This is one of the most overlooked aspects of creating cycles, but you'll see when we get into this cheat how problematic "eyeballing" a cycle actually can be.

The easiest way to calculate stride length for a walk cycle is to pose a character taking a step using just the root control and one foot. The character should look like he is taking a comfortable step, and isn't too stretched out. Then simply observe the value in the foot's Translate Z channel, and double it to get your stride length. From then on, you will be doing multiple calculations with this number, confident that, armed with stride length, your cycle will loop perfectly for eternity.

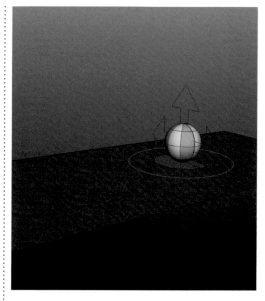

1 Open stride_start.ma. This is a bouncing ball animation, in which the ball is taking leaps forward. A good way to think of this for the purposes of stride length is that the ball is a uniped (one footed), and the "foot" is the entire character.

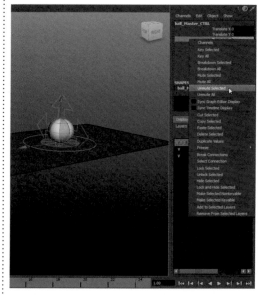

4 Play back the animation. Looks great, right? Now expand the timeline to 480 frames. Play back again. Still looks fine, so what's the problem? Go to f01. Select the ball_Master_CTRL, and right click on the Translate Z channel. Choose "Unmute Selected".

214

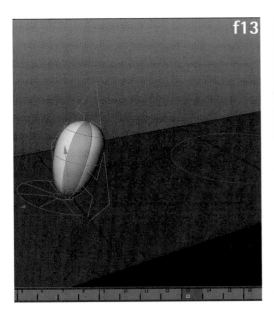

f13

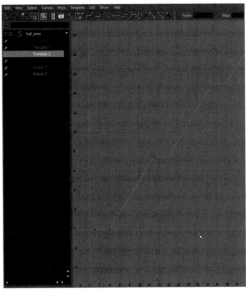

stride_start.ma
stride_finish.ma

2 He does one complete leap and landing every 24 frames. All that's left is animating the Translate Z channel to give him forward motion. Select the ball_anim control. On f13, translate it forward to about where the next edge in the ground plane is showing. (If the edges are not showing click on Shading > Wireframe on Shaded.)

3 On f24, with the ball_anim control still selected, hit **S** to set a key. Open the Graph Editor and change your Translate Z to linear interpolation like the one above. Now select the curve and change the Post-Infinity interpolation type to "Cycle With Offset".

HOT TIP

The stride length method presented here is the simplest, but it's also possible to animate stride length with an inverse method: by translating the root control forward, countering a cycle that has been animated in place. See the additional content on the How to Cheat in Maya website for a Walks chapter where that method is demonstrated.

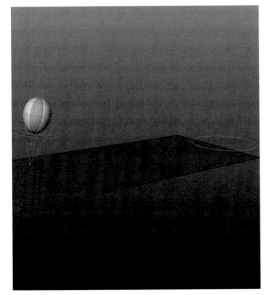

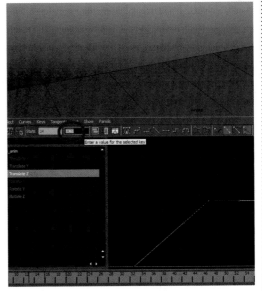

5 The master control is counter-animated against the ball_anim control to keep it in place while we work. It is moving backwards according to a set stride length, but since we eyeballed the ball's Z movement, it moves further away from its home position every cycle that goes by.

6 Let's investigate why our cycle is getting off of center. Select the ball_anim control and open the Graph Editor. Select the two keyframes on the Translate Z channel that are on f13 and f24. Look up at the value box to see what value is on these frames. Mine is 7.365.

Stride Length (cont'd)

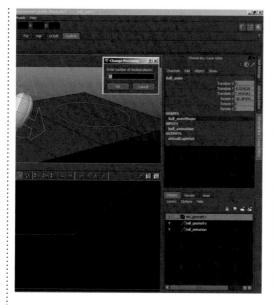

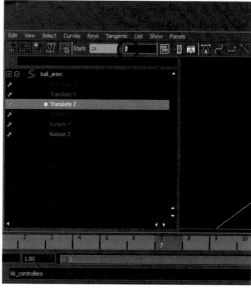

7 Is it really 7.365? Go to f13 in the time slider and then in the Edit menu in the channel box, click Settings > Change Precision. Type in 15 (the maximum) in the box and hit enter. Now look at the Z value. Mine is 7.364636278760326!

8 It turns out that when you eyeball poses in panel, Maya puts very precise values on keyframes that are nowhere near clean, integer values. Since our stride length is supposed to be 7 units, in the Graph Editor select the Translate Z keys on f13 and f24, type in "7" in the value box and hit *Enter*.

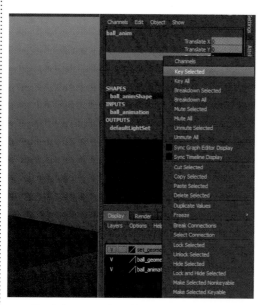

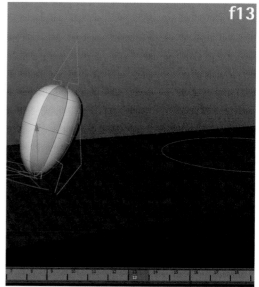

11 Now let's set some keys. On f01, type in "0" on the ball_anim control's Translate Z channel. Right-click on the Translate Z channel and choose "Key Selected". We're going to be careful not to add any keys on channels that we don't need to.

12 Advance to f04. Right-click on the Translate Z channel and choose "Key Selected". On f13, move the ball forward using only the Z axis on the translate tool, and try again to line it up with the edge on the ground plane ahead of the start position.

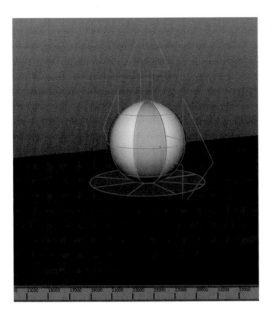

9 Now the stride length is perfect. If this were a character, all of the legs would cycle correctly knowing the stride length. Let's be totally sure; expand your timeline to 50,000 frames. Notice how the ball is still cycling perfectly in place.

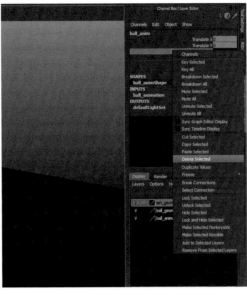

10 A more common workflow is to eyeball the stride length in panel and correct it later. Select the ball_ anim control and right click on the Translate Z channel in the channel box. Choose "Delete Selected". On f01, select the ball_Master_CTRL Translate Z channel, right click and choose "Mute Selected".

Making your stride length close to an integer value makes keeping the stride equal on all controls easy. But you may have to do a little bit of math: if the stride is 8 units, and the root starts at Translate Z=0, then it obviously moves to 8. But if one foot's Translate Z starts at -3 and the other at 6, then they need to finish at 5 and 14, respectively.

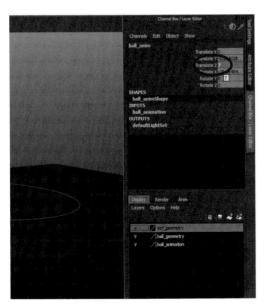

13 Pros will eyeball a pose and then choose nice, round numbers for their stride lengths. After you've set a controller's position, type a value in the channel box. Notice that even with 15 decimal places of precision, when you type it in, it is EXACTLY the value you chose. Type in 7 in Tz, right-click on the Tz channel and choose "Key Selected".

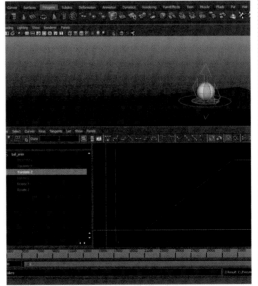

14 Set another key on f24. In the Graph Editor, make the Tz curve interpolation linear, and the Post-Infinity curve type to "Cycle With Offset". By eyeballing and then correcting, we have a workflow that gives us fast, accurate stride lengths. Unmute the Tz channel on the ball_Master_ CTRL and check the animation on frame 50,000 for fun!

217

Walk Cycle

W E ARE GOING TO LEARN how to find the stride length of a walk cycle quickly. This will be invaluable to your workflow, because a good animator should know how to put together an accurate, looping walk cycle in a short amount of time. Use this cheat whenever you start any looping animation that needs to travel in Z; for walk cycles that stay in place without having a master control counter-animated against the world IK controls (like in games), you need only make sure that, as the animation cycles, there are no visible pops in the animation.

Remember, the stride length is the distance that a character travels in one complete cycle. For a biped, this means two steps. We are going to assume a 20-frame walk cycle, meaning 10 frames per step. Also, the first and last frame need to be the same so we're going to be doing a lot of copying keys, and a lot of math input in the Graph Editor's stat boxes (see the Graph Editor chapter for detailed info on the math operations). However, knowing our stride length, this is a simple process and will quickly become an indispensible part of your workflow.

We are not going to animate the full cycle, only find the stride length and animate the feet accurately (see the additional content at howtocheatinmaya.com for a complete walk cycle tutorial). The rest of the animation on the body that doesn't travel in Z is very simple to make cycle: copy the first frame to the last frame of the cycle, and make sure the Post-Infinity curve type is just "cycle"! Let's give it a shot.

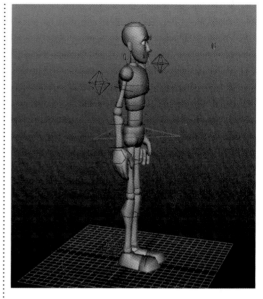

1 Open walk_start.ma. Goon is standing still, ready to animate. Remember that we're going to be using a lot of math operators in the Graph Editor, so open it up in preparation for this.

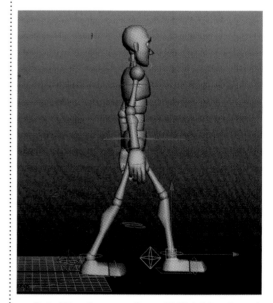

4 Go to f10, and now pose Goon with his left foot forward, along with the root moving forward as well. Keeping everything exact is not important because we're going to be typing in the Z values once we've found our stride length.

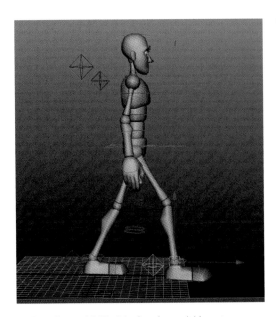

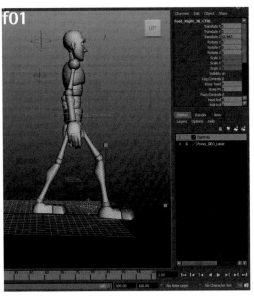

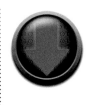

walk_start.ma
walk_finish.ma

2 Pose Goon with his right foot forward, his root comfortably between his feet and a little bit downwards in Y. We normally make a "milestone" f01 of a cycle, like the foot planting, as we've done here.

3 Set a key at f01 on all of the world IK controllers that are moving in Z. These are his left and right feet controls, and his root. Take note of what the value is on Goon's right foot. Mine is 10.967.

HOT TIP

You can also make your cycles accurate by changing each Translate Z value to an integer as you go instead of applying the math function at the end. Our first step was 10.976, so we could have made our first value 11, and then known right away that our stride length was 22. Just another time-saving cheat to get perfectly looping walk cycles!

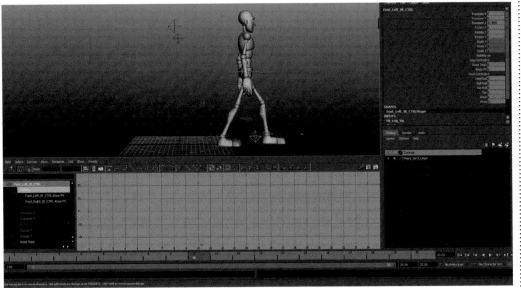

5 Now look at the translate Z value on the left foot. Mine is 21.96. Hey! That is roughly double the first value we had. We now can approximate our stride length. The nearest, nice, integer value is 22. Voila! We have our stride length.

Walk Cycle (cont'd)

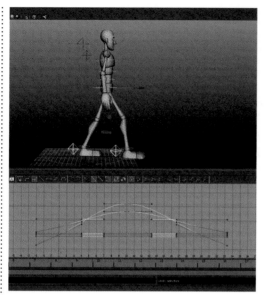

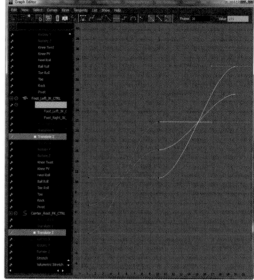

6 On the timeline, MMB-drag and copy f01–f20, with both feet and the root selected.

7 Now select the Translate Z channel in the Graph Editor on all three controllers (both feet and root). In the value stats box, type in "+=22". The last key has now been adjusted to reflect our stride length. Using a math operator means we know the values are exact.

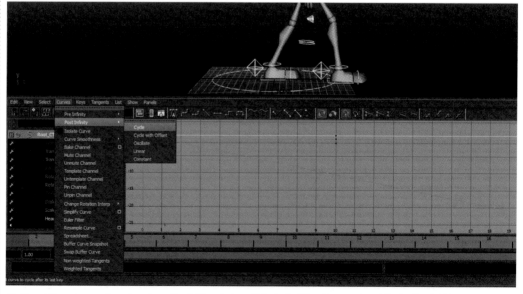

9 Now let's make sure these keys have the right cycle type. Select all of Goon's controls and in the Graph Editor, go to Curves > Post Infinity > Cycle.

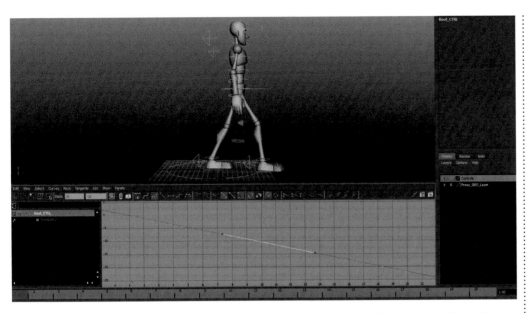

8 Flat all tangents in the Graph Editor. Now select the root_ctrl on the ground at Goon's feet. Set a key on f01 and then on f20, set a key on Translate Z on -22.

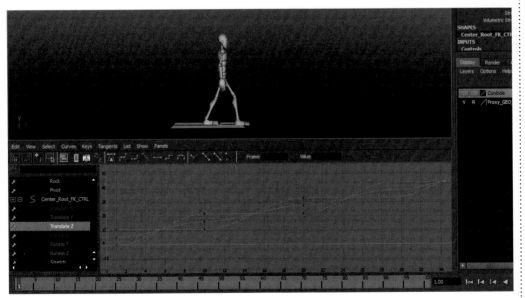

10 Now select both foot controls, the center root, and the ground root control. In the Graph Editor, select only the Translate Z channels. Go to Curves > Post Infinity > Cycle with Offset. Expand your timeline and watch Goon cycle perfectly in place! The rest of the cycle now comes easy.

HOT TIP

To quickly isolate specific curves on multiple controls in the Graph Editor, just select the channel you want to see in the channel box, such as Tz, and click the Isolate Curve Display button in the Graph Editor (looks like a squiggly line – make sure Classic Toolbar isn't activated in the Display menu). This saves tons of time scrolling through the attribute panel selecting specific curves.

Flying Cycle

FLYING CREATURES are a popular item in games, a major portion of the animation industry. Flying characters also find their way into popular feature films, TV shows, and commercials. From cartoony characters to the ultra-realistic, a flying cycle is an interesting exercise in the art of offsets. To cycle a flying creature, we are going to be taking advantage of some of Maya's great tools that we learned about in Chapter 4, Graph Editor. We're going to want to be able to see immediate results in the panel from making minor adjustments in the Graph Editor.

The first and best thing for an animator to realize about a flying cycle is that downward motion (thrust) of the wings will produce upwards motion in the body. It seems common sense, but we're going to make sure this concept is deeply engrained in your process by creating the wing motion and body motion together, then practice offsetting again.

We'll start with a demon version of Goon, with horns and bat-like wings added to our familiar rig to demonstrate fly cycles. It's worth mentioning that a hovering fly cycle like the one we are going to create has application in many different situations, from butterflies to dragons. However, you will quickly find that the principles of bird flight (simply put, forward motion creates the lift in the wings) are wildly different. It will take very extensive research and reference gathering to accurately create any realistic flying cycle. That said, though, the workflow cheats presented here will serve you in all your flying animation.

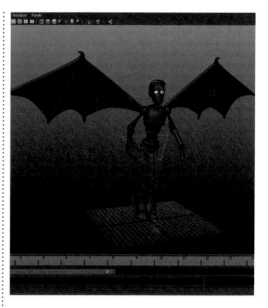

1 Open flyCycle_start.ma. With flying cycles, keying the extremes and offsetting is a quick and easy way to get the motion you want. We will create poses for the up and down wing positions, and then offset the keys on the different controls to get a more natural bend on the wings.

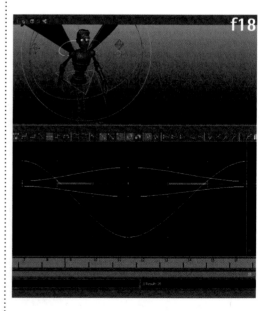

4 Remember that a cycle needs the same first and last frame. Select all of the wing controls, and from f01 on the timeline, MMB drag to copy the key to f18. Let go of the MMB, and hit **S**. Open the Graph Editor and make sure the frame was copied; then flat all tangents.

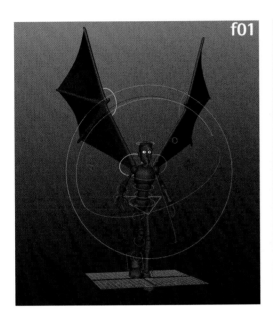

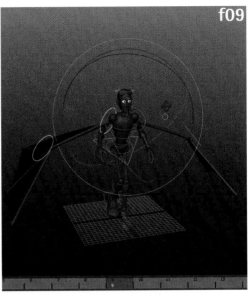

2 First make a pose with the wings up. This can be done entirely in-panel. Using the round controls on the wings, set a key on f01 with the wings in an upward position. I like this.

3 Now let's make the down pose. It looks really cool if the wings are curled under the body for big creatures. Key the wings down on f09 (we're making an 18 frame fly cycle).

HOT TIP

If you are working in games, it is common that the game engine will need all of the keyframes to fall within the set cycle frame range, and not have Maya interpolating Pre- or Post-Infinity Curves. No problem! In the Graph Editor, click Curves > Bake Channel, and then delete outlying keys to change your interpolated frames into true keyframes.

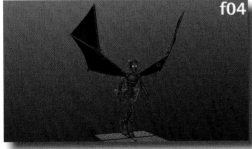

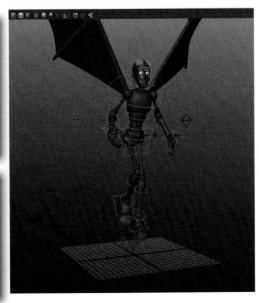

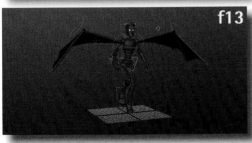

5 To make the breakdown poses for flapping wings, we need to remember that the wings are not flapping in a vacuum – they're pushing air! So on f04, key the tips of the wings bending upwards as if they are being pushed, and on f13 key the tips down.

6 Now it's time to key the up and down motion of the character. We're going to get some great practice doing offsets here. Go back to f01 (we're going to create all of our poses on f01 and f09 and then offset). Key the root_CTRL at Translate Y=5.

Flying Cycle (cont'd)

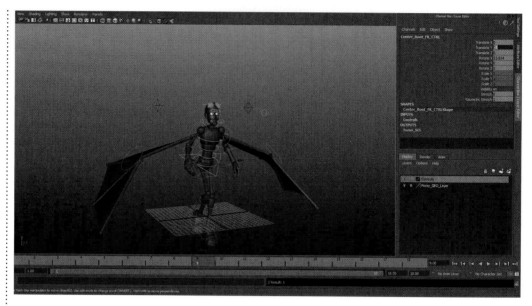

7 Select all of the controls in the body and set another key on f09. Translate the root control down in Y to about –5.

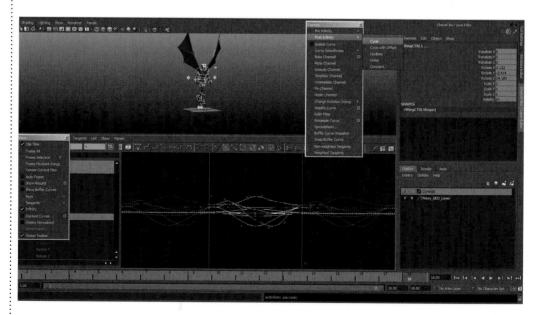

9 Select all of Goon's controls, and in the Graph Editor, select Curves >Post Infinity >Cycle. Also click Curves>Pre Infinity>Cycle. Remember this setting tells Maya to cycle the animation on any frame before our first and after our last set keyframe. View these curves by clicking View > Infinity in the Graph Editor.

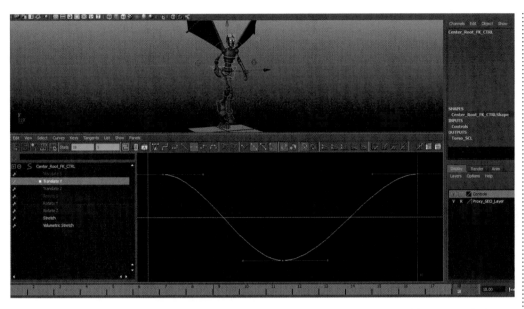

8 MMB-drag and copy f01-f18 in the time slider, open the Graph Editor, and flat all tangents. Noticing a pattern in the workflow yet?

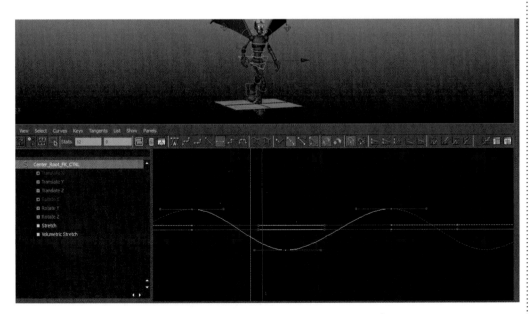

10 Let's offset! Select Goon's root control, and select all of the curves in the Graph Editor. One awesome feature of Maya is that you can make a change in the Graph Editor while the animation is playing and watch the result. Hit play on the timeline and move the selected curves backwards 6 frames in the Graph Editor.

HOT TIP

When creating cycles, experiment with making sections of the cycle slightly different lengths to get a more organic feel. For instance, sometimes in a walk you can make the right foot's step take 9 frames and the left foot 10 frames. Small differences that you imperceptibly feel but don't see can make an animation feel more lifelike.

Flying Cycle (cont'd 2)

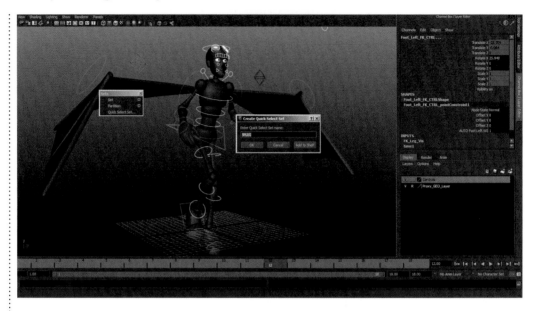

11 Cool! It now looks like his wings are thrusting him in the air! Let's build another layer of offset animation. Since we'll be selecting Goon's spine and legs a lot, let's make a quick select button. Select his spine and leg controls, and click Create > Sets > Quick Select Set. Name it "SPLEG" and click "Add to Shelf".

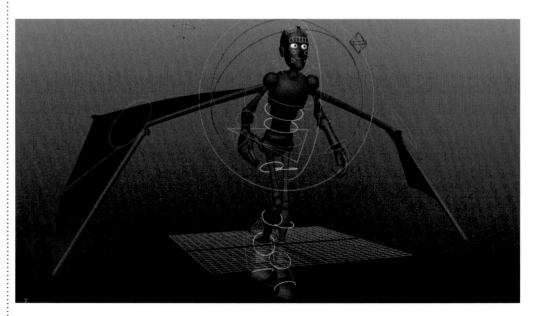

13 On f09 key Goon's spine bent forwards, and his legs slightly extended. Click the SPLEG shelf button, and copy f01–f18 by MMB-dragging in the time slider like we've become used to. We have our timing engrained in our mind by now, so creating animation on set intervals and offsetting is super easy!

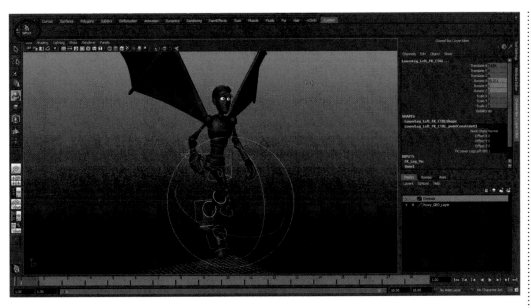

12 Now you have a handy button that selects these controls for you. Deselect everything, then click on the SPLEG button. Now on f01, key Goon's spine bent slightly backwards, and his knees slightly bent like above.

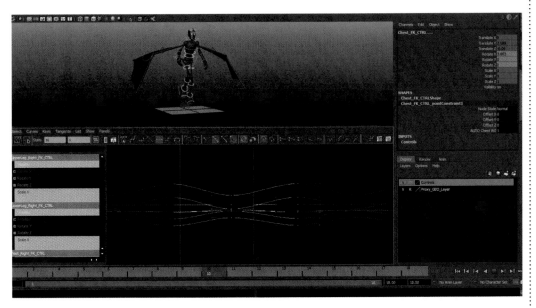

14 In the Graph Editor, set the Pre- and Post-Infinity curve types to "Cycle" as before. Select all the curves, flat all tangents, and offset! Drag his spine and leg curves backwards two frames. Play back your animation and adjust if necessary. Awesome!

HOT TIP

Don't stop working with your offsets after sliding the curves around. Keep subtly working more in by having the wings flap a frame or two apart from each other. Then use the tangent handles to give each wing a slightly different spacing through their individual flaps. Lots of little tweaks will add up to a big difference!

9 Cycles

Quad Cycles

QUADRUPEDS ARE PREVALENT in games and feature VFX. Knowing how to quickly block a walk cycle is an important skill for an animator. Finding stride length is an extremely important cheat to have mastered when it comes to quads; any trouble you can get into with two legs is doubled for four!

While teaching a full quad walk is outside the scope of a cheat, you will clearly be able to see the use of offsets throughout the body of this quad walk presented here. Take a few moments to click on a few different controls and go into the Graph Editor. You will see that the animation is cycled for 24 frames on all controls, but offset greatly. This is the fastest way to cheat a cycle, and it applies just as much to quads as it does to flying or walking.

We're going to do another kind of offsetting with this cycle; offsetting VALUES instead of offsetting TIME. We need to do this because we are going to copy the ¬animation from the left front paw to the right. You can save a lot of time by copying animation across a character's body, but as you'll see, we need to offset the values to make the animation work.

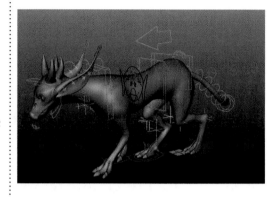

1 Open "quad_Start.ma". We have a blocked quad cycle that you can look through later, but for now we're going to take a look at copying the animation from the front left paw to the front right.

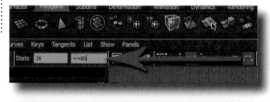

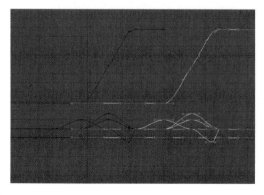

4 Let's offset the right paw. In the Graph Editor, select all of the curves, and slide them 12 frames forward in time. With the curves still selected, go to Curves>Pre Infinity>Cycle. Also select the frontLeg_CON Translate Z channel and go Curves>Pre Infinity>Cycle with Offset.

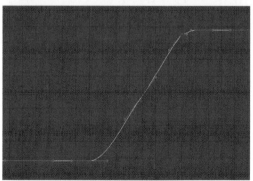

5 Now let's offset the value of the Translate Z channel. Putting the right paw 12 frames behind, put it HALF A STRIDE behind. Select the curve, and in the type-in transform box put in "+=80". (Half of 160 – our stride length.) Now the right paw is moving where it should.

228

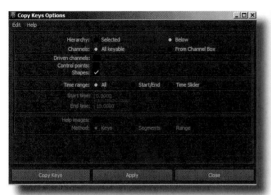

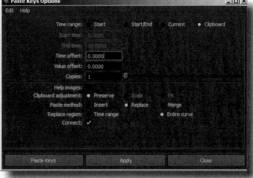

quad_Start.ma
quad_Finish.ma

2 Select the front right paw and go to Edit>Keys>Copy Keys □. Make sure your settings match mine.

3 Select the front left paw and go to Edit>Keys>Paste Keys □. Copy my settings once again. Now the front paws (and toes) have identical animation now. Select the front right paw and all of the toes for the next step.

Remember with cycles that your stride length should never change. We offset values by moving the ENTIRE curve, not individual keyframes. Doing so could result in different stride lengths for different limbs, and problems down the road.

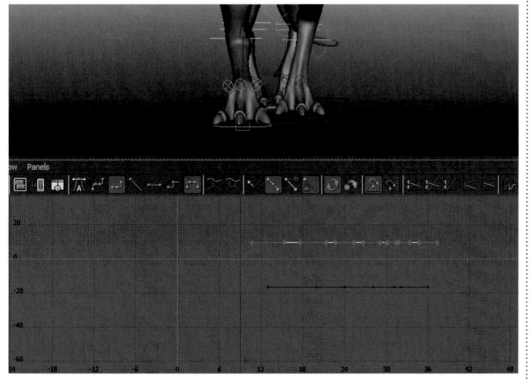

6 Finally, you'll notice that the right paw is sticking out to the side. This is the same X translation that is on the left paw. Select the Translate X curve in the Graph Editor, and watching the result in the panel drag it upwards until the two paws look the same.

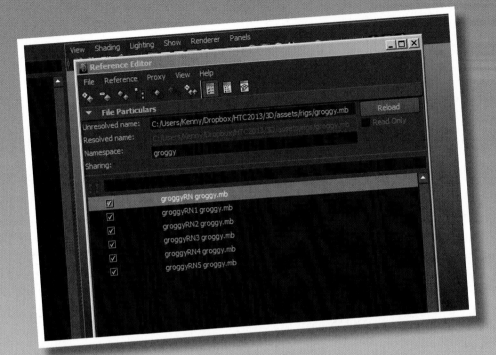

■ Referencing is a major part of a studio pipeline. Knowing how it works and ways to make it work better are essential to a professional workflow.

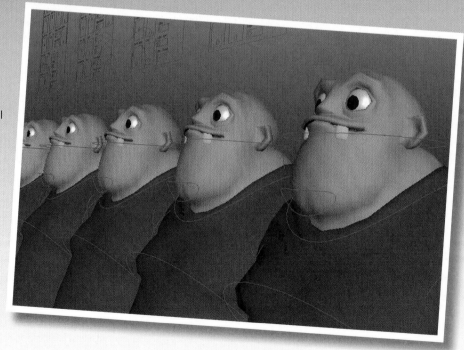

10
Referencing

UP UNTIL THIS POINT, WE'VE BEEN USING scene files that have all of the rigs imported into the shot. The reason we've done that is to make sure that you are focusing solely on the cheat at hand, and not trying to overcome any technical hurdles unrelated to the chapter.

Now, we're going to dive right in to referencing and hopefully be able to use referenced scene files from now on without leaving any readers behind. Our referencing cheats will surely make your animation a lot more efficient (at the very least) and possibly save your entire project. It's time to take advantage of the power of referencing!

Referencing Basics

REFERENCING HAS BEEN A PART OF MAYA for many versions, and even before the system was perfected, artists and technicians realized the value of re-using assets in multiple scenes. The concept is simple; instead of having unique copies of frequently used assets in every single scene, create "links" instead to the source files. This way, changes to the original file will propagate down to the multiple scene files, and you will save immensely on scene overhead and file size. It is not uncommon for an animation file with dozens of referenced rigs (all between 20-50mb) to still be only 1-2mb or so when finished.

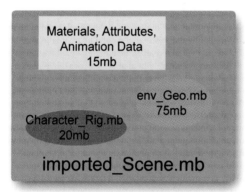

Materials, Attributes,
Animation Data
15mb

env_Geo.mb
75mb

Character_Rig.mb
20mb

imported_Scene.mb

Total = 110mb
(Without Ability to Propagate Changes)

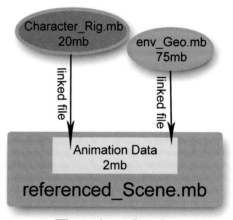

Character_Rig.mb
20mb

env_Geo.mb
75mb

linked file

linked file

Animation Data
2mb

referenced_Scene.mb

Total = 2mb
(WITH Ability to Propagate Changes)

1 Instead of importing characters and sets into a scene, we're going to reference from now on. In an imported scene, the data from all of the imported scenes combines to create a lot of scene overhead. In the referenced scene, the only data that is saved is changes to attributes, like animation curves for instance. The result is a far slimmer scene with less overhead, smaller file size, and the ability to make changes to assets and have those changes propagate into all of your referenced scenes.

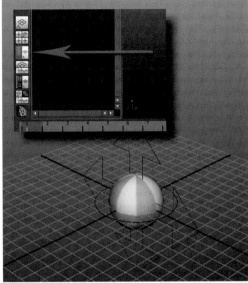

blank_Scene.ma
blank_Scene_finish.
ma

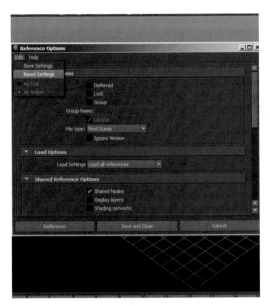

2 Open "blank_Scene.ma". Go to File>Create Reference
□. In the Options box scroll down and make sure
"Shared Nodes" and "Display Layers" are both checked. Click
"Reference" .

3 Choose "ball_Rig.ma" in the file dialog that appears.
Maya will load the file as a reference and bring you back
to your panel. It looks like it's imported but let's take a closer
look. Open the Outliner/Persp panel layout by clicking it's
icon in the toolbox.

HOT TIP

You can change
the namespace
in the reference
editor, which is
recommended
if your filename
is very long –
shorten the
namespace to
something more
manageable.

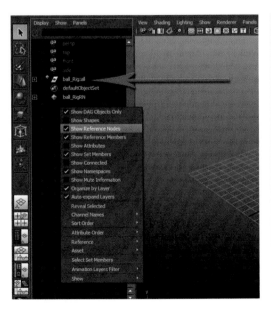

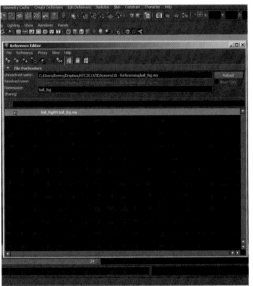

4 See the blue diamond next to the ball_Rig:all group?
That means the node is referenced. You can see all of
the reference nodes by right clicking in the Outliner and
checking the "Show Reference Nodes" box.

5 Go to File>Reference Editor. This box will give you
control over adding, substituting, and removing
references from your scene. It is also where you might go to
troubleshoot a reference.

233

Referencing Basics (cont'd)

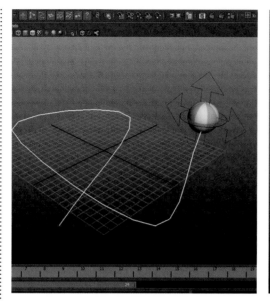

6 Close the Reference Editor, and select the ball rig's ball_Anim control. Set some random keyframes, moving the ball around the scene between f01 and f24.

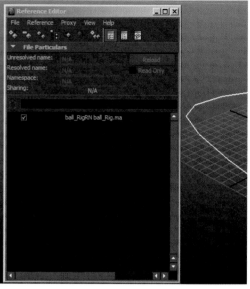

7 Open the Reference Editor. Uncheck the box of the reference node. This unloads the reference, so the ball disappears. The reference is still there, it's just temporarily not in the scene. Check the box again and play back your animation.

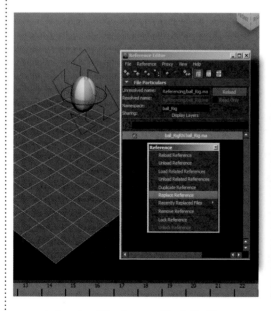

10 Let's replace this reference with a ball with a different color. Go to File>Reference Editor, select the rig, and click File>Replace Reference. Choose "ball_Rig_Yellow.ma". Since the naming and hierarchy is the same, the animation stays intact.

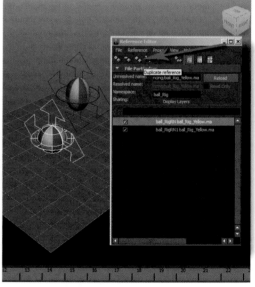

11 In the Reference Editor, click the Duplicate Reference button. This is handy if you want to populate a scene with multiple references of the same file, but as you'll notice, animation isn't copied because it is considered an "edit" done in this scene.

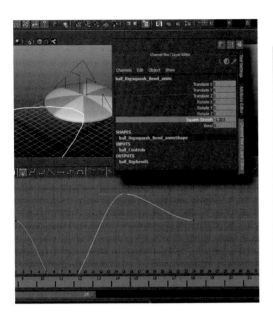

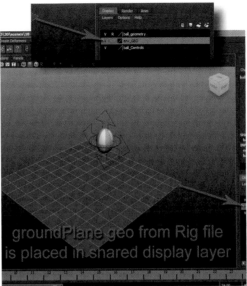

8 Notice that the Squash and Stretch attribute is animated. This animation is in the rig file itself. Up until now, you were unable to make any changes to animation curves on referenced objects. Now you can!

9 blank_Scene.ma has a display layer called "env_GEO". Our rig file has the same layer, and so objects in the referenced file are loaded into this layer when you check "Display Layers" in the reference options. Turn the visibility of this layer on and see.

HOT TIP

Come up with a standardized naming convention for your display layers and you'll find that you can get away with having as little as 4 or 5 that will allow you to handle hiding/showing all the objects in your scene!

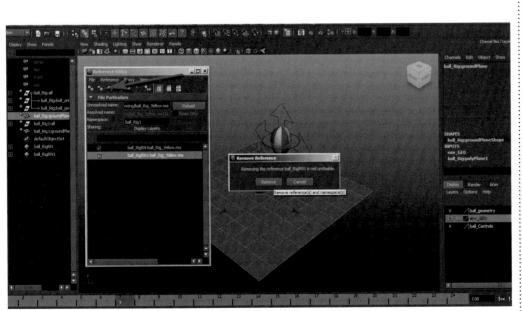

12 Notice how the display layers are still shared even when you duplicate a reference. You want to make sure your reference settings are correct before you duplicate anything. In the Reference Editor, select this new reference and remove it by hitting the Remove Reference button.

235

Offline Edits

THE REFERENCE PIPELINE IS DESIGNED to give artists the ability to manage a massive number of scenes, first and foremost. Most of the functionality built into referencing is geared towards this goal. Even the tool we're going to use now, "Export to Offline File," is geared towards being able to make edits to multiple scenes. We're going to cheat by using it as yet another way to export animation.

Reference edits come in all shapes in sizes, literally. Modifying an objects components, changing a texture's color, scaling the rig, even setting a keyframe is considered an edit. By allowing animators to export Reference Edits to an offline file, Maya 2014 has actually created a robust, and rock solid way to export animation. In fact, this method is by FAR the most full-featured and fool-proof method to export animation in Maya now.

Why? Exporting animation via AnimExport, Copy keys, and even the relatively new AtomExport only exports channels that have keys on them. Since changing ANYTHING is considered a reference edit, this Offline File you export from the Reference Editor contains all attributes that have changed in your scene, even if there are no keyframes on it. I can't tell you how many times I've tried to import animation from an animator's scene only to discover they did not put any keyframes on the master control. I then have to go into the animation file, put a keyframe on all controllers (even unchanging ones) to be fully sure I am importing the entire performance. Not any more. In fact, this Offline File will even recreate nodes that are related to the changes to your reference file, meaning constraints, layers, EVERYTHING. This tool was meant for propagating changes to multiple files, but we're going to cheat and use it as our favorite animation export tool.

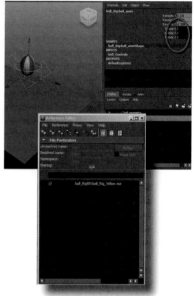

1 Open ref_Offline_start.ma. You will recognize this file as we just made it! Select the ballAnim control and notice there are no keyframes on the rotation channels. In rotation X, Y, and Z, put values of 1, 2, and 3, respectively.

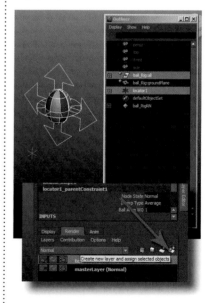

3 Let's also add the locator and the ball rig to a new render layer. In the Outliner select "locator1" and "ball_Rig:all group". In the Layer Editor's Render tab, click the New Layer from Selected button. Name this layer "testLayer".

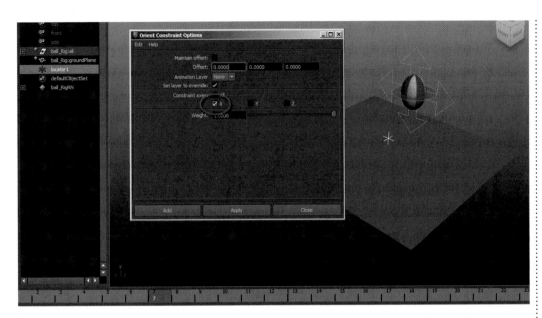

ref_Offline_start.
ma
ref_Offline_finish.
ma

HOT TIP

We added a
locator that
controls a
channel in our
referenced file
using an orient
constraint. If
the direction
was reversed
(the referenced
file controlling
an object in
the scene) then
exporting the
reference edits
would NOT
include the
locator.

2 Now we're going to get fancy. Go to Create>Locator. Hit F2 to get to the Animation menu set. Select the locator1, **Shift**-select the ballAnim control, and go to Constrain> Orient □. Make sure just X is checked, and hit "Add". We want to see if exporting the edits includes these new nodes.

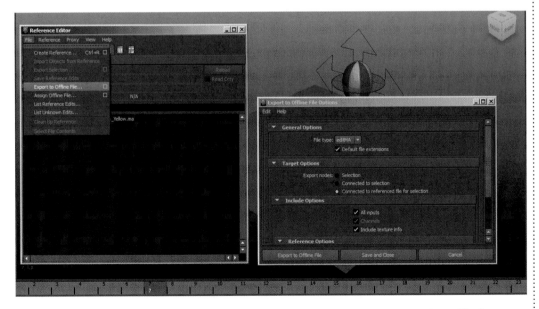

4 Now we export the Reference Edits.. Open the Reference Editor, select the ball rig reference, and go to File>Export to Offline File □. In the export dialog go to Edit>Reset Settings. Hit "Export to Offline File", and name it "ball_anim. EditMA".

Offline Edits (cont'd)

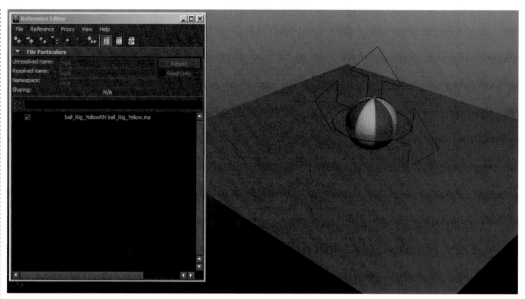

5 Remember we're hoping that not only the animation was exported, but also the relating nodes like render layers, the locator, and parent constraint. Create a new scene, and hit **ctrl**+**R** to load a reference. Choose "ball_Rig_Yellow.ma".

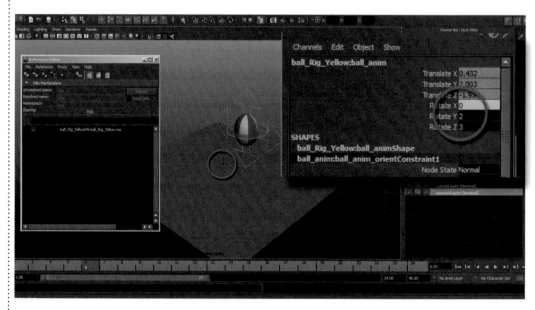

7 Check it out! First play back the animation and you'll see the animation has transferred. Also notice the locator1 has been brought into the scene as well. Select the ballAnim control. The constraint is in place, and the values of 2 and 3 in Y and Z rotation have come through too, even though there are no keyframes on those channels.

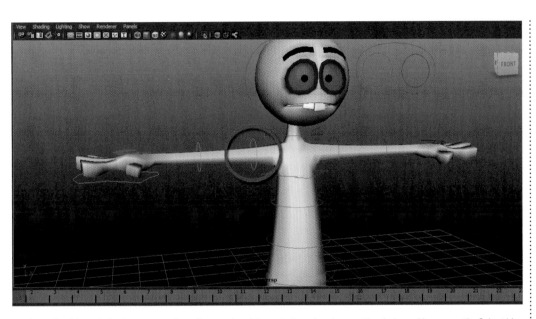

edits_Start.ma

2 Now that Moom is in the scene, we're going to select his controls and make sure the rig is working correctly. Select his right upper arm FK control.

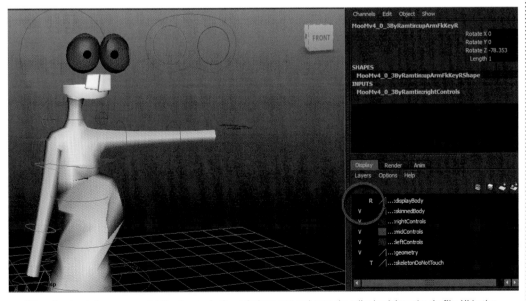

4 Yikes. He clearly has some weighting issues. Let's work these out and save the edits back into the rig file. Hide the display layer named "displayBody" and show the layer named "skinnedBody". This geometry is the one we'll do the weight painting on.

Saving Reference Edits (cont'd)

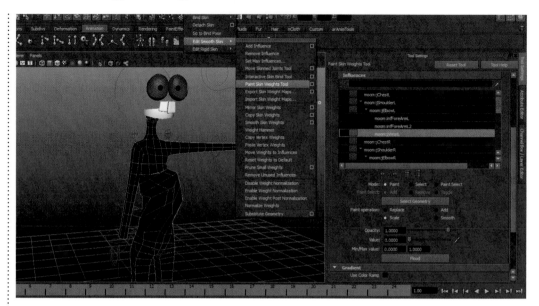

5 Select the body geometry and in the Animation menu set (F2), go to Skin>Edit Smooth Skin>Paint Skin Weights Tool.

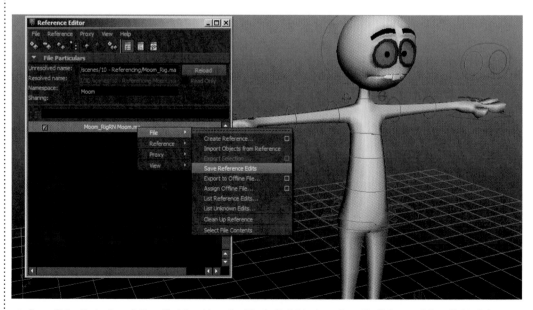

8 Turn off the display layer "skinnedBody" and turn the "displayBody" back on. Open the Reference Editor. Right click on the Moom reference and choose File> Save Reference Edits. It will inform you that you cannot undo this change. Choose "Save".

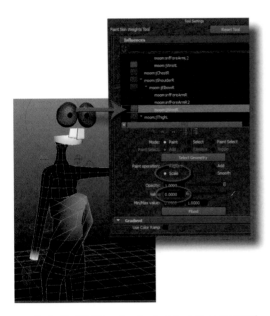

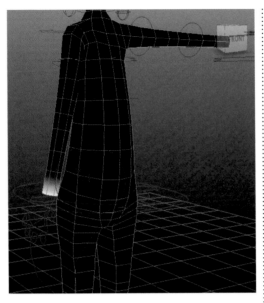

6 In the Tool Settings Panel, select the influence named "moom:jWristR". You will know it's the right one if the wrist AND the body turn grey to show there is influence on it. Change your paint tool to "scale" and the value to "0".

7 Paint the zero weight on the body to remove the wrist's influence. Once all of the influence is removed from the body, select the upper arm control and rotate it around to check and see. If you see body vertices moving, repeat steps 5-7.

HOT TIP

You have to make sure you are not sharing any layers when you load your references if you want to be able to save reference edits. A good idea might be to load references without anything shared to begin with, then switch to shared layers when you are sure you are past making edits.

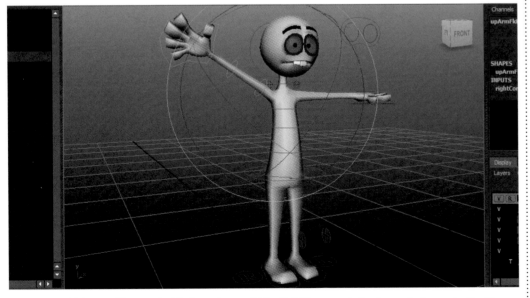

9 Let's test it! Open up Moom.ma in this chapter's scene folder. Grab his arm control and move it all around – the skin weights are now working correctly!

243

Planning Cartoony Shots

by Kenny Roy

WHEN PLANNING CARTOONY SHOTS, WE ARE SOMETIMES LEFT a little underwhelmed by the tools at our disposal. Our bodies cannot stretch and move the way that we want them to. It can be frustrating to have a dynamic, wild idea in your mind only to turn on your video camera and remember that, in fact, real world physics can be so boring. So how do we make the most of the tools at our disposal, and really get some valuable reference for our cartoony shots? It starts with knowing what makes animation cartoony in the first place.

See, most beginner animators think that cartoony animation, is simply exaggerated animation. Turn up the Squash and Stretch to 11, and bam, cartoony. This could not be further from the truth. In actuality, cartoony animation stems from our ability to give a strong impression on the audience. Cartoony animation is thus, impressionistic animation. For instance, we can normally come up with visual similes that describe the cartoony action that we are trying to create. Like, after the Coyote gets flattened by the anvil, he floats to the ground like a piece of paper. Or, after his arms are stretched 50ft long when holding onto a falling piano, his arms flop to his sides like wet noodles. In both of these examples, and all of the examples you could come up with, we describe parts of the body that resemble other visuals. Notice, however, that we are always referencing real-world things. And, we have PLENTY of reference for these real-world things.

We know what a spring that is pulled too far looks like, what a water balloon looks like dropped from a third floor window, and how an arrow vibrates when it sticks into a bullseye. If those are the images that you are referencing when you animate a character, you will be creating strong impressions. Instead of trying to animate a character unrealistically, animate these images TOTALLY realistically, just use the character's body to do it. Put that spring in the arms and legs, create the huge rubbery squash of a water balloon in the spine controls, and animate the whole body vibrating like an arrow when the character comes to a very sudden stop. Even though it seems like cartoony means we are animating very silly things that have never been seen before, it will be how closely we can match the real world THROUGH our characters that will be our measure of success.

So, now that we have identified that we are thinking of real-world objects, the world of video reference opens back up to us. YouTube, Rhino House, and other resources are back on the list of possible sources of great video reference. Your job then becomes to animate the character's body in a way that gives a strong impression of the real-world thing you are referencing. Using a lot of reference, you can't go wrong. If you are animating a character that is flapping his feet and hovering off the ground, then search for butterflies, birds, anything that the real world offers that you can then turn into body movements. If you are animating a character that is doing a zippy almost like being shot like a rubber band, then you should gather all of the rubber band footage you can get your hands on. This is what I had to do for the scene that you see in the Workflow chapter.

What about putting it all together? Is there a way that you can assemble the reference you've gathered or determine the real beats and timing of the shot? My favorite way is to 'perform' the action with my hands. For starters, you can use your hands to puppet actions much quicker and snappier than you can with your full body. Also, it is much safer to do these actions with hand puppets than it is to throw your body around the room. Last, combined with your voice cues, the resulting video reference with your hands serves as an AMAZING timing tool . We talk in the Workflow chapter about using this reference far into the lifespan of your shot.

Regardless of the level of 'cartooniness' you are trying to achieve, you need to approach the problem head-on or you will flounder when researching your shot. Remember, cartoony animation is not achieved by merely exaggerating your entire shot, or going overboard on the fundamentals. Instead, cartoony animation is the result of getting the audience to see familiar dynamics within the character's performance. If you can successfully do this, you will get laughs every time.

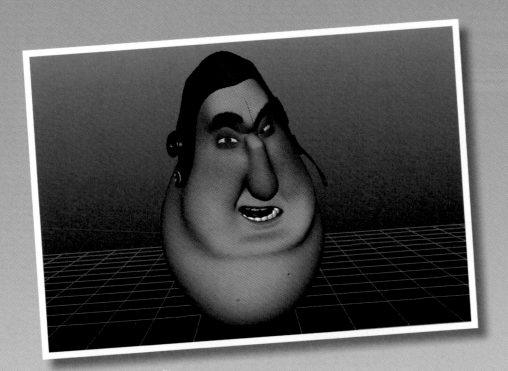

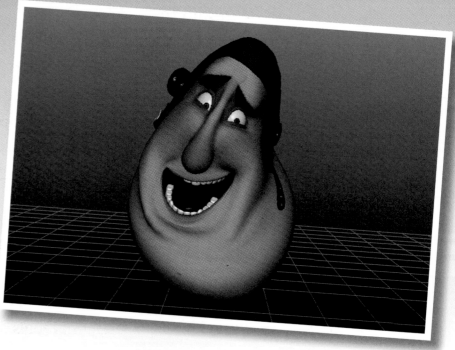

What's his motivation? The face is a huge part of conveying this clearly and convincingly through a performance.

Facial Animation

ANIMATING A CHARACTER'S face is one of the most interesting and enjoyable parts of the animation process. We can convey much with the body poses, but this is the really good stuff: the detail that literally breathes life into our characters. The drama and emotion that the face contains really makes us look inside ourselves and seek to understand and identify with a character. If animating the body makes us entertainers, then animating the face makes us actors.

Facial animation could fill many volumes on its own, but here we'll get into the bread-and-butter techniques that give us a great starting point. No two animators work through the face the same way, and you can build your own dramatic philosophies on the essential tools in this chapter.

Planning and Prep

W E ARE GOING TO WORK THROUGH some facial animation techniques using a simple example of a typical close-up shot. This keeps the staging simple and makes it easy to focus on just the face, while also being a very common shot style found in film, TV, and games. To make the exercises as straightforward as possible, the body has been blocked in for you, so you only need to worry about the face.

When doing any kind of dialog shot, it's important to thoroughly plan your animation. Don't just dive right in and start keyframing. Listen to the audio by itself, over and over, until all its accents and nuances are thoroughly ingrained in your mind. Also think about the context of the line, along with the character's internal thought process and motivation for saying it. It's quite possible to animate a line in completely different ways, yet when played in context with the surrounding shots, only a specific approach will ring true.

In our case, we don't have a context, just a single line to use for practicing some animation technique. For the sake of consistency, we'll pretend that the ideas in this planning section are what a director has instructed us to do. In the real world, this planning and prep would have been done before the body was animated, as it would influence our decisions in that regard as well.

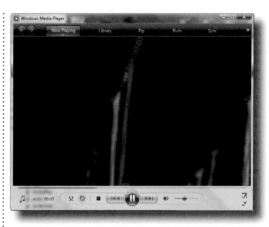

"I have nothing to say."

1 In the Sounds folder in this chapter's project directory is a .wav file with a short dialog clip (nothingtosay.wav). Open it in your favorite media player and listen to it on looped playback. Use headphones if possible. Write down the line and listen to its nuances.

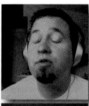

"I have..."
-slow blink on head raise
-head tilts back
-eyebrows raise

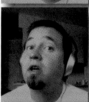

"...nothing to..."
-eyes flare slightly
-upper lids still touch iris
-head tilts more
-make brow pose asymmetrical

"...say."
-head comes down
-tilt is opposite of up position
-brows lower some
-eyelids stay lowered

4 Reference is always a good idea. Act out the line and create some video reference for yourself. Make notes on the brow poses, eye darts, blinks, etc. You can also make thumbnails, have a friend act it out, whatever you find useful in determining what you will animate.

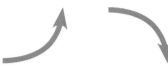

"I have nothing to say."

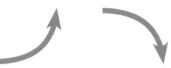

"I have nothing to say."

FaceAnimation_
START.ma
FaceAnimation_
END.ma

attitude: uncooperative, resistant, possibly hiding something, knows more than he is saying
subtext: "I have nothing to say to you, I don't want you to find out what you are asking me."

2 I hear two distinct accents in the line, on the "noth-" (first syllable) in "nothing", and on "say". The pitch goes up to "nothing" and down on "say". This is also reflected in the body animation. Mark the accents down in your notes.

3 Next I think about the tone of the line and the subtext it may be communicating. The way he says it sounds like he's being uncooperative. It feels like he means "I have nothing to say to you in particular", to whomever he's speaking to. This is more material for our notes.

HOT TIP

To import a sound file into your scene, go to File > Import and select the audio file. Then right click on the timeline and choose the file from the Sound menu.

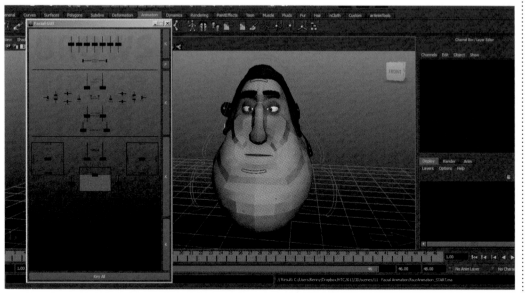

5 Once you've decided on the acting choices and know why you've made them, it's time to start working on the face. Some animators do the lip sync first, while others do it last. I find it helpful to first do a few full face poses to use as a structure. Open FaceAnimation_START.ma. The main head control has animation, but the face is stuck in its default blank stare, which we'll fix soon enough!

Core Poses

I T'S VERY FEASIBLE to animate the face in a layered fashion, but I've found I get better results when I first block in some initial expressions to use as a foundation. The accents we indicated in our planning stage create a perfect framework on which to base these poses. This also helps make the work stronger, since we can focus on just a few expressions and not worry about making fluid motion yet. We'll put in four poses in total: the accents on "nothing" and "say," the anticipation pose on "to," and the starting pose. Things will get moved around a little when we refine them, but you'll likely find that these core poses really help keep you on track.

Cenk is a very powerful and versatile rig. We're also going to try to make sure to take a very simple approach to the facial posing so that we don't get inundated with keyframes early on in the process. You will also notice we are referencing the Cenk rig into our scenes now, so don't forget the great referencing cheats from last chapter!

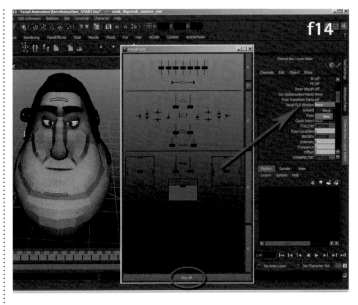

1 Open faceAnimation_START.ma. Select Cenk's master control and in the channel box, select "Facial GUI Window" and select "View". Now change the time slider to f14 and hit the "Key All" button on the facial GUI.

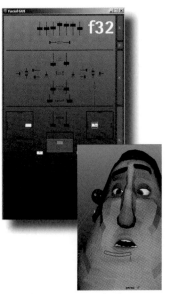

5 At f32, set a key on the face controls. Bring the brows down, lift the lids some, and expand and shape the mouth for "say".

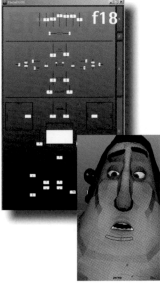

6 Copy f14's pose to f18 by selecting all face controls and MMB dragging in the timeline to f18 and setting a key. This will hold that pose for five frames.

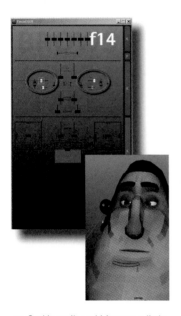

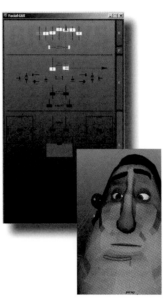

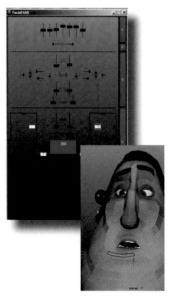

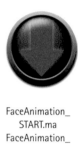

FaceAnimation_
START.ma
FaceAnimation_
END.ma

2 Cenk's pupils and irises are a little small. By scaling them up he will be more appealing. Make the iris size 1, and the pupil size .5.

3 Start with the brows, raise them and make the shape slightly asymmetrical. Raise the lower lids a bit and make the L eye upper lid slightly higher to complement the higher L brow.

4 For the mouth, bring the corners down and inward. It's roughly the mouth shape for "ha-", but we don't need to be concerned with it too much right now. Curl the lips out a bit and shape the mouth.

HOT TIP

In the timeline's right click menu, go to the sound options box. There you'll find an offset attribute if you need the sound file to start a given number of frames earlier or later.

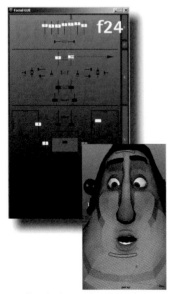

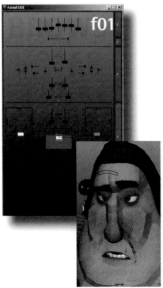

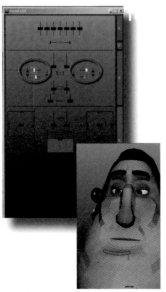

7 Key the face at f24. Raise the brows even more, lift the lids, and shape the mouth for the "to" sound.

8 Key the face at f01 and create the starting pose. We want to convey him being slightly defiant. Lower the brows, but not enough so he looks angry.

9 A slightly open frown helps show that he's displeased about the situation, but not gruff or stewing.

Lip Sync 1 – Jaw Motion

WITH THE CORE POSES COMPLETED, we're in a good spot to start on the lip sync. As we've seen time and time again, the approach of starting broadly and adding detail in phases will work beautifully here. We won't worry about mouth shapes yet, just the jaw movement. Once that is working, everything else usually falls into place pretty smoothly. It's easy to overlook the variety of timing in the jaw movement. In a given line of dialog, there is usually a wide range of sharp and smooth movements. One trick that helps make them a bit more tangible is to say the line while holding your hand underneath your jaw. You'll be able to feel the words with sharper timings and then translate that into your curves. I found that the biggest accents were on "I", "nothing", and "say".

Normally rigs come with a "face cam" that is used for animating lip sync. This is especially useful in scenes where the character is moving all over the place, doing twists and turns, etc. Cenk does not come with a face cam, partly due to the fact that he is basically one giant face to begin with. If you want to create one, simply create a camera and position it in front of his face. Then select his head head_local_con and parent constraint the camera to it.

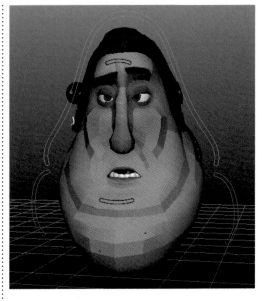

1 Start with the scene you just animated, or from my corePoses.ma.

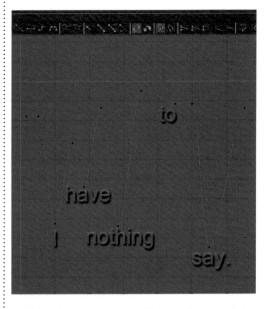

4 This is the curve I came up with for the first pass. Notice the accents on "I," "nothing," and "say", while "have" and "to" are much smaller.

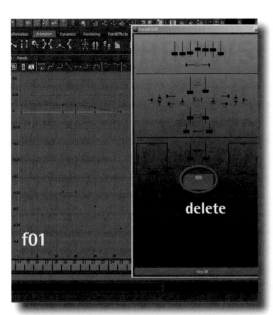

delete

f01

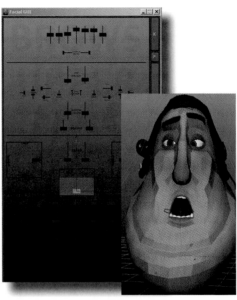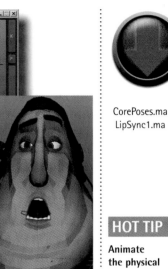

2 It will help to start fresh with the jaw animation. Select the "Jaw" control in the facial GUI, and in the Graph Editor, delete all of the keys except the one on f01.

3 Do a first pass just to add the open/close movement. Just get the general timing for now. Do an open/close for each open mouth shape, or four total. Keep in mind that you want the open to be a few frames before the actual sound.

CorePoses.ma
LipSync1.ma

HOT TIP

Animate the physical movement of what's being said, rather than simply basing it on the words. If you open/close every syllable, the mouth will chatter pop. Analyze yourself saying the line and only put in what you actually see.

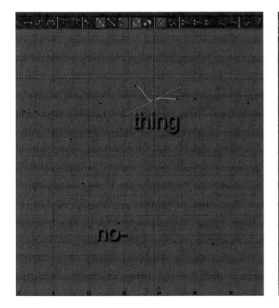

thing

no-

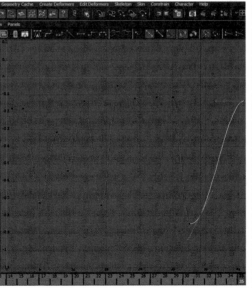

5 Tweak the timing and get the little bump that happens on "-thing". I like to save these secondary bumps for after the main accent so the mouth doesn't get too chattery.

6 Work on the timing of "say", which he draws out longer in the clip. I added a key to hold it open longer, and a longer ease in at the end.

Lip Sync 2 - Mouth Corners

THE JAW IS JABBERING AWAY, so it's time to work on the mouth corners. With this rig, the corners are accessible using the left_Mouth_Con and the right_Mouth_con in the facial GUI. The four directions are labeled Smile, Frown, Narrow, and Wide. The two directions we're focusing primarily on in this pass are Narrow and Wide. Other rigs might have more controls for the mouth shapes, but the idea at this point is the same: add another level of detail without going overboard. There's plenty of passes left to refine, so we don't need to do everything at once. Because the mouth rig is so simple, we're basically only worrying about if the corners are in or out at a given time. As for up and down, they will stay in a downward frown position for the entire shot. This is the point where we can start thinking about basic mouth shapes and phonemes. If you're new to animating lip sync, there are plenty of charts online and in classic animation books to study extensively. For this exercise, we'll just walk through the ones we need for the dialog. Remember, we're not doing the full mouth shapes yet, just the positioning of the corners to get us on the right track.

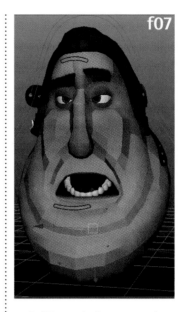

f07

1 At f07, move both corners out for the "I" sound.

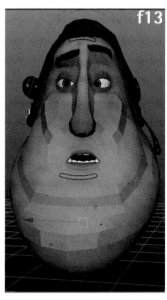

f13

2 Move to f13 and bring them in some for the "ah" sound in "have".

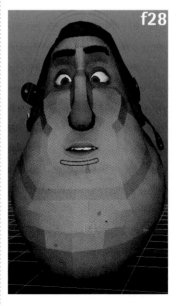

f28

6 At f28 bring the corner back in for the "to" sound.

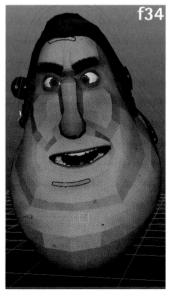

f34

7 Hold that shape until f34, then at f40 the corners come out again for "say". Bring out his L corner more to give a nicer shape on this last word, so it has a slight drawl to it.

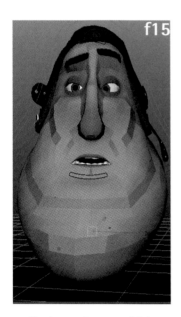

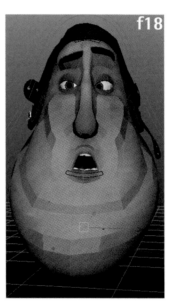

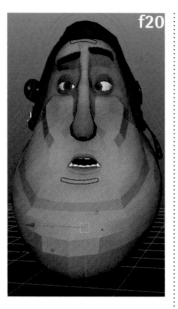

LipSync2.ma

3 Key the mouth corners slightly wide on f15 to get a good read of the "N" of "nothing".

4 On f18, we need an "O" shape for "nothing".

5 Copy the key from f18 to f20, and on f24, give him a nice wide shape.

HOT TIP

Don't forget to animate to the camera primarily, rather than the face cam if your shot has one. Use the face cam as a helper, but ultimately the shapes need to look their best in the shotCam.

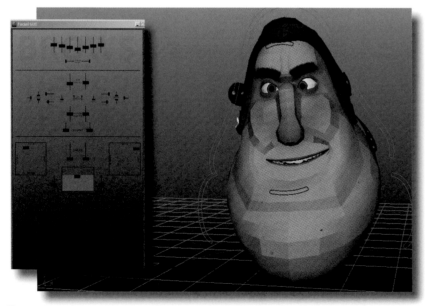

8 Finally, we want a nice ease in to the ending pose as the mouth relaxes into his final expression.

Lip Sync 3 - Mouth Shapes

LET'S CONTINUE REFINING our lip sync by fleshing out the mouth shapes. This is one of the more organic parts of the process, where you need to experiment a little and do some back and forth to get things working. The following cheat is a guideline, rather than a step-by-step process.

Remember that less is normally more. With the jaw open/close pass working with the lip corners narrow/wide pass, we generally are about 85% of the way done. These two passes need to be really close to perfect in order for the lip sync to read well to an audience. By adding this pass of custom shapes, we're getting much closer to the final performance.

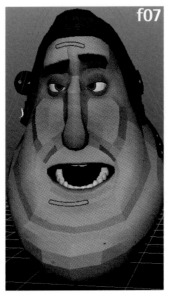

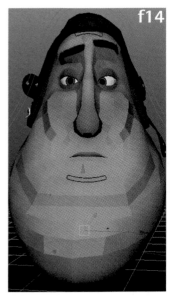

1 I removed the keyframe on the jaw on f03, and on f07, the corners of the mouth need to be wider to get the "I" shape.

2 On f14, create the "F" shape by using the bottom lip roll slider in the facial GUI.

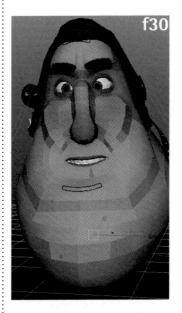

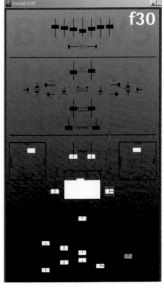

6 Key the lip up/down controls, as well as the jaw and sneer controls on frame 28, then build a nice, toothy, snarly "S" shape on frame 30.

7 I keyed all of the mouth controls on frame 30, then slid all of the keys starting on frame 31 3 frames forward. He needs to hold the "S" longer.

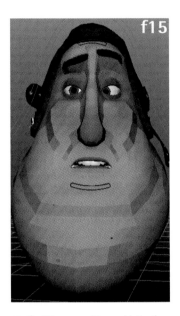

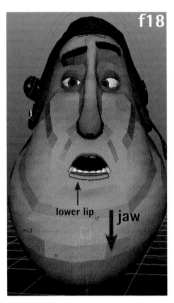

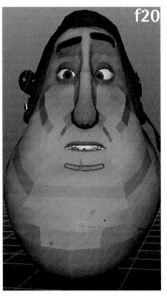

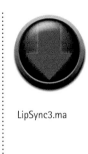

LipSync3.ma

3 On f15, we need to see his teeth a bit to get a read on the "N" of "nothing." I used the lip up/down controls and a bit of sneer.

4 The "O" shape was a little too overdone on f18. I toned it down.

5 Let's get another nice read on the teeth on f20.

HOT TIP

Be sure to give any closed shapes at least 2 frames. Ms, Bs, Ps, Fs, Vs, etc. all need to be held at least that long to not look like mistakes or hitches.

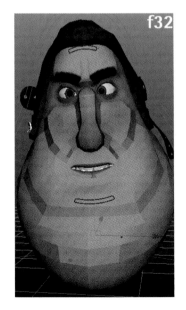

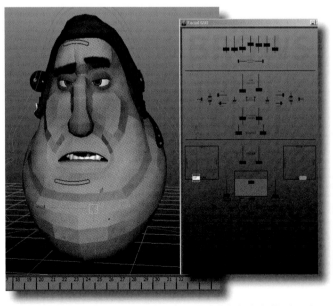

8 Finish that hold on the "S" by MMB-dragging the key on f30-f32 on all mouth controls except the jaw.

9 Watching the animation back a few times, it definitely feels like there is too much of a pose change in the corners of the mouth at the very beginning. I think this wider start pose feels better.

257

Lip Sync 4 - Tongue

T HE FINAL STEP TO REALLY SELL the lip sync is getting the
tongue moving on the right sounds, in particular "no-"
and "-thing", the "T" sound on "to", and the "S" sound on "say".
Unless it's an extreme close-up or something like that, the
tongue mainly just needs to be seen when it's touching the top
of the mouth, such as on "N" sounds, and when it moves back to
the lower palette. Otherwise it generally just needs to stay out of
the way.

   We can get away with a lot of cheating when
keyframing the tongue. Again, since a viewer will normally only
see the tongue peripherally when watching the animation, we
can build a tongue "flick" and copy to the correct frames later.

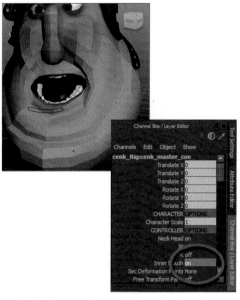

1 On f37 (because the mouth is open), select the master
controller and turn on the Inner Mouth controls by
either typing in "1" or "on" and pressing *Enter*.

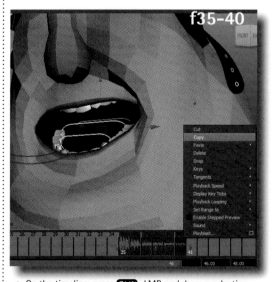

4 On the timeline, press *Shift*+LMB and draw a selection
from f35-f40. Right click on this range and choose
"Copy". Now anywhere we need this tongue "flick", we can
paste it.

LipSync4.ma

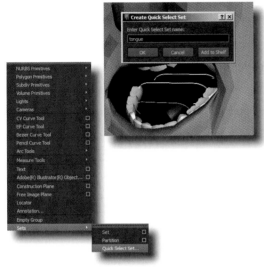

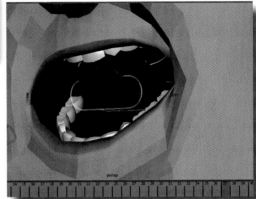

2 Select all 3 tongue controls and make a quick select set by going to Create> Sets> Quick Select Set. Type in the name "tongue" and choose "Add to shelf". This makes it really simple to select the tongue.

3 On f35 and f40, hit **S** to set a key with the tongue in default position. On f37, key the tongue in an upward pose like this. The tongue controls can be translated as well as rotated.

HOT TIP

Most of the time you don't need to get crazy detailed with the tongue for lip sync, unless it's an extreme close-up or realistic style animation. If it's at the top of the mouth when it should be, and we see it travel down when it needs to, that's usually enough to sell it for many situations.

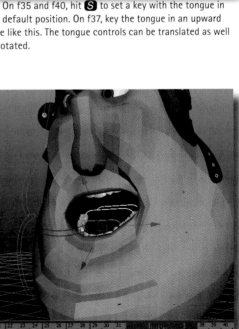

5 On f14 (2 frames before we need the tongue in the up position), right click on the timeline and hit Paste>Paste. All 3 keys are pasted and are still in the clipboard for us to paste again.

6 Paste this animation again at f20, and f27. Delete the animation on f35-f40 and paste your clipboard again on f32, or, if you feel comfortable, in the Graph Editor, delete the keys on frame 35 and slide the keys on f37 and f40 backwards 3 frames.

259

Blinks

BLINKS ARE A VITAL PART of facial animation and acting, and a great way to add more life and interest to your character. Before we continue with the lip sync animation, let's take a look at doing a typical, standard blink. This is a common approach to doing them, but you want to make sure you don't do all your blinks this way. There are many different kinds of blinks – fast, slow, half blinks, fluttering eyes, takes, disbelief, etc. The approach you use will be dictated by the emotion and thought process of the character. Nevertheless, this is a tried and true way to get a nice, organic-looking blink and is a great starting point for building a "blink library" in your animation toolset.

Remember we've learned some great ways to copy keys to the clipboard and export animation, so you can take a blink that you create in one file and use it throughout your animations over and over. Just be sure to add some customization and 'flavoring' of each blink to match the scene.

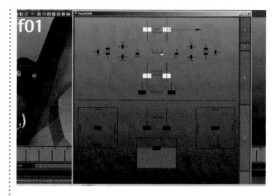

1 Open Blinks.ma and switch to a front view. Select the eyelid controls, and at f01 key the upper and lower lid controls where they are.

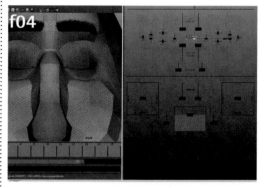

4 On f04 the lids are closed. Normally the upper lids come down about 75% and the lower lids 25% - on the Cenk rig, we control this contact point with the "Eye Height" control.

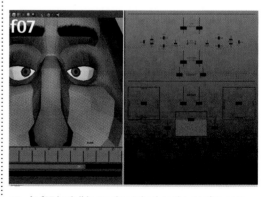

7 At f07 both lids are almost back to the starting pose. Unless the eyes are completely open or closed, I generally like to keep the lids touching the irises on the way up or down, as it makes the blink feel smoother.

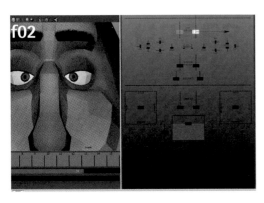

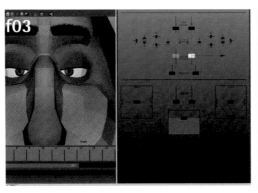

2 On f02 key the upper lids down slightly to create a slight ease out.

3 At f03 bring the upper lids down so they touch the top of the pupil, and start bringing the lower lids up slightly.

Blinks.ma
Blinks_End.ma

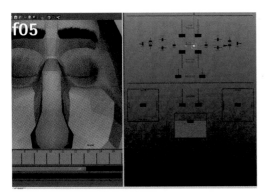

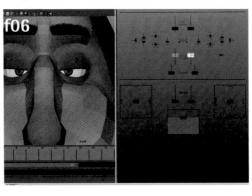

5 We'll hold the eyelids closed for 2 frames, but move the contact point down just a bit. Use the "Eye Height" control to key this.

6 At f06, the eyes are opening back up. For a standard blink, I like the upper lids to be around halfway past the irises on the way back up. The lower lids start to go back down as well.

HOT TIP

Another nice touch for blinks can be adding some very slight up and down in the brows. It depends on the situation, but sometimes adding a barely perceptible amount of motion here can help make things more organic.

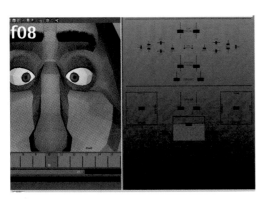

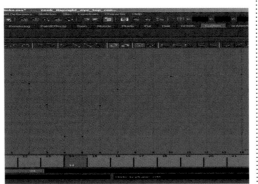

8 Instead of ending on f08, do a nice ease in from f07-f10 to cushion into the pose and make it feel more organic.

9 For an extra bit of polish, do another 4 frames of very subtle ease in cushioning on the upper lids. This is what the curves look like. Look at Blinks_End.ma for the final result.

Facial Animation
Blink & Brows

L ET'S REFINE THE BROWS and add a blink to our face
animation. We'll have Cenk blink when his head raises, since
its speed fits well with the motion we have going. We'll keep it
fairly close to a standard blink, except that the closing will be
a bit slower since that fits his uncooperative, slightly indignant
attitude. Then we'll tighten up the timing of the brows raising,
and add an accent in the brows and eyes to bring out the final
word of the shot, "say".

     You may find that you are doing a little bit of back
and forth with the timing of lids and brows. Indeed, you need to
have a workflow that allows this process to happen so you can
'discover' the best performance within. We'll go through adding
some blinks and brow movement to the scene, but experiment
with some different values and timings in your own shot to get
the best result.

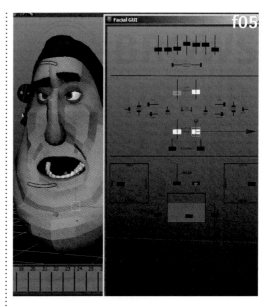

1 Start the blink on f05. Key the upper and lower lids in
their current position.

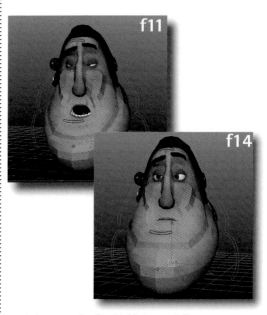

4 A slower opening fits this blink as well. The eyes start
opening at f11, and at f14 the tops and bottoms of the
irises are still touching the lids.

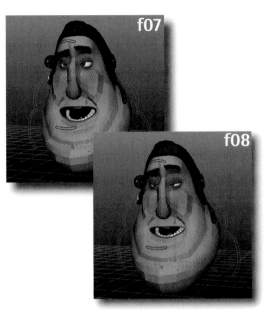

f07

f08

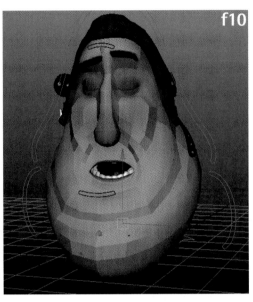

f10

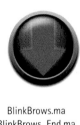

BlinkBrows.ma
BlinkBrows_End.ma

2 Let's make the transition down into the closed pose a total of 4 frames. Here are f07 and f08. Notice that we always see part of the iris when the eyes are open any amount.

3 On f09 and f10 we have the closed pose.

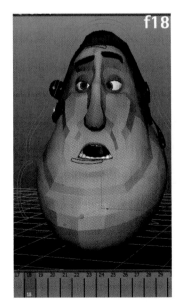

f18

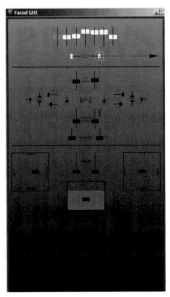

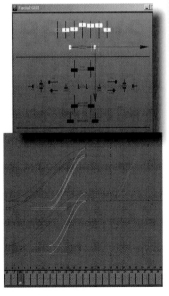

5 The eyes continue to ease into their pose at f18.

6 Now let's work on the brows during the blink. We want to have some overlap, with the brows going up leading the eyes opening slightly. Select all the brow controls.

7 Move the start of the brows' motion to f08, right before the eyes are closed at f09. At f14 they should hit their up pose.

Blink & Brows (cont'd)

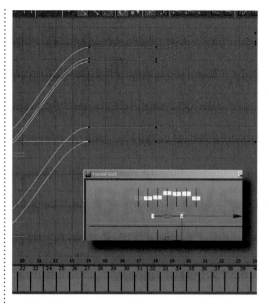

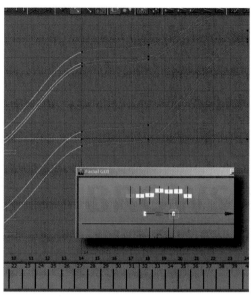

8 A quick trick for doing cushions for the flat curve sections is to move to the frame before they hit the pose, in this case f13.

9 MMB-drag in the timeline from f13 to f14 and set a key. Now f14 is almost the same value it was, but drifts through to f19. Fix the tangent handles and you instantly have a nice subtle drift to make things more organic and not frozen for a stretch of frames.

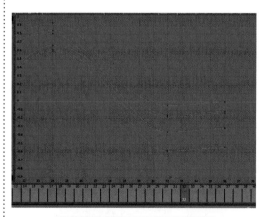

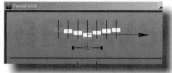

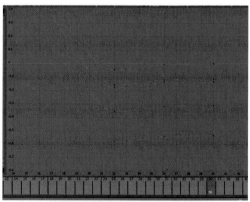

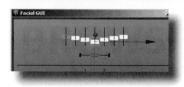

13 At f36, set a key on the brows so they have the same pose as f32. Then at f32, pull the brows down just a small amount to create a little overshoot.

14 Key the brows at f40 and add a little cushion starting at f36.

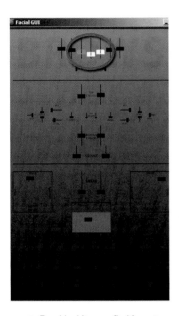

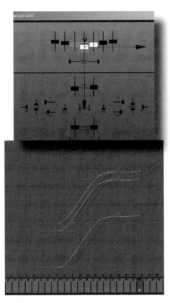

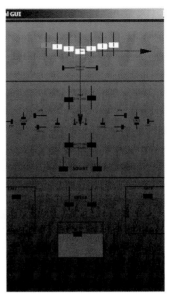

10 To add a bit more fleshiness to the brows, I often like to make the apex lead the rest by a frame. Select the 3 brow controls shown here.

11 Those are the apex of the brow pose, so select their keys at f08 and f14 and slide them one frame earlier to lead the rest of the brows. It's subtle but a nice little touch.

12 Let's move to the end of the animation, on the word "say". Right now the brows and eyes just stop on that last pose at f32, so let's add a little accent. Select the brow controls.

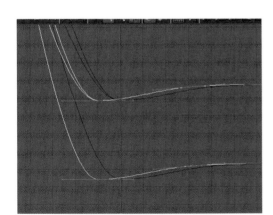

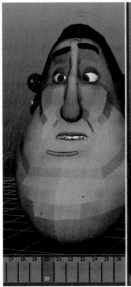

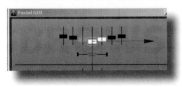

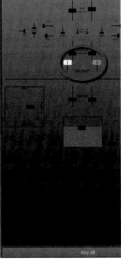

15 Select the 3 middle brow controls and move from f32 onward one frame earlier so they lead the rest of the brows.

16 Make a very small complementary squint with the eyes that trails the brow by a frame. It will help feel that his face is working as an organic unit, rather than an assembly of moving parts. See BlinkBrows_End.ma for the end result.

Eye Darts

ANOTHER IMPORTANT ELEMENT of organic facial animation is eye darts. They're often used for "keep alive" moments, where a character isn't really moving much but needs to still look like they're living beings. They show that a character is thinking about something and that they have an internal monologue happening. And on just a practical level, our eyes rarely stay focused on the exact same spot for more than a second or so, and usually less.

Eye darts can definitely go deeper than that, however, and should be thought about with as much attention as any other element in a character's performance. An eye dart at the right moment can communicate things that nothing else could. A character's eyes darting away as they're trying to convince someone of something can convey them thinking, "Are they buying this?", or show worry, realization, doubt, or any other internal emotion. This is something that we as animators need to be constantly thinking about.

We'll go through a simple eye dart workflow, but keep in mind it's a starting place. Your decisions about eye darts ultimately involve what you need to communicate about the character's internal mental state.

Rather than bouncing them around randomly, it helps to create a subtle pattern with the darts. Shapes like triangles, rectangles, etc. can be good guides for plotting the path the darts make, provided you don't make them too obvious. Varied timing and amounts of movement can help with this. Shapes make sense because we often look back and forth between a person's eyes and mouth when we're conversing. For this exercise, we'll do three darts, and form a triangle shape with their path. They're traced in the example as they're very hard to see in still pictures. Be sure to follow along with the Maya file.

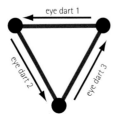

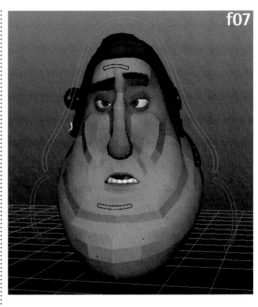

1 Open EyeDarts_Start.ma. If your eye control is not visible, select the master control and change the "eyes" attribute to "on" or "1". Then switch to the front panel to key this action. Hit **S** to set a key on f07.

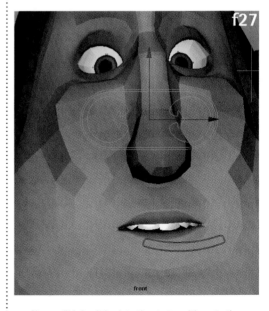

4 Now we'll bring it back to the start position, starting on f25 and ending on f27. You can even MMB-drag the key from f7 to f27 to be sure.

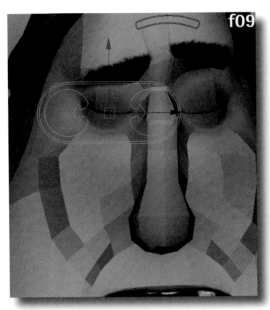

f09

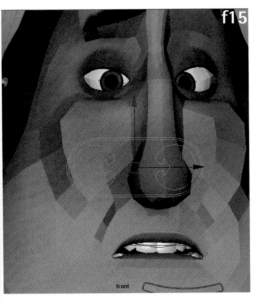

f15

EyeDarts_Start.ma
EyeDarts_End.ma

HOT TIP

Our eyes tend
not to smoothly
track things,
at least not
without turning
our head with
it. If the head
isn't moving,
it's common to
do a series of
sequential darts,
rather than a
smooth pan
across.

2 Eye darts are generally 2 frames long at 24fps, so on f09, move the eye target slightly to the left in the front panel and hit **S**. It's ok that his eyes are closed – in fact eye darts work just as well hidden within blinks.

3 Now do another dart, this time downwards. Key the eyes where they are on f13, then move the eye target downwards and slightly back towards the middle on f15.

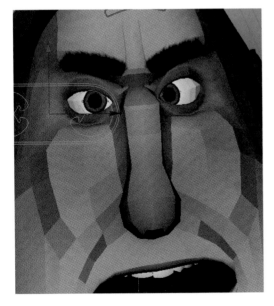

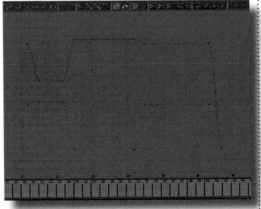

5 I did one more eye dart from f38-f40 from right to left. Often our eyes dart between the eyes of the person we're speaking to, so this last dart reinforces the idea Cenk is talking to someone directly.

6 Here's what the curves look like for these darts. Our eyes move VERY quickly, so it's not necessary to spend too much time cleaning this up. Watch EyeDarts_End.ma for the final result.

Final Touches

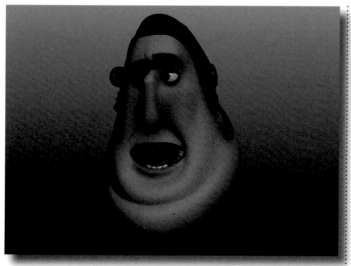

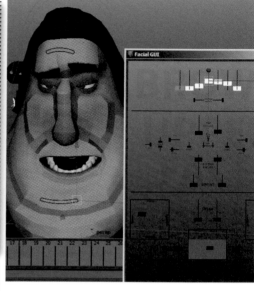

1 The first thing to do is give a slight anticipation down before the brows move up. It's another detail that will help things feel less mechanical and more organic. Select the brow controls.

W E'RE AT THE HOME STRETCH with this face animation! All that's left is some tweaks and polishing to make it look as good as possible, which we'll go over in this cheat. No matter what kind of facial rig you run into throughout your career, the principles remain the same. The face is working as an organic whole, yet some parts are influencing others (brows can influence the lids, mouth corners can push up the cheeks, etc.) From ears to nose flares to a dozen lip controllers, modern production rigs are capable of most any expression possible. Remember, the face has to support the body animation.

Most novices get very excited when they first encounter a sophisticated facial rig, like Cenk. The result is normally a very finely tuned face performance on a lackluster body. Do not do this! The great thing about Cenk is that he is a bouncing ball, so there is no reason that your 'body' performance shouldn't be really solid before moving on to the face. And when you venture out into the animation world and use different characters, remember the basics you learned with Cenk. Happy animating!

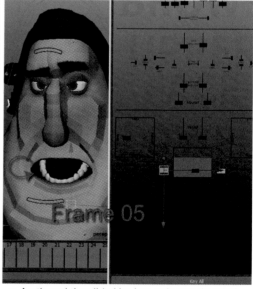

4 Another subtle polish thing is to make sure the mouth corners have nice little arcs in them when moving in and out. It's another one of those details that isn't obvious, but just helps everything feel a little nicer.

faceAnimation_
END.ma

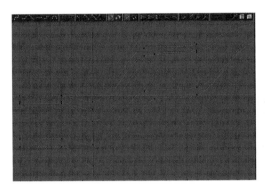

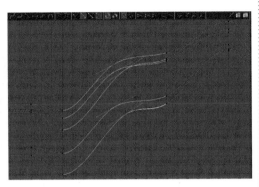

2 I added a key to f03, and on f08 brought the eyebrows all down together slightly. Notice how nice and fleshy this makes the face feel.

3 On second look, it looks like the up pose at f14 is still hitting a bit too hard. Select the keys at f13 and f14 and pull them down to make the cushion a little bigger. Now they won't stop so quickly and will look more natural.

HOT TIP

Always have a reason for everything you're doing when it comes to acting choices. If you can't justify something by what the character is thinking, you probably don't need it (or need something else).

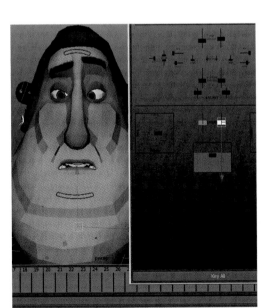

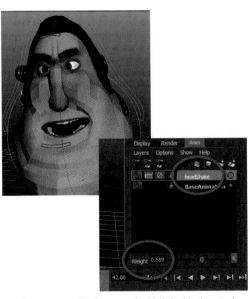

5 I added more snear to the "N" of "nothing". The nose is easy to over-animate, so be careful when doing your own.

6 For some very final texture, I added the head control to an animation layer and animated a little shake on the word "nothing". I animated it just a little too big, and then used the weight parameter to dial it down until it looks nice and subtle. Watch the final in faceAnimation_END.ma.

Is This a Business Worth Getting Into?

by Kenny Roy

I WOULD BE REMISS IN MY DUTIES IF I WERE TO NOT at least mention the turmoil that has befallen our beloved industry. With all that is happening right now, is it even a good idea to become an animator? I say whole-heartedly yes, but let me explain.

For years now, VFX houses have found it increasingly hard to compete with shops set up in countries such as India, China, Korea, and others where government subsidies make business more lucrative for them. Add on top of that the fact that most of the aforementioned countries have labor much cheaper than the US, and you are not only getting substantial tax benefits for sending your work overseas, but your budget stretches even further. Finally, and perhaps the scariest issue facing us as artists, is that labor laws surrounding the VFX industry are weak. Long hours and little stability are the norm.

So why would I still advise entering this industry? Because I truly believe that we are on a cusp. I believe that in the next few years, methods of independent digital distribution will offer small teams of artists the outlets they need to reach an audience and make a living producing their own content. Already, many of my friends have opted to work with programmers and web developers to create online content, mobile games, and interactive applications. ITunes and Google Play Store level the playing field; when you are not competing for billboard space against a major movie studio, things change. Small teams of artists collaborating on projects, communicating and working over the internet, can accomplish what it took hundreds of people to do only ten years ago. And recently, major studios have acquired YouTube channels for sums in the millions. It goes to show that you can be successful if you are prolific and consistent, and can build a following for your content.

This might be the best time to be an animator! Sure, it would have been amazing to be in Walt Disney Studios in the years surrounding *Snow White*, again in the last 80's and early 90's with the new Masterpieces, or up at Pixar to be a part of *Toy Story* in 1995. These high points in our past may have been exciting, but only now is the most valuable change to the industry in full effect: individual artists have the ability to produce and distribute content all on their own, with the potential for literally millions of people to see their work.

At every point up until now, the act of distributing content has been left up to very time- and labor-intensive processes. The complexity of logistics would baffle (and bankrupt) individuals trying to do it all on their own. Not anymore.

You may not be as inclined to want to create your own animated content, but this is a great time for animators still. Why? With the way things are going, it looks like major VFX houses may try to restructure the current business to make filmmaking much more collaborative between studios and VFX houses. This change will mean that, fundamentally, there will be more work, and better understanding and planning of the process, which will all hopefully lead to improved conditions for all digital artists. If studios are involving the VFX houses at the very beginning of a project, then we will surely gain a foothold in the approval process (the main point of contention that forces VFX houses to go to great lengths to deliver more work for a fixed bid). When project expectations are communicated clearly at the beginning, then everyone can be held accountable.

We may have seen some ugly things recently; major VFX houses closing or moving countries just to stay afloat, huge snubs by directors and the Academy in the Oscars' broadcast in 2013, and a general lack of understanding from the public and the government alike.

All that said, we are lucky enough to be animators during the major paradigm shift in entertainment. A shift away from traditional distribution and towards digital means. A shift away from a huge barrier to entry for content creators and towards both the hardware and software being affordable for all. A shift away from the studios pitting VFX houses against each other and towards long-term partnerships to produce amazing visuals together. I don't know about you, but I can't think of a more exciting time to be right in the middle of it all.

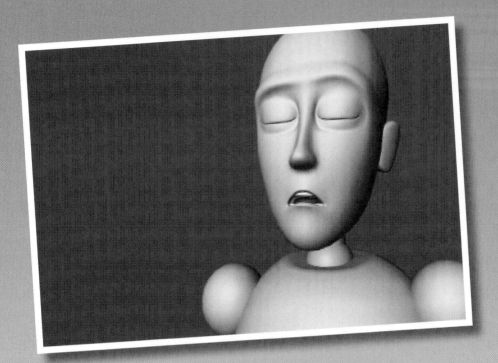

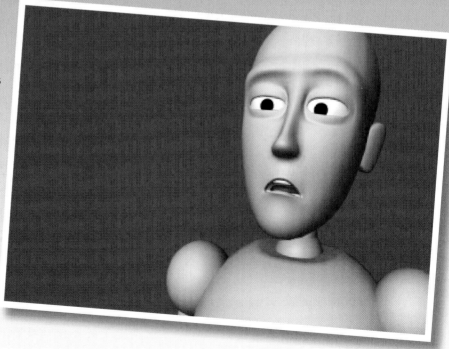

■ Undecided? Animation layers will let you organize and create unlimited variations in your work. Much like layers in Photoshop, you can control what curves are playing where and how much they influence the final result. Mix and match to your heart's content and come up with new ideas.

272

12
Animation Layers

SINCE THEIR INTRODUCTION, animation layers have
been one of the most powerful tools yet in computer
animation. They exponentially increase the ease of
creative tasks like trying different approaches and
variations, and they make working with curves much
simpler and more compartmentalized.

However, they're still a relatively new tool in Maya.
I've met many professionals who don't even know they
exist, yet their benefits can't be overstated. They allow a
flexibility and simplification of animation curves that is
completely on another level from how many of us learned
Maya. This chapter will show you how to employ this
incredibly powerful feature into what will likely evolve
into a new and vastly improved workflow for you.

How Animation Layers Work

Animation Layers

I F YOU'VE USED GRAPHICS PROGRAMS like Photoshop, then understanding Maya's animation layers will be a short leap from there. Layers let us stack multiple versions of spline curves on top of each other, which Maya then mixes together the way we want. This default behavior is one of two available layer modes, and is called Additive mode. A simple example would be two layers for the Translate Y attribute:

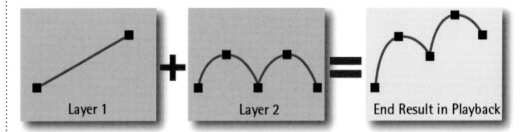

You can see how the two Y curves are mixed together for the end result. While this alone can make working with curves simpler, particularly with more complex examples, the real flexibility is how we can adjust the weight of each layer, much like opacity in a graphics program.

Instead of editing the curve itself, simply turning the weight of Layer 2 down to 50% reduces its influence on the final result by half. It looks like this:

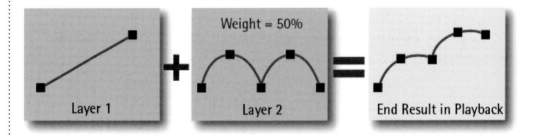

Likewise if we switched that concept, and reduced the weight of Layer 1 to 50%, we get this:

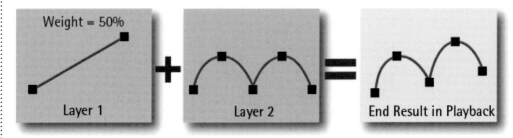

Since the weight is just a slider, we can instantly experiment with any ratio of weights, giving us exponentially more options with no extra spline editing.

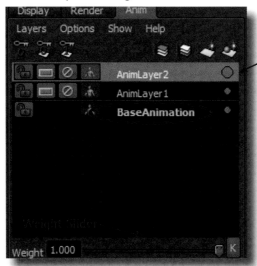

Green = layer currently being keyed (possible for multiple layers to be keyed simultaneously)

HOT TIP

When working with layers, lock the BaseAnimation to keep it from getting accidentally keyed.

When we use layers, any animation we've done before the first animation layer was created will be labeled as BaseAnimation in the editor. BaseAnimation is not actually an animation layer, so we can't adjust its weight or turn it off.

Creating animation layers stacks them on the base layer. As far as Additive mode layers go (which is the default), the order doesn't really matter and the results should look the same. Override, the other mode, does take the order into account. When we set a layer to this mode, it essentially mutes any animation on layers below it that share the same controls/attributes. Animation above an verride layer will be added into the end result.

Override Layer (bold)

Display   Render   Anim

Layers   Options   Show   Help

AnimLayer2

AnimLayer1

BaseAnimation

Weight 1.000

275

Animation Layer Basics

N OW THAT WE UNDERSTAND how animation layers work, let's see in Maya the example that was just illustrated. The Translate Y curves are exactly the same as the previous pages' example to keep things consistent. You'll be able to experiment for yourself and see how the weighting of a layer affects the animation. Weighting can also be animated just like anything else, so curves can have different amounts of influence throughout an animation, continuing to expand the possibilities. Finally, layers offer some nice organizational colorizing, complete with different colored ticks in the timeline, which can be a lifesaver if you're using many layers.

After this cheat, we'll revisit the facial animation we did in the previous chapter and continue to improve it, as well as create some new variations.

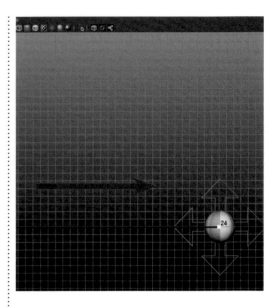

1 Open layerExample.ma and switch to front view. Right now only the BaseAnimation is active, which is the ball translating in X from left to right.

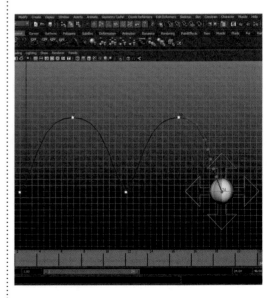

4 Re-mute Layer 1 and unmute Layer 2. You can see the Translate Y curve from Layer 2 in the illustration at work.

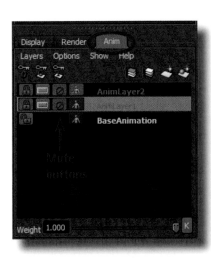

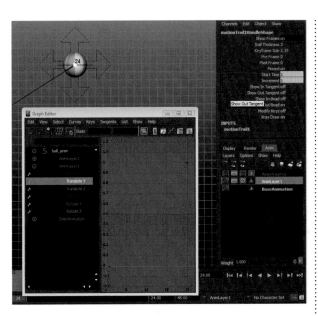

layerExample.ma

2 In the Layers panel, switch to Anim layers. There are the two layers above the base, with the same animation as in the example we just talked about. Currently both layers are muted.

3 Click the Mute button for Layer 1 to unmute it. Our Translate Y curve from the illustration is now active and the ball travels upward. Muting is a great feature for comparing how different curves affect the end result.

HOT TIP

If you have lots of layers and the Graph Editor is getting crowded, right click in the Graph Editor's left panel and select Animation Layers Filter > Active. Now only the active layer's curves will appear.

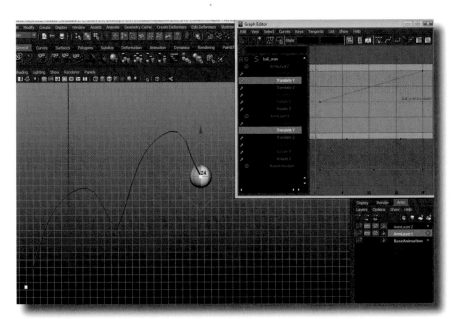

5 Unmute both and they are added together in the final result. You can see that there are two separate Translate Y curves in the Graph Editor, separated by their layers.

Anim Layer Basics (cont'd)

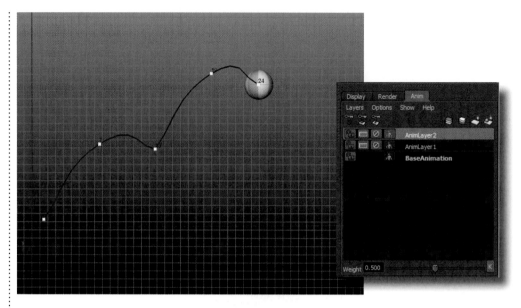

6 Select Layer 2 and move the weight slider down to .5, or 50%. Now the peaks of the Layer 2 Translate Y curve are half of what they were. Remember that we haven't changed the actual curve at all, only the amount of it that is combined into the final result.

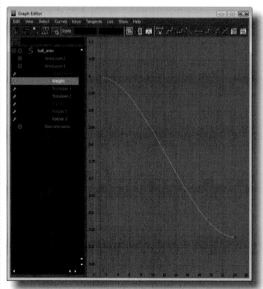

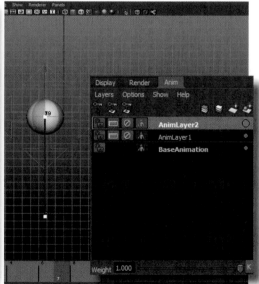

8 The K button next to the weight slider keys the weight attribute. You can set a layer's weight to different amounts throughout an animation. Once you set a key on it, a curve called "Weight" will appear under the layer's name in the Graph Editor, which you can edit as normal.

9 Right click on Layer2 and select Layer Mode > Override. The name turns bold and the ball only moves up and down. Override causes a layer to not evaluate the layers below that have the same controllers. Since the ball's move control is animated in everything below, they are overridden.

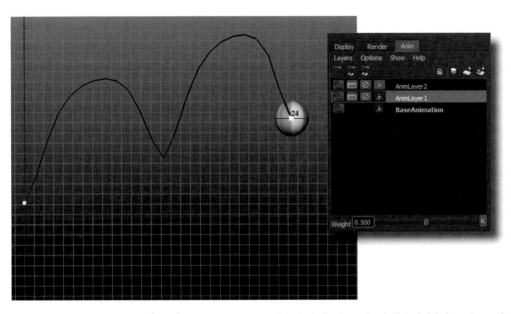

7 Set Layer 2's weight back to 1 (100%) and slide Layer 1 to .5. Now the ball only reaches half the height it used to at the end, but the bounces are back to their full amount.

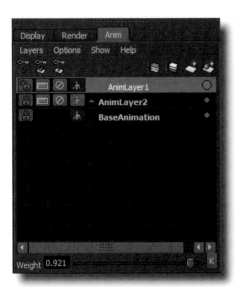

10 MMB- drag to reorder layers, and the lock button protects them from being keyed or changed.

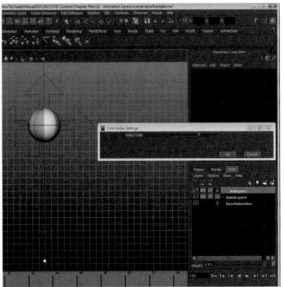

11 Right click on the colored Ghost button to set the layer's color. This will make all the key ticks for that layer in the timeline the color you choose. Clicking on the Ghost button will also enable ghosts for that layer in the color as well.

HOT TIP

A layer in override mode mutes any layer below that has the same controller/ attributes, including the BaseAnimation. You can put variations on separate override layers, and mute back and forth to compare.

Cheating a Cycle

MAYA'S ANIMATION LAYERS HAVE COME a long way in terms of stability and ease of use since their introduction. A very exciting new use for layers is to animate the weight of the layers to create some variations in cycles. We can use a layered approach to creating animation and then isolate layers for some custom movement. In doing so, we will "break up" the repetitive look of a cycle without having to delete the cycle, bake the keys, or alter it in any way. This is a fantastic new way of working. Now is a good time to start playing with layers to see if they have earned a spot in your workflow.

In this cheat, we're going to look at how planning a scene with a walk cycle using layers can give you new flexibility to create some great results in a short amount of time. We will look at how easy it has become to split animation up on the body into layers and then how easy it is to mix and match those layers to create unique results in your scene.

If you are still on the fence about layers after this cheat, then just imagine how many of your scenes that used walk cycles could have been done, and done better, using these cheats. It may be time to rethink your Workflow...

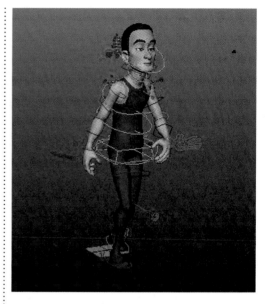

1 Open layer_Walk_Start.ma. You will see Morpheus walking in a cycle. This will be the animation we start with.

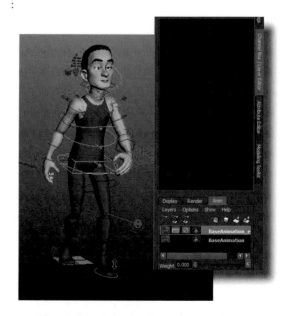

4 Select the Base_Animation_Extract layer, play back the animation and notice how you can slide the weight slider for this new layer and remove the movement in the torso as the character is walking.

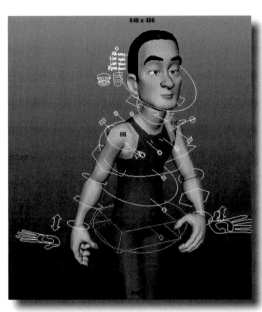

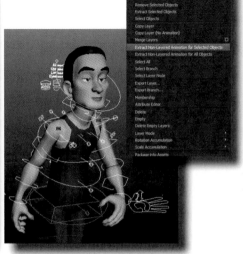

2 A great new feature is the ability to extract animation and put it on a new animation layer. Select all of the controls of Morpheus from the waist up. Do not select his root or hips.

3 In the Anim Layers tab (Channel Box/Layer Editor, then Anim tab), click on Layers>Extract Non Layered Animation on Selected Objects. Maya will create a new anim layer with the torso animation in it.

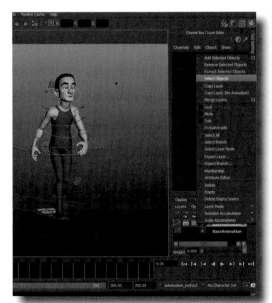

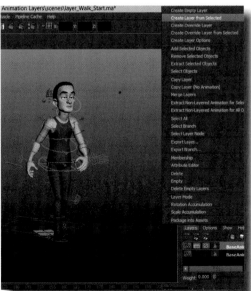

5 Now let's create a new layer for the custom animation. Right click on the new animation layer and click on Select Objects.

6 Click on Layers>Create Layer From Selected. Select the new layer, which should be called "AnimLayer1".

281

Cheating a Cycle (cont'd)

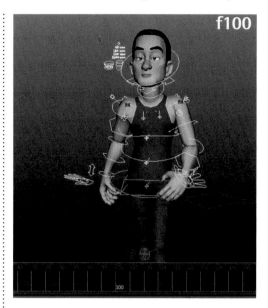

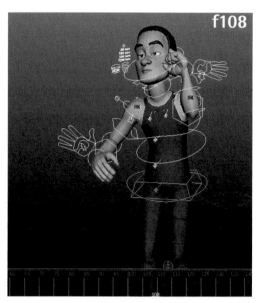

7 Making sure that the weight on the Base_Animation_ Extract layer is at zero so it does not distract you, set a key on all the controls on f100.

8 On f108, create a pose similar to mine, this is an anticipation pose for a finger point.

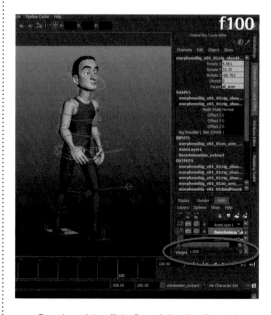

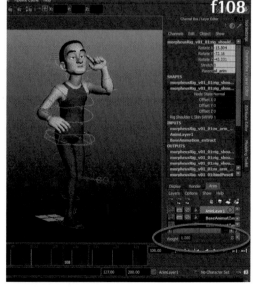

11 Turn the weight off the Base_Animation_Extract layer to 1. Go to f100 on the timeline, and key the weight of this anim layer. Key the weight of AnimLayer 1 to 0.

12 On f108, key the weight of the Base_Animation_ Extract layer to 0, and key the weight of AnimLayer1 to 1.

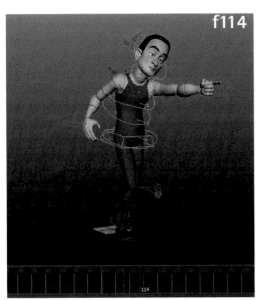

f114

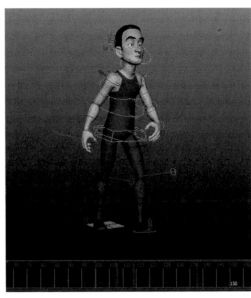

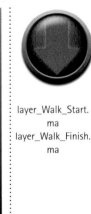

layer_Walk_Start.
ma
layer_Walk_Finish.
ma

9 On f114, create a pose similar to mine. Key all of the controls again on f138 so that he holds this pose for 24 frames.

10 Select all of the controls and MMB drag on the timeline from f100 to f150 to copy the neutral pose of Morpheus, then hit **S**. Now turn this anim layer's weight to 0.

HOT TIP

If rethinking
your scenes
in a layered
approach is too
disruptive to
your workflow,
remember you
can always
create your
animation
normally and
then just extract
the layers like
we did in this
cheat.

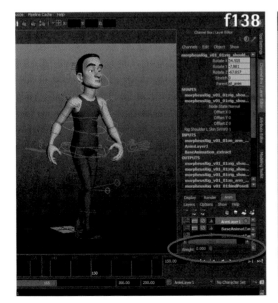

f138

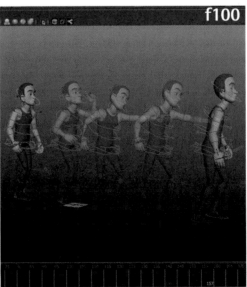

f100

13 On f138, key the weight of both anim layers as is. Finall on f150, key the weight of AnimLayer1 to 0, and key the weight of Base_Animation_Extract layer to 1.

14 Play back the animation and watch your cycle take an interesting turn on f100, only to return perfectly to the cycle when Morpheus has done his point!

Layers for Texture

THE ANIMATION IS LOOKING quite a bit better with our recent additions, and we can instantly go back to the original version at any time. Such is the power of layers. Yet it still needs a little something. A little shake when he raises his head and closes his eyes will add a nice bit of texture.

Creating layers to add in texture is a technique that can save you tons of work, especially if working for a picky or indecisive director. It's easy enough to add in the headshake as normal, but if you're then asked to tone it down or take it out, you have to go back in and edit the original curve quite a bit. Using a layer for the shake, you can simply turn the weight down until they're happy. And best of all, it makes your curves simpler to work with. If you were asked to start with the head rotated further in Y, you can simply adjust the original curve while the head shake stays the same in its own layer, rather than having to tweak where Rotate Y starts and all the shaking keys after it.

In short, layers have lots of uses and you'll figure out plenty more as you continue to use them and tailor them to your workflow. Happy (easier) animating!

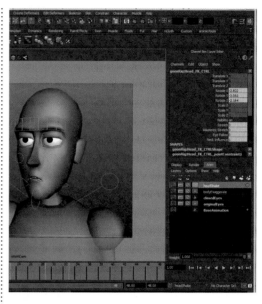

1 Open texture_start.ma and select the head control. In the Anim layers click the Create Layer from Selected button. Name it "headShake" and give it a unique color.

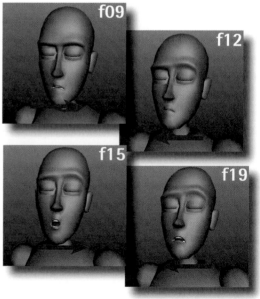

4 The subtle shake.

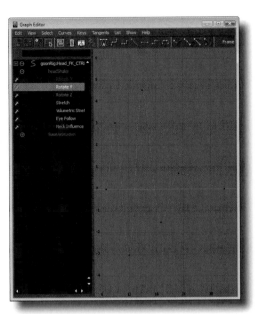

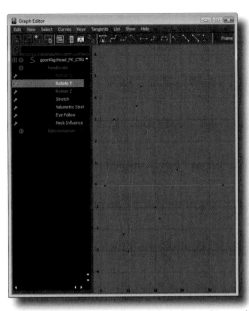

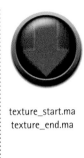

texture_start.ma
texture_end.ma

2 In the headShake layer, starting at around f07, rough in a back and forth "No" movement in Rotate Y as he raises his head.

3 Work with the curves until the shake looks good to you. I added some more ease in on some of the shakes.

HOT TIP

Layers can be parented to other layers. This isn't like parenting with props or anything though. It's simply Maya's way of organizing layers, like folders in Photoshop.

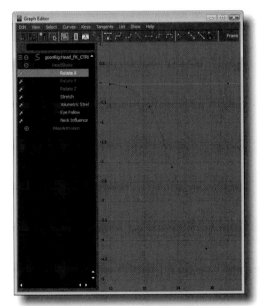

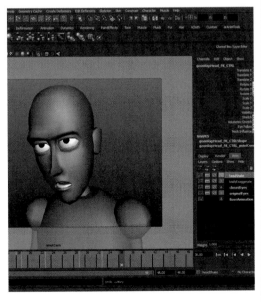

5 With the bigger movement in the body, I noticed his head needs to drag more in Rotate X. Add that in on the headShake layer, or put it on a new layer if you like.

6 Now you can really tweak things to your heart's content. Using the layers and their weights, experiment with different amounts of head shake, body exaggeration, eye versions, and anything else that you want to try!

The Final 5%

By Kenny Roy

AT THE VERY END OF WORKING ON A SHOT, we turn to the final polish stage. Of course each shot is different, but many have enough in common that you should have a clear list of tasks to look for to be sure that your work is complete. I have always advocated for the practice of writing down one's workflow. If you have enough experience, you can probably get away without a written list. Whatever the case, I thought that it would be helpful to you to have an extensive list of some of the things that professionals look at when they are trying to get a shot out the door.

By no means is this a complete list, and conversely there may be many items on this list that don't apply to your current scene. Take this list as much as an indication of the level of detail that feature film and high-end commercial work demands, as a complete rubric for success. The list is also basically ordered from head to toe, as every animated shot will need polish in different areas and so any other ordering might be confusing.

Without further ado, here's the list:

1. Make sure anything attached to the head that is keyable has good overlap and secondary movement. Floppy hats, pony tails, and antennae come to mind.
2. Make sure that the ears, if keyable, have a little bit of life to them, perhaps perking up when the character hears something. A tiny bit of wiggle in the tips is good too.
3. If any dynamics exist on the head, turn them on and adjust the settings.
4. Add a tiny bit of micro movement to match the inflection of the dialog.
5. Check that the eyebrows and eyelids do not take on any unharmonious poses.

6. Add some overlap and overshoot to the eyebrow movement.

7. Add some micro darts to the eyes.

8. Untwin the keyframes of the eye blinks and eyebrow movements.

9. Key the cheeks and squints if they haven't been touched yet.

10. Key the sneer and nose controls if they haven't been done already.

11. Add a tiny bit of puff to the cheeks on m, b, and p syllables in the dialog.

12. Key the tongue if it has not been done already.

13. Add asymmetry to the mouth shapes in the dialog.

14. Cheat emotional face shapes like smiles and frowns towards camera.

15. If there are lip puff controls, add them to m, b, and p shapes.

16. If there are controls to keep the lips stuck together as the jaw moves downwards, add a pass of that now for words in the dialog that start with b and p, especially after a long pause.

17. If there are swallow or breathing controls for the neck, add those.

18. Check arcs are clean and smooth on all the head movements.

19. Add breathing movement to the chest.

20. Relieve a little bit of the distress in the neck and shoulder by keying the clavicles if they haven't been keyed already.

21. Check arcs on chest and upper torso.

22. Check arcs of elbows.

23. Make sure the pole vectors are animated – we don't want Maya deciding where our elbows are pointing.

24. If this is a character with wings, add the stretching of the wing membranes against the flow of air.

25. Check wing poses for good silhouette.

26. Refine and nail down overlap amount on wrists.

27. Add and refine overlap on fingers.

28. Break up finger animation timing.

29. Add contact of fingers on any props the character holds or touches.

30. Refine and nail down any IK/FK switching by matching the pose and movement perfectly.

31. Add moving holds to hand poses and finger poses.

32.   Add micro movements to hands and fingers.

33.   Make sure the spine controls are not counter-animated against each other and that each spine pose is explicit and meaningful.

34.   If there is a stomach bulge control, use it in conjunction with the chest controls to further refine the subtle breathing movements.

35.   Add secondary movement and overshoot to stomach bulges and fat.

36.   Refine the hips by doing a pass where you look closely where the weight is distributed.

37.   If the hips and lowest spine control both have IK movement, make sure there is no counter-animation between them.

38.   Refine arcs on the hips.

39.   Make sure all of the main body movements have a weight shift in the hips to allow the legs to come off the ground.

40.   If you are working on a dog-legged character, make sure the femur and the foot bones stay parallel at nearly all times.

41.   If there is a tail, smooth the movement on the tail by reducing keys.

42.   Add overlap and some bounce on the tail.

43.   If the tail is prehensile, make sure there are no penetrations with props or the set, and add contact poses if it touches objects.

44.   Remove pops in the knee by refining the height of the root, or by using the stretch control on the legs very sparingly.

45.   Key knee pole vectors.

46.   Add micro movements on the knees to indicate when a huge amount of force is applied, especially on large creatures.

47.   Make sure the knees line up with the foot in general.

48.   Avoid bow-legged poses or knees pressed together.

49.   Key foot roll.

50.   Key toe roll, and a little bit of overlap on the foot and toes.

51.   Key sliding and micro movements on the feet, even on a static character.

52.   Fix any penetrations that are happening between the ground and feet.

53.   Make sure all of the curves on the feet fast-in to the ground in

TranslateY – we don't want the feet to slow-in to contact poses.

54. Make sure any FIK/IK switches on the legs are cleaned up nicely.

55. If you are working on a barefoot creature, key the toes splaying as the weight is applied to the foot.

56. Do an overall silhouette pass and make sure there are no unattractive slivers of light in the negative space, or messy silhouettes.

57. Take once last look at your thumbnails, and reference and compare your golden poses.

58. Watch the animation back with the lip sync moved one frame earlier to see if it improves the readability.

59. Watch the animation play backwards to see any pops or hitches in the animation that you couldn't see before.

Phew! Of course on a per-shot basis, you could go on forever. Hopefully this list will inspire you to create your own, and to integrate a regimented polish pass into your workflow. Good luck animating!

Darrin Butters

DARRIN BUTTERS HAS BEEN AT WDAS for 16 years. He was born and raised in Nebraska. His wife, Lorelei, and daughter, Julia, live in Glendale, CA.

WHAT IS A WORKFLOW CHANGE YOU'VE MADE THAT HAS HELPED YOU TO CREATE GREAT ANIMATION?

On the shot I'm working on right now, I posed it out, splined it, made some offsets, then pinned everything down on twos. Everything. I'm working on it like a traditional scene. Weird, right? Every shot I work on has a different workflow. Because I'm crazy.

WHO IS YOUR FAVORITE ANIMATOR? WHY?

Tony Smeed. His shots are always incredible and perfect. He's generous and extremely humble. And he's funny and kind.

IF YOU COULD HAVE BEEN THE ANIMATOR THAT ANIMATED ANY CHARACTER IN FILM HISTORY, WHICH CHARACTER WOULD THAT BE? WHY?

I love Captain Hook. He has ONE purpose. He has an all-consuming fear. He is a really good liar. He is smart. He is elegant. He is a barbarian.

WHAT ARE SOME OF YOUR INTERESTS OR HOBBIES BESIDES ANIMATION?

I perform and teach improvisational theater. Some of the principles from that art translate well to animation. Yes - and, mirroring, sharing, listening, group dynamics, all can be applied to the animation process. Abandoning your idea, and accepting another without hesitation is a principle we can all use every day.

WHAT ARE SOME TIPS FOR GETTING INSIDE A CHARACTER'S HEAD, UNDERSTANDING THE MOTIVATION AND THE SUBTLETY OF A SCENE?

Find the want. Find the want. Find the want.

HOW DO YOU KNOW WHEN YOU'VE FOUND THE "RIGHT" IDEA FOR A SHOT?

If I can do something unique and original WITHIN the director's needs for the shot. The idea is clear in the blocking or reference. And when you show it, they laugh and say "keep going".

TELL US ABOUT YOUR FIRST JOB IN ANIMATION.

I was hired as an assistant for *Dinosaur* (2000) There was such a long pre-production schedule for it that I made it through my apprenticeship and became an animator soon after we started production shots. I cried when I saw my name in the credits.

IF YOU HAD TO GO BACK AND LEARN ANIMATION ALL OVER AGAIN, WHAT ONE THING WOULD YOU DO DIFFERENTLY?

There are SO many things I'd do differently. But I think I learned about "Golden Poses" too late. Those poses that the viewer remembers from your scene. Those poses that you linger on to show the appeal and essence of that character.

IF YOU HAD TO GIVE ONE PIECE OF ADVICE FOR A DEMO REEL, WHAT WOULD IT BE?

Show your best stuff first. Don't assume that the reviewer is going to watch more than 20 seconds of your reel before making a decision. That awesome stuff at the end may never be seen.

DO YOU HAVE ANY ADVICE FOR ANIMATORS?

Show your work to others, often. Embrace criticism. Embrace changes. Shoot reference for everything, even if you don't use it, you may learn SOMETHING from studying it.

Keith A. Sintay

KEITH SINTAY HAS BEEN A PROFESSIONAL CHARACTER ANIMATOR for 18 years. He has worked as a traditional (2D) animation artist at Disney Feature Animation, as well as at Dreamworks Feature Animation, Sony Imageworks, and Digital Domain. He lives in southern California with his wife, Connie, and five dogs.

TELL US A LITTLE BIT ABOUT HOW YOU USE MAYA IN YOUR EVERYDAY JOB.

In my "everyday job" I work as a Senior Character Animator. I use Maya daily to not only create a performance using CG characters, but often to set up cameras and create (model) props for those characters; even if the props are temporary and will be fleshed out by the modeling department later on.

The performance animation I do can range from full character lip sync and acting to digital stunts. It also ranges from biped to quadruped; and from human to alien depending on the project.

WHAT ARE SOME OF YOUR FAVORITE TOOLS IN MAYA?

Maya has many tools that I use so frequently, that they come as second nature now and I have to stop and think about how I am actually using them. I guess a big part of why I like Maya is the quick interface and how you can arrange the windows. It allows for amazing workflow, which is very important in CG animation. I use the timeline for all of my timing; only using the Graph Editor for gross timing changes. One of the newer tools in Maya that is essential to a VFX artist working with live action background plates is the ability to zoom and pan in 2D using the \ key. That is a LIFE saver when you want to get in close to a detail, but you need to maintain perspective - such as when you are looking through your shot cam.

WHAT IS A WORKFLOW CHANGE YOU'VE MADE THAT HAS HELPED YOU TO CREATE GREAT ANIMATION?

A HUGE change that I made after my first movie was not letting the computer dictate what my characters were doing - but rather create it all myself. In other words, I control not only the breakdowns but the in-betweens as well. I do this by animating in linear (or stepped if I am asked to do so), and getting the animation in the workspace to look as close to final as I can without going into the Graph Editor to manipulate tangent handles etc. I work with non-weighted tangents, and by working in linear, I can watch my arcs and movements by scrubbing the timeline; much as I used to do as a traditional (2D) animator by flipping my drawings. I can see the movement evolve. It is only after I am satisfied with how it looks in linear (maybe animated down to two's in some cases) that I will go in and use "auto tangent" or "plateau" to give some ease in and out to the keys. In this way, the frames are like the drawings in 2D-, if I didn't draw it, it won't be there. If I allowed the computer to create my in-betweens, they would all be halves, and the breakdowns in an arc would be flat.

WHAT ARE SOME TIPS FOR GETTING INSIDE A CHARACTER'S HEAD, UNDERSTANDING THE MOTIVATION AND THE SUBTLETY OF A SCENE?

Learn all that you can about the character. If you are only given a name, and nothing about the back story, figure out their role in the story and how they will fit into the narrative. Ask yourself how that character would react in hypothetical situations. Often, even if a character is a CG model, I will draw it a few times in various poses to become more familiar with how it will move. It is more organic for me that way (much like thumbnailing a scene).

I look at what the previous scenes were and any that might follow my shot and determine what is needed to move the story along; often you will get notes from the director telling you what they want, so you always have to stay within certain parameters. Sometimes, when acting out a scene for reference, I will also ask a friend to act it out as well. This is because often, your friend will come up with a different movement or gesture that you, yourself had not thought of.

DO YOU EVER HAVE TO WORK WITH MOTION CAPTURE? DO YOU THINK THAT MOTION CAPTURE WILL CONTINUE TO GROW AS A LARGER PORTION OF ANIMATION IN MOVIES IN THE FUTURE?

I have worked with motion capture, and my experience with it has been fair at best. Sometimes I think of it like inheriting a scene from a really bad animator. If the motion capture curves are wonky and all over the place, using several controls in various combinations from one frame to the next, you have to go in and prune and edit that motion before you can even animate on top of it. As a keyframe animator, I would prefer that motion capture remain for crowd milling, battle and other large scale shots. I don't like it in close-up so much; the movement starts to edge toward the uncanny valley, especially if the characters have cartoony bodies/faces and the movement is too realistic, like in *Monster House* or *Polar Express*.

DO YOU RELY ON A SPECIAL SCRIPT OR PLUGINS IN YOUR EVERYDAY JOB? DO YOU THINK BEGINNER ANIMATORS SHOULD TRY TO LEARN WITHOUT SCRIPTS AND PLUGINS?

The only script I use and LOVE is called Auto Tangent by Comet Cartoons. That is an amazing curve manipulator for the Graph Editor. It gives just the right amount of ease in and ease out without adding or allowing any "over-shoot".

I definitely don't think beginners should use scripts or plugins when they are starting out. The number one reason, is that often you will work at a studio that won't allow outside plugins or scripts to be used. If you become accustomed to using these tools, you will be handicapped without them. I have seen it happen. At Dreamworks we became reliant upon a script that would actually create a timing chart like we used to use in 2D animation. It was a real crutch for us coming from traditional animation and moving into CG. Well, it was fine to do your timing and inbetweens that way at Dreamworks, but once I went to another studio, I was suddenly without that tool and had to learn very fast how to work without it.

TELL US ABOUT YOUR FIRST JOB IN ANIMATION.

My first job in animation was at Disney Feature Animation in Florida. I was hired after my internship to work as a clean-up in-betweener on *Pocahontas*. I was more thrilled than you can imagine to be working on a Disney film, knowing that so many millions of people would actually see my drawings up on the screen.

HAVE YOU EVER THOUGHT ABOUT GIVING UP? IF SO, WHAT MADE YOU STICK WITH IT?

I have never thought of doing any thing else. I love to take inanimate things, whether they are lumps of clay, drawings or CG wire-frame models, and make them come alive. The whole process of animation still keeps me learning, even after almost 18 years.

IN TODAY'S INDUSTRY, ARE ANIMATORS A DYING BREED?

In the bigger studios, I think you can still specialize, but in smaller studios, from what I have seen it is more efficient to be a "generalist" and know more than just one discipline. I don't know if animators are a dying breed. I teach animation, and from where I sit, there are still plenty of eager young people who are just as fascinated by creating, if you will allow me, an "illusion of life" as I am.

IF YOU HAD TO GIVE ONE PIECE OF ADVICE FOR A DEMO REEL, WHAT WOULD IT BE?

I would leave off anything that you are not 100% sure of. That is a vague statement, but really, if you aren't sure it is good, leave it off. If it might offend someone, leave it off. If it is good, it doesn't matter if you did it ten years ago or yesterday, good is good. I don't like it when I am looking at reel and the owner of the work says, "Oh, that is old, I did that back in school". Never qualify your work like that. It is either good or it isn't. This same advice goes for a portfolio of drawings.

ARE WE IN THE GOLDEN AGE OF ANIMATION? IF YES, WHY DO YOU THINK SO? IF NO, WHAT WAS/WILL BE THE GOLDEN AGE OF ANIMATION?

I think we are in the Golden Age of multimedia. I don't know that animation itself is in a golden period. I think a second "golden" era could describe the time of *The Lion King* and the several movies that surrounded it (ie *Beauty and the Beast*). But that era has passed. We came into a Pixar age of animation, which is still ongoing, and is brilliant. But, there are also massively popular video games and other platforms that animators are finding tremendous success with.

DO YOU HAVE ANY ADVICE FOR ANIMATORS?

If you are a CG animator, I suggest you take some drawing classes to learn anatomy and physiology. Take acting classes and improv classes if you can. Learn as much as you possibly can about movement: what propels an object, why it behaves the way it does, etc.

John Nguyen

JOHN NGUYEN IS A 17-YEAR VETERAN of animation and visual effects. He has worked at many major studios, on blockbuster movies. He is an artist, a father, a husband, and loves to make people laugh.

WHAT ARE SOME OF YOUR FAVORITE TOOLS IN MAYA?

I use the Dope Sheet, the middle mouse copy/paste keyframe function in the timeline. And the copy/paste key tool. But one of the tools I use the most is the anim layers. They allow me to add animation without the risk of losing what I had originally.

WHO IS YOUR FAVORITE ANIMATOR? WHY?

Glen Keane. His work transcends the mechanics of animation. It goes beyond the techniques of animation and had a spirit, a soul. That comes from him, his talent, his choices, his understanding of the medium. It is true animation, which is more than just movement.

WHAT ARE SOME TIPS FOR GETTING INSIDE A CHARACTER'S HEAD, UNDERSTANDING THE MOTIVATION AND THE SUBTLETY OF A SCENE?

Understand the biography of the character. If you are not given one, then form one. What is his background, what happened to him, what is his motivation? What are the physical limitations? So often an animator is concerned with "what" actions or motions a character will do, that they don't think of "why" they would do it. The bio answers the "why." If they are angry, happy, weak, or obsessed, these things will influence them. They are why they choose certain actions and not others.

DO YOU HAVE ANY PERSONAL PROJECTS THAT YOU'D LIKE TO TELL US ABOUT?

I am currently working on a short film/pilot.

HOW DO YOU KNOW WHEN YOU'VE FOUND THE "RIGHT" IDEA FOR A SHOT?

When an idea makes me smile, and excited to animated. When I don't know exactly how it will end. Then I know I'm on the right track. Also, I want my shorts to have a real story, not just repetition of an action, i.e someone trying to open a box that is locked. Or trying to catch something that alludes him. These aren't stories, these are just parts of stories.

DO YOU RELY ON A SPECIAL SCRIPT OR PLUGINS IN YOUR EVERYDAY JOB? DO YOU THINK BEGINNER ANIMATORS SHOULD TRY TO LEARN WITHOUT SCRIPTS AND PLUGINS?

There are about three scripts that I use on a regular basis, but not every day. I do recommend that young animators do not rely on scripts and plugins. Because, if/when they go to another studio, they won't have access to those tools. They should be more focused on basic animation principles, and achieving them not matter what tools they have.

IN TODAY'S INDUSTRY, ARE ANIMATORS A DYING BREED?

Somewhat, but not because of generalists, but because there are fewer and fewer studios, fewer positions, so animators are forced to learn to do other jobs.

IF YOU HAD TO GIVE ONE PIECE OF ADVICE FOR A DEMO REEL, WHAT WOULD IT BE?

Be critical of yourself, and only put on your best. Just because something is finaled, doesn't mean that it is good enough for your reel.

DO YOU HAVE ANY ADVICE FOR ANIMATORS?

Stick with the fundamentals. Remember the 12 principles of animation, and use them to bring characters to life, not just to move them.

Jacob Bergman

JACOB HAS BEEN WORKING IN THE LOS ANGELES animation industry for 15 years on episodic, commercial, and some feature productions. He has worked for many large and small studios, and has run his own shop briefly. He is looking forward to what the next 15 years brings to this industry!

WHAT ARE SOME OF YOUR FAVORITE TOOLS IN MAYA?

I love nCloth and its ability to add that extra level of detail and finish to my animations.

WHAT ARE SOME OF YOUR INTERESTS OR HOBBIES BESIDES ANIMATION?

Playing music. I find that timing, quick creativity, and discipline helps my animation immensely.

DO YOU RELY ON A SPECIAL SCRIPT OR PLUGINS IN YOUR EVERYDAY JOB? DO YOU THINK BEGINNER ANIMATORS SHOULD TRY TO LEARN WITHOUT SCRIPTS AND PLUGINS?

Yes, work within the software without custom tools and setups as much as you can. As a freelancer you will move around a lot- to be able to just sit down and start working right away is key to you staying there.

DO YOU EVER HAVE TO WORK WITH MOTION CAPTURE? DO YOU THINK THAT MOTION CAPTURE WILL CONTINUE TO GROW AS A LARGER PORTION OF ANIMATION IN MOVIES IN THE FUTURE?

Absolutely. Automation is the future of our industry, "artificially intelligent" rigs will drive your character's performance. You will simply tell it what to do much like a director and actor work together to create a believable performance.

HOW DO YOU KNOW WHEN YOU'VE FOUND THE "RIGHT" IDEA FOR A SHOT?

Usually, when I bounce it off other people and watch their response, if they "get it" the first time they see it, I know its on the right track.

TELL US ABOUT YOUR FIRST JOB IN ANIMATION.

I worked on recreating television characters' facial performances, spent a lot of time copying video reference, it was a great experience. I love rotoscoping as you will find natural nuances that you could never make up.

HAVE YOU EVER THOUGHT ABOUT GIVING UP? IF SO, WHAT MADE YOU STICK WITH IT?

It seems that just when things look bleak or quieten down, something will come around to work on. In down times I would help friends on their personal projects to keep busy and maintain contacts.

IN TODAY'S INDUSTRY, ARE ANIMATORS A DYING BREED?

In commercial production, the "animation only" artist is less in demand. I prefer hiring animators who can rig and model a bit, and know a bit about the other ends of a pipeline (modeling and lighting). This helps them deal with issues that come up rather than waiting on someone else to move forward.

DO YOU HAVE ANY ADVICE FOR ANIMATORS?

Don't pigeonhole yourself, be flexible, learn as many styles and aspects of animation as you can and you will never be out of work.

Greg Kyle

GREG WAS RAISED IN THE GREAT WHITE NORTH to be a hockey player. After getting into Sheridan, he interned for Chuck Jones Film Production before working at SquareUSA, ILM, and Laika. He has worked as an animator, CG supervisor, and manager, and plans to retire at Laika.

WHAT ARE SOME OF YOUR FAVORITE TOOLS IN MAYA?

I'm simple. I love Graph Editor, Dope Sheet, and auto tangent.

IF YOU COULD HAVE ANY ANIMATION TOOL IN THE WORLD, WHAT WOULD IT BE?

A good character picker saves me a lot of time. ABX is a decent one.

WHO IS YOUR FAVORITE ANIMATOR? WHY?

Milt Kahl. He was such a great draftsman. He brought such character to his animation. Shere Khan is the most powerful antagonist. He was limited to only a few scenes but he is one of the most memorable characters from that movie.
    I love *Looney Tunes*, as well. Had to say that.

WHAT ARE SOME TIPS FOR GETTING INSIDE A CHARACTER'S HEAD, UNDERSTANDING THE MOTIVATION AND THE SUBTLETY OF A SCENE?

I think about the history. Where a character has come from will often tell you how a character will act and react. If there isn't much of an established history, then I make something up that I thinks fits.

HOW DO YOU KNOW WHEN YOU'VE FOUND THE "RIGHT" IDEA FOR A SHOT?

It just feels and looks right, but mostly it's when the director nods and smiles.

DO YOU RELY ON A SPECIAL SCRIPT OR PLUGINS IN YOUR EVERYDAY JOB? DO YOU
THINK BEGINNER ANIMATORS SHOULD TRY TO LEARN WITHOUT SCRIPTS AND PLUGINS?

Nah, I'm a minimalist. I do think there is a value to learning without all the bells and
whistles.

I think students shouldn't have access to a facial library. They should have to
make their own. They need to learn how to create aesthetically pleasing shapes on their
own.

HAVE YOU EVER THOUGHT ABOUT GIVING UP? IF SO, WHAT MADE YOU STICK WITH IT?

Nope. Sure, I've had bad days, but never thought about throwing it all away. In the real
world, animation is a cushy career.

IN TODAY'S INDUSTRY, ARE ANIMATORS A DYING BREED?

Nah, good animators aren't appreciated, but no, not a dying breed.

IF YOU HAD TO GIVE ONE PIECE OF ADVICE FOR A DEMO REEL, WHAT WOULD IT BE?

Lead with your best stuff with NO filler.
Oh, and make sure your link works.

DO YOU HAVE ANY ADVICE FOR ANIMATORS?

Work your butt off.
Be yourself. But if "yourself" is a jerk - change.
Pay attention in dailies.

D

W

Y

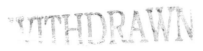